LITERARY
TOPICS

ISSN 1526-1549

LITERARY TOPICS

Volume **6**

The Southern Renaissance

Thomas L. McHaney
Georgia State University

A MANLY, INC. BOOK

GALE GROUP

Detroit
New York
San Francisco
London
Boston
Woodbridge, CT

THE SOUTHERN RENAISSANCE

Matthew J. Bruccoli and Richard Layman, *Editorial Directors*

ISBN 0-7876-4471-4

ISSN 1526-1549

Printed in the United States of America

10 9 8 7 6 5 4 3 2 1

ADVISORY BOARD

Matthew J. Bruccoli
> Jefferies Professor of English
> University of South Carolina

Denis Donoghue
> Henry James Professor of English and American Letters
> New York University

George Garrett
> Henry Hoyns Professor of Creative Writing
> University of Virginia

Trudier Harris
> J. Carlyle Sitterson Professor of English
> University of North Carolina at Chapel Hill

Hugh Kenner
> Franklin Professor and Callaway Professor
> University of Georgia

Alvin Kernan
> Senior Advisor in the Humanities
> The Andrew W. Mellon Foundation

Richard Layman
> Vice President
> Bruccoli Clark Layman

R.W.B. Lewis
> Neil Grey Professor, Emeritus
> Yale University

Harrison Meserole
> Distinguished Professor of English, Emeritus
> Texas A & M University

TABLE OF CONTENTS

THE SOUTHERN RENAISSANCE

A NOTE TO THE READER

Gale Study Guides are designed to be helpful by being informative, by removing tedious and unnecessary obstacles, and by pointing you toward further thought. They are also designed to be responsive to the changed conditions of reading literature which have arisen in the past fifteen or twenty years in schools, colleges, and universities. What are these conditions?

by Denis Donoghue, Henry James Professor of English and American Letters, New York University

They are mainly imposed by Theory. There was a time when students read literature—and were instructed to read it—without a theory of reading or a theory of literature. Even a critic as far-reaching as William Empson seemed to play it by ear and to trust to his hunches. It was assumed that everybody knew what a work of literature was and what reading such a work entailed. Teachers tried to offer a persuasive interpretation of the work, and that was that. One interpretation might be more interesting than another, but both interpretations were in the same field of assumption and reference. These assumptions don't hold any longer. If we say that such-and-such a book is a work of literature, we have to explain what we hold a work of literature to be, why it is such, and how it has become such. No attribute of the book can be taken for granted. Theory asks not, primarily, what the book is or what it means or how it works but what are the conditions under which it has come into being. Those conditions are deemed to be social, political, economic, linguistic, formal—and perhaps most insistently, cultural. A novel, a play, or a poem is said to be a work of cultural production. What does that mean? It means that many diverse forces have come together to produce the book, not just the intention of an author.

One result of this emphasis is that the context of a work of literature is not deemed to be a static "background" or scene. In a celebrated essay called "The Historical Interpretation of Literature" (1941), Edmund Wilson assumed that "history" could be called upon to steady the work of literature, to curb its mobility, and to ground it in some value more ascertainable than the author's intention or the formal properties of the work. History is no longer thought to provide such a ground. If there is a contemporary sense of history, it features rather the conviction—or the fear—that history itself is partly fictive. There are histories, but there is no single or stable History. A history of the French Revolution is not a sequence of characters and actions, transcribed. What or who is the real Julius Caesar? In the second chapter of James Joyce's *Ulysses* Stephen Dedalus asks himself: "Had Pyrrhus not fallen by a beldam's hand in Argos or Julius Caesar not been knifed to death?" and in answer to himself he murmurs: "They are not to be thought away. Time has branded them and fettered they are lodged in the room of the infinite possibilities they have ousted." Yes: in some sense, yes. But it is hard to establish "Julius Caesar" as an entity independent of my sense of him, or your sense of him. Granted that he was knifed to death. But that is not enough to establish him or to remove from the image of him the taint of fictiveness. The philosopher E. M. Cioran asserted, in *Précis de décomposition* (1949), that "history is merely a procession of false Absolutes, a series of temples raised to pretexts, a degradation of the mind before the Improbable." We are not obliged to agree with Cioran, but we can't shrug off his skepticism or assume that we are free to invoke History, as Wilson did, without misgiving. The concept of History is, as we have been schooled to say, problematic. History may be everything that is the case, but the force of fictiveness in constituting it can't be ignored.

So a question arises: is literary history possible? If it is: is it necessary or desirable? Why do we talk about literary movements and schools, if the very concept of History is questionable? Was there ever such a thing, for instance, as Romanticism or Modernism?

There was, but not in any fixed or steady sense. Writers who live at a particular time often feel a certain commonality of purpose. They respond in similar ways to the conditions they face. They share, in some degree, a conviction of the expressive possibilities. The revolutionary writers are those few who intuit or divine, among those possibilities, the ones that clamor to be fulfilled. T. S. Eliot saw the possibility of putting fragments of verse together in a seemingly arbitrary or at least unofficial way which would make a rather esoteric kind of sense: the result was *The Waste Land,* a kind of poetry no other writer thought of writing. It soon began to emerge that *The Waste Land,* Ezra Pound's *Cantos,* W. B. Yeats's *The Tower,* Hart Crane's *The Bridge,* and a few other poems had something in common—a distinctive sense of their time—despite their formal and rhetorical differences. The concept of Modernism seemed to be called for, to note similarities of purpose among such writers: Eliot, Pound, Valéry, Yeats, Rilke, Joyce, Proust. This does not mean that these writers thought of themselves as associates. Pound and Eliot did, but not Eliot and Yeats. The concept of Modernism is a worthy one, provided we deal with it flexibly: it is not a place of residence for the writers it designates. Differences, then, persist and have to be acknowledged; but they are folded within a grand sense of "the modern spirit" or Modernism. So we can still use this word. It is more useful to think of a certain consanguinity of purpose among various writers than to assume that one writer is utterly separate from other writers.

So too with the concept of the author, another once-steady notion that has come into question. Of course Shakespeare or Emily Dickinson or F. Scott Fitzgerald or James Dickey wrote the book, but not in utter freedom or sky-blue autonomy. They had to deal with the exigencies of cultural performance: specifically, with questions of language, communication, ideology, audience, readership, money patronage, publishers, genre, literary form, the social forces issuing in taste. Not that any one of these was absolutely coercive. Pierre Bourdieu has maintained, in *A Theory of Literary Production* (1966), that "a writer never reflects mechanically or rigorously the ideology which he represents, even if his sole intention is to represent it; perhaps because no ideology is sufficiently consistent to survive the test of figuration." Otherwise put: the force of an ideology is not irresistible; it must yield in some degree—bend if not break—to the force of the language, the figures of speech and thought, which are entailed by writing in English, French, Greek, Latin, or another language. Total freedom is not available in the production of literature. Writers may proceed as if such freedom were available. They would be wise not to capitulate to the social, economic, or cultural forces at large. A certain measure of resistance is possible. Kenneth Burke maintained, in *Counter-Statement* (1931), that the motto of the imagination is: "When in Rome, do as the Greeks." But it's not quite as straightforward as that.

It is hoped that these *Gale Study Guides* will help you to negotiate these and other issues. They won't tell you what to think about, say, *The Great Gatsby*, or dictate the limits of your experience in reading that book; but they will open up new possibilities.

ACKNOWLEDGMENTS

This book was produced by Manly, Inc. R. Bland Lawson is the series editor and the in-house editor.

Production manager is Philip B. Dematteis.

Copyediting supervisor is Phyllis A. Avant. The copyediting staff includes Brenda Carol Blanton, Allen E. Friend Jr., Melissa D. Hinton, William Tobias Mathes, Nancy E. Smith, and Elizabeth Jo Ann Sumner.

The index was prepared by Alex Snead.

Layout and graphics series team leader is Karla Corley Brown. She was assisted by Zoe R. Cook and Janet E. Hill, graphics supervisor.

Permissions editor is Jeff Miller.

Photography supervisor is Paul Talbot. Photography editors are Charles Mims and Scott Nemzek. Digital photographic copy work was performed by Joseph M. Bruccoli.

Systems manager is Marie L. Parker.

Typesetting supervisor is Kathleen M. Flanagan. The typesetting staff includes Mark J. McEwan, Patricia Flanagan Salisbury, and Alison Smith.

Following is a list of the copyright holders who have granted us permission to reproduce material in this volume of Gale Study Guides to Great Literature. Every effort has been made to trace copyright, but if omissions have been made, please let us know.

COPYRIGHTED MATERIAL IN *Literary Topics, Vol. 6: The Southern Renaissance,* **WAS REPRODUCED FROM THE FOLLOWING SOURCES:**

Cleanth Brooks. "What Deep South Literature Needs." *Saturday Review of Literature* (19 September 1942); reprinted in *Defining Southern Literature: Perspectives and Assessments, 1831–1952,* edited by John E.

Bassett. Madison & Teaneck, N.J.: Fairleigh Dickinson University Press / London: Associated University Presses, 1997.

Cash, W. J. "The Mind of the South." *American Mercury,* 17 (October 1929): 185–192.

Justus, James. Foreword to *Southern Writers at Century's End,* edited by Jeffrey J. Folks and James A. Perkins. Lexington: University of Kentucky Press, 1997.

McHaney, Thomas L. "Literary Modernism: The South Goes Modern and Keeps on Going." In *Southern Literature in Transition: Heritage and Promise,* edited by Philip Castille and William Osborne. Memphis: Memphis State University Press, 1983.

Mencken, H. L. "The Sahara of the Bozart." In his *Prejudices: Second Series.* New York: Knopf, 1920.

Singal, Daniel Joseph. "Coda." In his *The War Within: From Victorian to Modernist Thought in the South, 1919–1945.* Chapel Hill: University of North Carolina Press, 1982. Copyright (c) 1982 by the University of North Carolina Press. Used by permission of the publisher.

PHOTOGRAPHS AND ILLUSTRATIONS APPEARING IN *Literary Topics, Vol. 6: The Southern Renaissance,* **WERE REPRODUCED FROM THE FOLLOWING SOURCES:**

Alabama tenant-farmer family singing hymns, 1936. Photo by Walker Evans. J. Paul Getty Museum, Los Angeles.

Armstrong, Louis. Max Jones and John Chilton, *Louis: The Louis Armstrong Story, 1900–1971* (Boston: Little, Brown, 1971).

Black maid ironing. Photo by Doris Ulman.

Brooks, Cleanth, in his early forties. Photo by Cameron King.

Cabell, James Branch. James Branch Cabell Library, Virginia Commonwealth University.

Cabell, James Branch, with Julia Peterkin. South Caroliniana Library, University of South Carolina.

Caldwell, Erskine. Wide World Photos.

Cash, W. J., 1936. Courtesy of Harry Ransom Humanities Research Center, University of Texas at Austin.

Country store and gas station, Alabama, 1936. Photo by Walker Evans. Museum of Modern Art, New York.

Davidson, Donald. Photo by Fletcher Harvey.

Faulkner, William, 1924. Special Collections Department, University of Virginia.

French Quarter House, New Orleans, 1935. Photo by Walker Evans. Estate of Walker Evans.

Fugitive reunion photo, 1956. Vanderbilt University Photographic Archives.

Glasgow, Ellen, 1902. Culver Pictures, New York.

Gordon, Caroline. Manuscripts Division, Department of Rare Books and Special Collections, Princeton University Library.

Heyward, DuBose. Courtesy of the South Caroliniana Library.

Hurston, Zora Neale. Photo by Carl Van Vechten. By permission of Joseph Solomon, the Estate of Carl Van Vechten.

Mencken, H. L., with Frances Newman in Atlanta, October 1926. Courtesy of the Enoch Pratt Free Library, Baltimore.

Mississippi farm, 1936. Photo by Walker Evans. Museum of Modern Art, New York.

Porter, Katherine Anne. Photo by George Platt Lynes. Courtesy of the Estate of George Platt Lynes.

Ransom, John Crowe.

Tate, Allen. Photo by Stephen Spender. Willard Thorp Papers, Princeton University Library.

Toomer, Jean. Courtesy of the Prints and Photographs Collection, Moorland-Spingarn Research Center, Howard University.

Warren, Robert Penn, as a student at Vanderbilt. Vanderbilt University Photographic Archives.

Welty, Eudora. 1955. Wide World Photos.

Wolfe, Thomas. Thomas Wolfe Collection, Pack Memorial Public Library, Asheville, North Carolina.

Wright, Richard. Special Collections, John Davis Williams Library, University of Mississippi.

ABOUT THE SOUTHERN RENAISSANCE

OVERVIEW

The term *Southern Renaissance* identifies a period of imaginative and critical energy that, starting in the 1920s, led to the production of a remarkable volume of excellent creative writing in the American South. The Mississippi native Hershel Brickell, a writer and editor in New York for much of his life, apparently first offered the term. In "The Literary Awakening in the South" (1927) he summarized the "evidences of a Renaissance" and noted that most of its writers were "at the outset of their careers."[1] Three years later the cultural critic Howard Mumford Jones, who had taught at the Universities of Texas and North Carolina before moving on to the University of Michigan, asked the question, "Is There a Southern Renaissance?" His essay of this title appeared in *The Virginia Quarterly Review* in 1930, after a remarkable first decade of achievement by modern Southern writers, and one suspects that Jones's question was rhetorical. Surveying the national literary scene, he decided that voices from the Pacific coast and New England were few and that the "renaissance of 1910" in the Midwest (now generally called the Chicago Renaissance) had essentially run its course. In the South, however, he noted,

> there is a distinct re-birth of letters. Southern names—Cabell, Mrs. Peterkin, Isa Glenn, Ellen Glasgow, Elizabeth Madox Roberts, Maristan Chapman—are high in the list of distinguished contemporary novelists; a southern dramatist, Paul Green, seems to some a writer who may one day stand beside Eugene O'Neill; and a distinguished group of books by DuBose Heyward, Howard Odum, Robert R. Moton, Mrs. Peterkin, E. C. L. Adams, Roark Bradford and others, has presented Negro life outside the usual conventions of sentimentality. Moreover, the southerners are also writing important biographies: Winston's "Andrew Johnson," John Donald Wade's "Life of Augustus Baldwin Longstreet," Allen Tate's "Jefferson Davis." In poetry and criticism the South, of course, is still behind, but there is ground for the pride which Dixie takes in its new writers.[2]

Prophesy is difficult, but can Jones be forgiven for neglecting to mention William Faulkner, whose remarkable fourth novel, *The Sound and the Fury,* was published in 1929, or Thomas Wolfe, whose first novel,

Newspaper story on the Fugitives, a group of Southern writers associated with Vanderbilt University, who helped launch the Southern Renaissance

Look Homeward, Angel, was published that same year? Both of these writers received praise in 1930 from the Minnesotan Sinclair Lewis, the first American to win the Nobel Prize in literature. Lewis took a few moments during his prize acceptance speech in Stockholm to acknowledge the work of these Southern writers.

Had Jones paid attention to Faulkner, in fact, he might not have concluded later in the same essay that Southern writing was "a little thin, a little lacking in ideas" and had not "revolutionized fiction" as had Marcel Proust and James Joyce.[3] Jones feared that the new Southern writers had put culture, community, and religion behind them, working nothing but the surface, and that they thus wrote without significant ideas: "It seems to me therefore that southern letters will remain merely charming and interesting, merely regional studies and topical books, until such time as the South again stands for a significant idea."[4]

Doubters such as Jones existed even among those who had helped to establish the South's new fame for literature. The Southern poet and critic Allen Tate, who as a college student at Vanderbilt University played a role in the first major phase of this movement, chose the Latin form of the term *renaissance* when in 1945 he reflected upon the "brilliant and unexpected *renascence* of Southern writing between the two world wars,"[5] but he doubted that it could be sustained because the South had no great cities or a publishing and reviewing infrastructure.

Tate was proved overly pessimistic. By 1949 even a widely distributed automobile tour guide for the South noted a "southern renascence" of creative and historical writing in the region,[6] and by 1953 there was a book on the subject, *Southern Renascence: The Literature of the Modern South.*[7] There was thus general agreement that the term expressed something true: that between the two world wars a revolution in the literary arts had taken place in the old Confederacy. Subsequently, dozens of books, hundreds of articles, and scores of conferences have kept the subject in discussion and debate. The number of writers who may be considered part of the Southern Renaissance has grown from some thirty principal figures identified by the 1940s to several hundred in the following years as a second, third, and perhaps even fourth generation of writers have declared themselves willing to be regarded at least as heirs of the renaissance of 1919–1941.

Whether one spells the word *renascence* or *renaissance* is a matter of personal preference. The term means *rebirth,* referring figuratively to a cultural revival, or blossoming, involving new vigor and achievement in the arts. *The Renaissance* is commonly used to denote the great rebirth of

PAST AND PRESENT

"What then was the Southern Renaissance? Put briefly: the writers and intellectuals of the South after the late 1920s were engaged in an attempt to come to terms not only with the inherited values of the Southern tradition but also with a certain way of perceiving and dealing with the past, what Nietzsche called 'monumental' historical consciousness. It was vitally important for them to decide whether the past was of any use at all in the present; and, if so, in what ways? Put another way, the relationship between present and past which the Renaissance writers explored was fraught with ambivalence and ambiguity. The 'object' of their historical consciousness was a tradition whose essential figures were the father and the grandfather and whose essential structure was the literal and symbolic family. In sum, the Renaissance writers sought to come to terms with what I call the 'Southern family romance.'"

Richard H. King

From *A Southern Renaissance: The Cultural Awakening of the American South, 1930-1955* (New York & Oxford: Oxford University Press, 1980), p. 7.

learning and artistic creativity that spread from Italy throughout Europe starting in the fourteenth century. The importance and familiarity of the Renaissance in England that reached a summit in the works of William Shakespeare gave this spelling of the word greater currency in Britain and the United States. It influenced such modern coinages as the Celtic Renaissance, applied to the flourishing of early-twentieth-century Irish literature during the early career of the poet William Butler Yeats, and the American Renaissance, which was the title of F. O. Matthiessen's 1941 study of the generation of Ralph Waldo Emerson, Henry David Thoreau, Nathaniel Hawthorne, Herman Melville, Emily Dickinson, Walt Whitman, and Edgar Allan Poe. Literary historians have since written about the Chicago Renaissance that narrowly preceded the Southern one and a Harlem Renaissance of African American expression that closely paralleled it.[8] One general study of the literary traditions of the American South, *The History of Southern Literature* (1985), uses the spelling *renascence*, perhaps because the chief editor, Louis D. Rubin Jr., used this spelling in 1953 when he coedited *Southern Renascence: The Literature of the Modern South*, but the invaluable—and more recent—*Encyclopedia of Southern Culture* (1989) uses *renaissance*, and so will the present survey.

The end of the Southern Renaissance has been predicted several times; indeed, some Southerners will even argue not only that the Renaissance is over but also that the South is irretrievably gone, a victim of American homogenization and standardization, from airports to hamburger shops. Admitting that the issue is still in hot debate and that the South's perception of itself, as well as its literary expression, is more subtle than it used to be—certainly more subtle than journalistic, movie, and television stereotypes ever allowed it to be—some students of society and culture still maintain that both the distinct South and a distinct Southern literature remain. Many people will insist upon this. A few will keep finding themselves—quite unconsciously—living within that culture and making new

Southern literature about it. In *Requiem for a Nun* (1951), one of his most experimental later novels, Faulkner has a character say, "The past is never dead. It's not even past."[8] The ways in which this statement speaks the truth have not been lost on subsequent Southern writers, who have benefited from meditating on the power of the past in the present and the force of the present on the reinterpretation of the past. As long as Southern writers can perceive the constant play of past and present in this way, even a South that becomes completely, in Faulkner's shorthand, "*was*"— absorbed, perhaps, into modern commercial society—will produce some writers who look forward by looking back, and the era of the Southern Renaissance will continue to exert its imaginative spell.

DEFINING THE SOUTH

To discuss the origins and place of the Southern Renaissance in the history of the South, one must first address the question, "What is the South?" One approach to this question concerns geography, a second concerns culture, and a third concerns history.

The editors of the *Encyclopedia of Southern Culture* make the point that their subject, "the South," is a "cultural" and not simply a geographical unit, but they nevertheless state that their focus is on the former Confederate states. There were, of course, Southern colonies at the time of the early settlement of America, though it has been argued that the early settlers of Virginia, for example, thought of themselves as English, not Southerners, and that the Southern colonies that revolted against England in the eighteenth century were fighting for national, not regional, identity.

In *A History of the South* (1956) Francis Butler Simkins argues that it was fifty years after the American Revolution before citizens of the South developed a sectional awareness. This awareness, he argues, was the result of an increasingly defensive position regarding the institution of slavery. The Missouri Compromise of 1820–1821 brought the slavery question into Congress for debate and made the South's adamant position nationally known. The rapid growth of the cotton economy and the expansion of Deep South cotton agriculture on former Native American lands in Alabama and Mississippi led to an enormous increase in the slave population of the South. This development sealed the region's fate not just as it moved toward secession and Civil War, but eventually even later, as it entered the modern era still addicted to a single cash crop and the sharecropping system. Southern self-consciousness, interests, history, and the strange codes of stringent but selective separation of the races lay behind the modern renaissance in literary activity in ways difficult to sort out from one another, but all these factors were clearly important.

A geographical definition of the South is also subject to a variety of interpretations. One such interpretation is found in *The American Guide: A Source Book and Complete Travel Guide for the United States* (1949), a multivolume guide derived from book-length individual guides to the American states created and published during the Great Depression. The WPA guides, as they are called, were researched and written mainly by local people under the sponsorship of the Federal Writers' Project, a program of the Works Progress Administration. In *The American Guide: The South, The Southwest,* the Southern states are identified as Alabama, Arkansas, Florida, Georgia, Kentucky, Louisiana, Mississippi, North Carolina, South Carolina, Tennessee, and Virginia. This reckoning omits Delaware, Maryland, Missouri, Texas, and West Virginia, each of which is historically connected to slavery and other aspects of the Southern past. Delaware, though a slave state at the outbreak of the Civil War, remained in the Union. Maryland, though like Delaware somewhat divided between supporters of the Union and of the Confederacy, also remained in the Union. Missouri, admitted to the United States through the Compromise of 1820–1821 as a slave state and balanced by the admission of Maine, a free state, also stayed with the Union during the Civil War. Texas was a slaveholding state that joined and stayed with the Confederacy, but it was relatively far from the central campaigns of the war and became increasingly identified in the twentieth century with the region known as the Southwest (the heading under which it is treated in *The American Guide*). West Virginia separated from Virginia during the Civil War and entered the Union as a free state in 1863.

The *Encyclopedia of Southern Culture* differs from *The American Guide* by including Texas and omitting Kentucky (which supplied soldiers to both sides during the Civil War but remained in the Union), taking as its geographical focus "the eleven states of the former Confederacy"—Alabama, Arkansas, Florida, Georgia, Louisiana, Mississippi, North Carolina, South Carolina, Tennessee, Texas, and Virginia. The editors point out that Delaware, Maryland, Kentucky, and Missouri, although omitted, nevertheless were also slave states at the beginning of the war, "and many of their citizens then and after claimed a southern identity." The editors of the *Encyclopedia of Southern Culture* discuss the problematical nature of studying "a" South, reporting that contemporary social scientists include Delaware, Maryland, Oklahoma, West Virginia, and the District of Columbia in their statistical investigations of the

South, while the Gallup opinion poll "defines the South as the Confederate states plus Oklahoma and Kentucky."[10]

Geography, culture, and history intertwine wherever humankind has settled, of course, but different perspectives on these three matters, turned into topics, themes, and even obsessions by Southerners, are especially important for the literature of the South. During the Southern Renaissance all three topics were subject to revisionary analysis in poetry, fiction, drama, essay, and biography. Whatever one believes has happened to the Renaissance, a process of revisionary analysis—rewriting the past in view of the present, rewriting the present in view of the past—has yet to end in Southern writing, and geography is as much subject to revision as history and culture.

Geography has entered the postmodern consciousness as the landscape defined and shaped by different human beings; culture has become cultures; and history is the lie one group tells about another. Study of each of these topics in and about the South has, of course, enjoyed a renaissance of its own. For the last three or four decades startling revisions and exposures of documentary evidence by historians of the South, cultural geographers, and others have altered the material on which imaginative writers often set to work.

Associated with the Southern Renaissance are many Souths within the borders of any and all of the Southern states, including imaginary ones created by Southern writers. Eudora Welty found in her grandmother's West Virginia home place and her life there materials so Southern that Welty simply moved those border-state events and people into the hilliest of the northeast Mississippi counties, Tishimingo, to create Deep South fiction out of mountain music. (Similarly, no modern reader would doubt, reading her stories and novels or even hearing her voice, that Rubin's West Virginia student Lee Smith is a Southern writer.) Conversely, contemporary author Richard Ford, who grew up near Welty in Jackson, Mississippi, and speaks with a cultivated Southern voice, denies that he is a Southern writer and sets his fiction in other regions of the country where he has lived. Not every writer from the South is a Southern writer, perhaps, while some writers from the margins and even outside the margins of the South find value in accepting a place in the Southern tradition of writing.

Each of the eleven Southern states for which *The American Guide: The South, The Southwest* offers information is, as the editors of the book remind its readers, different from the others, even in those districts that fostered a similar agriculture. Antebellum plantation cul-

Mississippi farm, photographed by Walker Evans in 1936

ture in South Carolina was quite different from plantation culture in Louisiana; its development in Virginia was different from its development in the Black Belt of Alabama or the Delta of Mississippi. The great plantation—so strong a part of the Southern myth—represented a relatively small percentage of the life of any one Southern state. Mountain culture varied not only state by state but even within single states. The inhabitants of different mountain enclaves cannot be subsumed under any single impression—and the general term "hillbilly" is no more applicable to people from the many different mountain and hill cultures than white farmworkers throughout the South can be defined as "white trash," "rednecks," or "crackers," all terms used to strip less affluent classes of their humanity.

The record of stripping some people of their humanity and giving an extra allotment of it to a ruling or elite class is a fact of history. But in the South, the impact of race and racism on agriculture, class divisions, politics, education, social life, language, and the arts were important for the Southern Renaissance. Southern race consciousness and race relations, as well as the consequences of racial division, are frequent subjects in the writing associated with the Renaissance. On the positive side, the literary consciousness of the modern South developed many characteristics from the inspired art, storytelling, and musical traditions of African Americans—blues, jazz, and gospel, for example—and from the folklore, expressive language, personal courtesy, and quiet social pressure emanating from African American culture. This is history, too, a history rarely told with honesty before such writers of the Southern Renaissance as Faulkner, Zora Neale Hurston, Julia Peterkin, Richard Wright, and Paul Green took an imaginative hand in the telling.

A revealing and somewhat unself-conscious view of the South—and of early modern writing in the South—appeared in the original, individual book-length guides to the Southern states prepared in the 1930s by the Federal Writers' Project of the WPA. The project to prepare state guides employed local researchers and writers, for the most part, though some final editing was done in Washington, D.C. Several Southern writers later known for their fiction took part in one way or another, though not always in their native states. Welty worked for the WPA as a publicity agent, covering the impact of WPA rural improvement projects in Mississippi, but three of her photographs made their way into *Mississippi: A Guide to the Magnolia State* (1938). Writers now less well known, such as Lyle Saxon of Louisiana and Pulitzer Prize–winning dramatist Paul Green of North Carolina, were researchers and writers in their states.

Researched in the 1930s, without an awareness that a literary "renaissance" was in progress, the "Literature" sections of the WPA guides reveal, in each Southern state, a steady history of fiction and poetry, much of it by names long forgotten, some of it by writers who remain well known. In the aftermath of the Civil War and Reconstruction, the guides record, the South slowly developed a varied and critical modern literature, even within a culture that was too often backward-looking and sentimental. Realism and naturalism were much in evidence at the opening of the twentieth century, and modernism appeared in the South as surely as it appeared in other conservative environments—for instance, Joyce's Ireland or the American Midwest of Lewis, Theodore Dreiser, and Sherwood Anderson.

The WPA guides were an advertisement, a stimulus, and a resource to writers and would-be writers in their states, whether they worked on the project or not. Faulkner borrowed freely from *Mississippi: A Guide to the Magnolia State* for *Requiem for a Nun,* and his short stories about the Snopes family were praised in the guide two years before they found expression in his novel *The Hamlet* (1940). For a young writer who worked on the project, the guides were potentially important as reminders of the everyday lore of relatively small places; Welty has written that as she traveled Mississippi for her WPA job, she saw places and people she would otherwise never have known, and that this experience helped her develop her passion and eye for fiction.[11] In addition to their sections on literature and their attention to landmarks of local and more general historical interest, the guides featured special sections on archaeology and history, religion and folklore, labor and handicrafts, agriculture and music, education and media and transportation, and even on African American life. Although the writers of the South who encountered these books in the late 1930s might have had to read a schoolbook history of their state when they were younger, the guides offered a refreshingly mature and inclusive addition to school histories. (Such histories in the South tended at this time to reflect the cultural position of the so-called Redeemers, those anti-Reconstruction white Southerners who took back control of their state governments at the end of the Reconstruction period.)

The local WPA projects coincided with and promoted concurrent national interest in regional folklore and its recovery. Hurston was collecting folklore in Florida in the 1930s and wrote several books from this enterprise, including the novel *Their Eyes Were Watching God* (1937). In the same decade Faulkner developed two of his most folkloric strains of writing, stories about the fictional rural hamlet Frenchman's Bend (in *The Hamlet*) and about African American life on a small plantation. He blended these latter stories with nearly legendary tales about hunting for *Go Down, Moses* (1942). Popular collections such as B. A. Botkin's *A Treasury of Southern Folklore* (1949) and *A Treasury of Mississippi River Folklore* (1955) were part of the phenomenon, as were the valuable field recordings made by researchers from the Library of Congress who traveled to the mountains, the Mississippi Delta, and other regions to record the origins of American folk music, black and white.

The WPA guide project did not begin until the mid 1930s, so the guides were not an initiating force of the Southern Renaissance, but they provide insight into the local sources of the movement, recording the kinds of things everybody in a community knew but that people in the next county probably did not. The guides were later a great stimulus to second- and third-generation writers of the Renaissance. They were even modernist in structure; that is, they were not conventional histories nor even conventional touring guides like those for European countries.

Their narratives were not conventional but juxtaposed sections on different topics in an apparently random order. The contents differed from guide to guide. The Kentucky and Georgia guides, for example, featured a whole section devoted to "The Negro" that was not found in the Arkansas or Florida guides, whereas the Mississippi guide, under "Mississippi Past and Present," balanced a section titled "White Folkways" with one called "Black Folkways." Following the introductory essays on various topics, the guides devoted a section to the larger cities and towns—of which there were few in the South at the time—and their special points of interest (more often scrap-metal yards, canning factories, or cotton oil mills than cultural institutions). The majority of the books were travelogues of what one could see following the few national highways, the improved state roads, and even some of the dirt tracks winding through each state in what was mostly a rural odyssey.

History is revealed in many ways in the WPA guides, ways that were doubtless known to many of the writers of the first Renaissance generation, and thus the guides offer an interesting insight into the kind of unadorned history of ordinary people and ordinary places that a writer growing up in the South was more likely to know than the academic histories that highlighted governors, generals, and tycoons. A random sample from one of the guides, *Arkansas: A Guide to the State* (1941), is worth quoting. Climbing with the guide from the Black River Valley at a town named Pocahontas, readers have their attention called to the remarkable contrast between valley and precipitous mountain roads, and the narrative adds,

> No less remarkable is the difference in the lives of the inhabitants. The valley farmer is often

A "FLOWERING OF SOUTHERN TALENT"

"Only a few years ago all eyes were on the Middle West, but the movement which centered in Chicago and produced a number of poets as well as realistic novelists has passed on. So suddenly has the South taken the spotlight that not many readers realize how much good writing has come out of a section which was scorned by the Corn Belt literati in the heyday of their glory.

"Just what causes are behind the present flowering of Southern talent is not easy to discover. The industrial revolution of the last few years has broken up old patterns of life, bringing a shifting of values; much new blood has come into the section, especially in the cities, introducing a needed haven of liberalism; dozens of Southerners of the oldest stock have taken to wandering up and down the earth with the rest of America; there has been a change in the general attitude toward the Negro because of his exodus to northern and western industrial centres.

"When one sets out to link these social and economic causes directly to recent literary production, the task grows very complicated. It would be relatively simple if the present output of writing were readily classifiable as to material and method. But what gives it such keen interest is its extreme diversity—the fact that there are no 'schools' and no group such as had its headquarters in Chicago in the old days."

Herschel Brickell

From "The Literary Awakening in the South," *Bookman*, 76 (October 1927); reprinted in *Defining Southern Literature: Perspectives and Assessments, 1831-1952*, edited by John E. Bassett (Madison & Teaneck, N.J.: Fairleigh Dickinson University Press / London: Associated University Presses, 1997), pp. 289-290.

menaced by floods, insect plagues, and market prices. The hill farmer, however, always seems to make out somehow with his corn patch, his few vegetables, his rifle, and fishing rod. This self-contained economy creates in the hillman a comparative disinterest in the world's affairs, along with a disdain of lowland ways. "I don't go to question the good Lord in his wisdom," runs the phrasing attributed to a typical mountaineer, "but I jest cain't see why He put valleys in between the hills."[12]

In *Mississippi: A Guide to the Magnolia State* the authors repeatedly point out the ruined or vanished landmarks of plantation culture, as in an entry for the town of Canaan, which "sits upon land that belies the promise of its name. The soil is fast washing away from the scattered farms, and erosion has marked the woods and farmlands with blood-red scars." In Slayden, some twenty miles away, the highway "passes a number of crumbling relics of antebellum culture. Before the war, when the now almost sterile soil was productive, planters grew rich on cotton and built homes in keeping with their prosperity. These houses, the majority of them Southern Planter in type, are ghosts of the past; but even with sagging blinds, columns, and chimneys, they are impressive."[13] The populations of the two towns, respectively, are seventy-five and fifty.

As a supplement to narrative histories of the larger movements of settlement, enterprise, politics, war, and recovery in the region that spawned the Southern Renaissance, the WPA guides are highly instructive about what young writers were actually seeing in their specific regions and subregions as they grew up. The guides are not always trustworthy, but they are remarkably direct. If they idealize the working man—part of the ethos of the New Deal clearly leaks into them—they are often frank, and their inclusiveness is remarkable, providing details of local life, communities, anecdotes, and folklore that only a native would notice. One can imagine how rich was Welty's experience of leaving her middle-class home in Jackson, the state capital, to enter out-of-the-way rural Mississippi in its many modes: from hill farm to river shanty to truck-crop lowland to the steaming Delta, and on to the resin-redolent piney woods and the breezy coast.

The subregional variety that Welty came to know and write about in her state is found in each of the Southern states, and thus when it is said that the Southern Renaissance occurred principally in the former slave states, one is still speaking of a remarkable diversity of landscape, agriculture, people, and customs. Geographical and human diversity fostered social, economic, and political diversity, and that made for historical diversity, which in turn made for relatively different material to be used by the human imagination. Young poets, writers of fiction, dramatists, biographers, and historians with diverse backgrounds naturally produced richly different kinds of literature in many different voices.

THE EVOLUTION OF THE SOUTHERN RENAISSANCE

ORIGINS: The beginnings of the Southern Renaissance in the 1920s are subtle, for the South lived with a great many contradictions, and it had a past that made it different from the rest of the country. It had literally codified a morally indefensible position regarding human freedom and justified this stance in terms of Old Testament religion. It had rebelled against the still-developing national union, lost a savage and costly war, suffered occupation and readjustment at the hands of a hated enemy, and saw much of its capital—which happened to be human beings—completely devalued and its means of production reduced or destroyed.

Thus, if the Southern mode of the modernist imagination was dependent on both the region's past and the discovery of the new international worldview, it had not one but two sets of contradictions with which it had to struggle. The shock of the new, as art critic Richard Hughes has described the advent of modern art, flashed into the mind's eye of young people who, like Faulkner's Quentin Compson in *The Sound and the Fury* and *Absalom, Absalom!* (1936) had to a large degree grown up with ghosts of the past. These specters included impressions of a gallant but bizarre ancestry; tirades from angry sentimentalists who were confused about the causes of the Civil War and why it was lost, such as Rosa Coldfield in *Absalom, Absalom!*; and crass, arrogant materialists such as Thomas Sutpen in the same novel. What Faulkner did with such material is instructive: at the beginning of *Absalom, Absalom!* Rosa summons Quentin to hear her story so that he will tell it to others. Quentin, however, does not reconstruct her story as she intends, and Faulkner does not tell Quentin's version in a narrative style recognizable to readers who wept into their copies of Margaret Mitchell's *Gone with the Wind*, which was published in the same year, 1936.

The discovery of all the causes of the Southern Renaissance may be as difficult as the discovery of the meaning of the history of the South, but the literary movement came about in part simply because Southern writers struggled, like Faulkner and his characters, to penetrate Southern stereotypes, even as they used them, in order to find a human as well as a local truth. In the opening pages of *Absalom, Absalom!* Faulkner even parodies what the writers of the Southern Renaissance could expect to face: Rosa reveals that she has summoned Quentin to hear her story

Dust jacket for William Faulkner's 1936 novel, which questions the myths of the Southern past

because she has heard he is leaving town to study at Harvard University:

> So I dont imagine you will ever come back here and settle down as a country lawyer in a little town like Jefferson since Northern people have already seen to it that there is little left in the South for a young man. So maybe you will enter the literary profession as so many Southern gentlemen and gentlewomen too are doing now and maybe some day you will remember this and write about it. You will be married then I expect and perhaps your wife will want a new gown or a new chair for the house and you can write this and submit it to the magazines.[14]

Cultural criticism abounds in this passage, even for a reader who does not know how difficult it was for Faulkner to publish serious work in magazines or to find an audience willing to pay for his demanding and unsentimental novels, especially *Absalom, Absalom!* Quentin's quandary, as it happens, is resolved when, after months of speculation on Rosa's story with his Canadian roommate at Harvard, he takes a research trip with the obsessed Rosa to the remote old Sutpen house, where he discovers living remnants of the truth. Quentin finds the unmistakable stamp of Sutpen's face in an African American child descended from Sutpen's abandoned and exiled first son. The encounter, which neither Quentin nor Faulkner specifically explains, apparently confirms Quentin's growing suspicion that the greed and fratricide of the Sutpen family history had their origins in racist hypocrisy and white arrogance, not in a noble Southern code of honor.

The broadest outline of the Southern Renaissance suggests, as literary scholar M. Thomas Inge has written in the *Encyclopedia of Southern Culture,* that it was the "culmination of a number of historic and cultural forces at work in southern society."[15] The South's experience of military defeat in the Civil War and the subsequent occupation by the triumphant national government, which instituted the postwar program called Reconstruction, is one source of the sensibility that produced reflective and creative cadres of writers. The federal program to both control and repatriate Southern society did little to make the

South like other parts of America, and it did not resolve the economic and social exclusion of the former slaves and their children, despite their being freed from the condition of slavery. The South did begin to embrace national economic values and to move from agrarianism to dependence on, and some participation in, capitalistic industrialism, but in fact the great wealth previously achieved in Southern states through agriculture was based on something much like modern industrial society: large-scale production using cheap exploited labor, marketed internationally through brokers and transported to industrial centers for mechanical processing.

The Southerner's reflections on the Civil War, its complex causes, its disastrous outcome, and its disagreeable aftermath, Inge argues,

> brought about a period of self-analysis and reflection on the values [the South] had fought to preserve and in some cases a reaffirmation of those values. . . . Resistance to cultural reconstruction intensified the traditional regional sense of identity and distinctiveness in which some [Southerners] took pleasure and from which others felt the need to escape. These tensions stirred the creative sensibilities of writers, who were instructed well by southern history in mortality and the inevitability of death—concerns that would bring their themes to a level of universal relevance.[16]

It might be added that the instruction in mortality involved not merely the death of human life but the death of cultural icons, economic hopes, long-developed self-images, and traditions.

Historian C. Vann Woodward has suggested that the South was differently prepared than the rest of America for the changes the modern era brought.[17] Other regions of America that contributed their fathers and sons to the war effort still did not experience the war directly, and they could justify their sacrifices in a holy cause on both moral and nationalistic grounds. The South tried to do the same, but it was a problem. Irony—the incongruity between what is expected and what occurs or between what is said and what is meant—was increasingly abundant in Southern culture after the Civil War, and where irony was thought to be absent, the new Southern writers began to supply it. One irony was that following the defeat and destruction of the single-crop slave-plantation system, with its large, economically dependent underclass, the postwar South simply began to waste its substance again and continued to deny economic and political opportunity to more than half of its people. After the war it constructed railroads into its abundant forests and watersheds so that they could be clear-cut, abused its agricultural lands by the practice of one-crop farming, shortchanged its abundant workforce to increase profits but thereby limited the development of local economies and capital, and sold its products on national and international markets through a host of middlemen from other places, who sold these products back to the South as processed goods, taking away potential Southern capital at every stage.

Interestingly, the notion of the "benighted" South coincided with the regional boosting of its success as a "New" South. The self-proclaimed heirs of Thomas Jefferson's dream of an agrarian republic made it increasingly impossible for the hardworking poor farmer, black or white, to rise into the ranks of those who owned property, received useful educations, or were able to vote in a democratic society. Southern Reconstruction following the Civil War thus took a rather different form than the Northern enemy and conqueror might have expected. This included not only the gradual resumption of power by the old ruling classes and the creation of local and state laws restricting African American freedom, but also the creation or redevelopment of elaborate cultural myths—even a myth about Reconstruction.[18] As the South used some of its restored wealth to memorialize the "Lost Cause," it also crystalized the primary Southern myth about what had preceded war and defeat. Those who had not experienced the rigors of the early Southern settlement, the hardships of its peoples (black and white) during the brief rise of King Cotton in the nineteenth century, or the horrors of the war wrote and read versions of a vague story about a Pan-Southern Golden Age. According to the story, genteel large-scale farmers, gracious and hospitable, and their idle, adoring spouses and polite children lived in spacious mansions served by a worshipful agrarian peasantry and loyal house staff—both composed of childlike people of African descent who thrived under the protective custody of the "peculiar institution" of slavery. The lesser neighbors of these elegant Southern grandees formed a sterling white yeomanry who lived on small independent farms and rarely owned, and never coveted owning, slaves. The South even adopted the cultivated-sounding Latin term *antebellum* (before the war) to refer to the period of slavery, and it remains the favorite adjective to describe the surviving mansions built by the wealth the slaves created.

There were—and still are—many Southern myths, but the powerful Golden Age myth about the pre–Civil War past strongly exercised the critical imaginations and the wary irony of the writers who are credited with initiating the Southern Renaissance. It was not too difficult for young people of the generation between the wars to perceive that the myth was specious. Having a fund of disabled and discreditable myths, however, proved a boon to writers of the Renaissance. The *Encyclopedia of Southern Culture* devotes an entire section, almost 150 pages, to discussions of more than 40 examples of the "Mythic South." The historian George B. Tindall, consultant for this section of the *Encyclopedia,* notes that the "complexity and contradictions of southern mythology, one can argue, make the mythology of the American west seem fairly simple by comparison."[19] Entries on the Fighting South, the Plantation Myth, the Reconstruction Myth, the New South Myth, the Cavalier Myth, and the Myth of the Lost Cause are especially useful for studying the Southern Renaissance and its writers. By and large, such myths were the first targets the new writers challenged and punctured, usually before historians and other scholars did.

This critical reaction came about as the reconstructed South began to educate its more privileged children and entered the modern era. Not surprisingly, cultural myths began to come under critical scrutiny as a new generation emerged for whom the privations of the past were genteel stories. Those young men who had experienced or merely paid close attention to World War I had some reason to doubt a chivalrous account of universal gallantry and decorous combat in the war fought by their grandfathers. Those young women who grew up in communities where evidence of sexual relations between white and black people was not merely anecdotal but daily visible, though hotly denied, felt less pressure to maintain the sanctity of a pure Southern womanhood. Sentimental views of Southern morality and purity were challenged in the backseats of automobiles as they had been challenged for decades in the cabins behind the big house.

In the twentieth century, as the recovery of the South reached a temporary apogee prior to the next tragedy—the Great Depression— some of the region's bright children could not help observing, whether they attended school outside the South or not, that the genteel Christian South that was portrayed as the cradle of Jefferson's agrarian democracy trampled many of its most trumpeted moral, religious, political, and economic principles. Children born late in the nineteenth century or early in the twentieth could not help noting that all over the South their elders proclaimed from pulpit, political stump, and club lectern a set of pieties as vulnerable to critical questioning as were those that writers such as Melville, Hawthorne, Twain, Dreiser, Lewis, Stephen Crane, Upton Sinclair, Edith Wharton, or Robinson Jeffers—to name a few from all sections of the country—had challenged in their own times and places for more than half a century.

A flashpoint for a homespun critical reappraisal of the South was a witty essay by the Baltimore-born and educated journalist H. L. Mencken. He started a lifelong career as a city journalist at the age of eighteen; read widely; wrote for and then edited an increasingly chic and adventurous New York magazine, appropriately called *The Smart Set;* cofounded another excellent small-circulation magazine, *The American Mercury;* and promoted modernist literature, including works by many of the writers important to the Southern Renaissance. Mencken, as Fred Hobson has pointed out, actually had a romantic view of the old culture of Virginia but believed that in the aftermath of the Civil War, Southern culture dried up. Hobson paraphrases Mencken's belief that "the worthless, depraved poor whites seized control and dominated every aspect of southern life. Fanatical preachers, corrupt politicians, and nostalgic poetasters made the South the laughingstock of the nation." As Hobson observes, the "antebellum South, in truth, was never so civilized—nor the postbellum South so barbaric—as the South of Mencken's imagination."[20]

In an essay titled "The Sahara of the Bozart," which was first published in the 13 November 1917 edition of the *New York Evening Mail,* Mencken took his battle against the mediocrity and false piety of what he called "booboisie Americana"—bourgeois or middle-class America—across the Mason-Dixon Line and led a charge against Southern culture. The essay was probably unnoticed by the new generation of Southerners in 1917, when World War I, or simply the completion of their adolescence, was more on their minds, but it was republished in the seminal year 1920 as a part of Mencken's essay collection *Prejudices: Second Series.* This publication came when the writer was already well known to many progressive young Southerners for his iconoclastic essays, his association with *The Smart Set,* and his championing of the Southern writer James Branch Cabell (whose 1919 novel *Jurgen* was considered obscene in some American circles). The republication of "The Sahara of the Bozart" also coincided with such exciting new American publications that year as Sinclair Lewis's novel *Main Street,* F. Scott Fitzgerald's novel *This Side of Paradise* and short-story collection *Flappers and Philosophers,* and T. S. Eliot's *Poems* (originally published in England that same year in slightly different form as *Ara Vos Prec*). In 1920 Mencken's essay fitted well with the worldly views of the new youth culture.

Mencken attacked the South in other articles besides "The Sahara of the Bozart." In "The Literature of a Moral Republic," published in *The Smart Set* in August 1913, he charged that the South, "an area three times as large as either France or Germany," had "not a single symphony orchestra, nor a single picture worth looking at, nor a single public building or monument of the first rank, nor a single factory devoted to the making of beautiful things, nor a single poet, novelist, historian, musician, painter or sculptor whose reputation extends beyond his own country. . . ."[21] In a 1917 editorial for the *Baltimore Evening Sun,* Mencken asserted that "There are whole areas in the South—areas quite as large as most European kingdoms—in which not a single intelligent man is to be found. . . . Its literature is that of the finishing school. Its philosophy is the naif supernaturalism of the camp-meeting, the wind-music of the chautauqua. It has no more art than Liberia."[22]

Inge has written that "Mencken's attack, of course, had nothing to do with initiating the [Southern] Renaissance," but its unmasking of the ironies of Southern culture doubtless coincided with less flamboyant discoveries of a similar nature by the young Southerners with literary ambition who went on to make up the generation of this particular renaissance. Characteristic of this generation was a group of young teachers and students at Vanderbilt in Nashville, Tennessee, who came to be known as "The Fugitives."

THE FUGITIVES: The Nashville group has received more credit than it deserved, or even than it ever desired or subsequently accepted, as an instigator of the Southern Renaissance. This is not because they were really the first to launch a renaissance in letters—they were not—but because the title of their little magazine, *The Fugitive,* created a memorable journalistic identity for them and because several of them became distinguished teachers and promoters of Southern writing. The core members of this group were both Tennesseans who had become instructors in English at Vanderbilt, where both had themselves received undergraduate degrees, John Crowe Ransom and Donald Davidson.

Both young men came from similar families in the upper South and from similar genteel (but not affluent) backgrounds. Davidson was the son of a rural schoolmaster and Ransom the son of a well-read Methodist minister, and both young men found it necessary to interrupt their college educations to teach in small schools for a year and earn money for tuition. Ransom later became a Rhodes Scholar at Oxford University, completing a degree there in 1913 and joining the Vanderbilt faculty in 1914. Davidson, several years younger, fought abroad in World War I in 1917 and 1918, coming to Vanderbilt in 1920 to pursue a master's degree and teach as an instructor. Ransom and Davidson met with a promising and, as it turned out, brilliant group of undergraduates to discuss philosophy, art, and literature. They gathered frequently at the home of Sidney M. Hirsch, a widely traveled young Jewish intellectual who had studied many of the world's mystic philosophies and a variety of languages. Soon they turned to writing examples of literature of their own, chiefly poetry.

In 1922 they joined the well-established tradition of the "little" magazine and established *The Fugitive,* a tiny journal in which they published a mild manifesto explaining what they were "fugitives" from. They also published their own poetry and essays, and writing by a widening circle of like-minded friends. The year 1922 was propitious for new American literature in several ways: it was the year of the publication of Lewis's *Babbitt,* Eliot's *The Waste Land,* and Joyce's *Ulysses.* Parts of Joyce's novel had first been serialized in another American "little" magazine, *The Little Review,* from 1918 to 1920, when publication was suppressed by the U.S. Post Office on grounds of indecency. The most promising of Ransom and Davidson's students were Tate and Robert Penn Warren, who went on to become two of the most distinguished men of letters in modern America; a young pair of equally brilliant and eventually successful men of letters, Andrew Lytle and Cleanth Brooks; and the physician-poet Merrill Moore. Other Southern intellectuals and literary artists, both older and younger, came into the circle, among them the poets John Gould Fletcher and Laura Riding, the playwright and drama critic Stark Young, the scholar John Donald Wade, and the litterateur William Alexander Percy (who, like Wade, owned and managed a considerable farm).

Why the title *The Fugitive?* In the first issue of the little magazine, this was the explanation: "THE FUGITIVE flees from nothing faster than from the high-caste Brahmins of the Old South. Without raising the question of whether the blood in the veins of its editors runs red, they at any rate are not advertising it as blue; indeed, as to pedigree, they cheerfully invite the most unfavorable inference from the circumstances of their anonymity."[23] Thus the group questioned, subtly, two strong aspects of the legend of the South: the caste system that put "Brahmins" (the "Cavaliers" or aristocrats) at the top and the code of honor. Hardly proletarians, but representatives of an educated and even idealistic yeoman stock, the editors were more innocent than one might imagine regarding Deep South racial codes, which they never mention in the foreword to the first issue of their magazine. Their origins were in the upper South, where slavery had been rare and few African Americans lived, and where sympathy for the Confederacy had not been uniformly strong even during the period of secession. The poetry the Nashville group wrote often did not even depict the South they knew, though in the work of Davidson and especially Warren and Lytle a growing attachment to Southern anecdote, history, folklore, and moral concerns soon appeared. Ransom moved toward philosophy and the dramatization of abstractions while Tate moved toward the moderns— especially, in his first decade as a poet, such powerful influences as Eliot. Tate came to meditate on Southern experience in a clearly universal, modernist mode, especially in his "Ode to the Confederate Dead" (1928), a title based in ironic disdain for all the sentimental odes written by local poets about the "Lost Cause" and portraying instead a modern, alienated Southerner who resembles Eliot's Prufrock in "The Love Song of J. Alfred Prufrock" (1917).

Tate's later remarks on his beginnings are interesting, not only because he was an instigator. He at first perceived the label *Southern Renaissance* in somewhat ironic terms, seeing in it several contradictions. He saw, correctly, that the emergence of a strong, new, and varied Southern literature in the 1920s was not an indigenous event, springing out of the culture and past of the region alone. Any Southern cultural renaissance in this time, Tate knew, was part of the broad international phenomenon in the arts associated with modernism. He was also at first doubtful that a truly *Southern* renaissance could occur in the region. In an essay titled "The Profession of Letters in the South" (1935) Tate observed that because "there is no city in the South where writers may gather, write, and live, and no Southern publisher to print their books, the Southern writer, of my generation at least, went to New York. There he was influenced not only by the necessity to live [which meant meeting Northern expectations] but by theories and movements drifting over from Europe." Thus, the "Southern writer was perilously near to losing his identity, becoming merely a 'modern' writer. He lost the Southern feeling which . . . informs the Southern style." The Southern writer, Tate believed, could be a "Southerner in the South"[24] only if a regional profession of letters and a regional literary infrastructure existed.

Tate did not foresee such an infrastructure coming into being in his native region, not even in its university towns, and he was to some degree correct. Yet, not only did the writing that had begun in the South continue to flourish, its volume and literary quality continued to grow

THE FUGITIVE

VOLUME I.   No. 4

PUBLISHED AT NASHVILLE, TENN.
Copyright, 1922, by the Fugitive Publishing Co.
Subscription Price, One Dollar a Year.

BOARD OF EDITORS

Walter Clyde Curry   Sidney Mttron Hirsch   John Crowe Ransom
Donald Davidson   Stanley Johnson   Alec B. Stevenson
James M. Frank   Merrill Moore   Allen Tate
Jesse Ely Wills   Ridley Wills

In absentia: William Yandell Elliott, William Frierson.

CONTENTS

Contents page from the fourth issue of the literary magazine founded by the Fugitives, featuring contributions by such key members as Donald Davidson, John Crowe Ransom, and Allen Tate

THE FUGITIVES

"As poets, the Fugitives had held the simple aim of developing a craft; but their dedication to that purpose had led them ever farther into an exploration of their heritage. They had found that their true task was not the creation of an ideal world but the discovery of a real one, independent of their own thinking; they had learned that a genuine culture, whatever its moral flaws, is an analogue of something nobler toward which the human spirit aspires but which it can grasp only through submission to the actual."

Louise Cowan

From *The Fugitive Group: A Literary History* (Baton Rouge: Louisiana State University Press, 1959), p. 257.

and change, even without such an infrastructure. Uncompromisingly Southern writers found publishers in New York and eventually an audience all over America and throughout the world. Even when the writing was done by authors who insisted on remaining "at home"—as Tate and many of his Fugitive friends did not—between the two world wars Southern literature had a warm reception from national magazines and publishers and from an international audience.

Tate's interpretation of the Southern Renaissance was that "the arts everywhere spring from a mysterious union of indigenous materials and foreign influences: there is no great art or literature that does not bear the marks of this fusion."[25] But in his view at the time, the success of Southern writing in the decade and a half from 1920 was going to be a short-lived phenomenon specific to the rapid changes overtaking the South, a rebirth much like the Elizabethan Renaissance in England that, in his opinion, played out quickly as soon as English society was transformed. Irreversible and conclusive social changes in the South, Tate wrote, "made possible the curious burst of intelligence that we get at a crossing of the ways, not unlike, on an infinitesimal scale, the outburst of poetic genius at the end of the sixteenth century when commercial England had already begun to crush feudal England."[26] Clearly, he expected commercial America to crush the feudal South, and perhaps he was right. The unexpected longevity of the Southern Renaissance may reflect, however, the relatively slow pace of social, political, and economic change in the region, a slowness that the conservative Tate did not anticipate, partly because he did not see how much some of the things taken for granted—such as the racial status quo—needed to change before the South could truly enter the modern era, either as victor or vanquished.

The year *The Fugitive* ceased publication, like the year of its founding, was significant for the Southern Renaissance. In 1925 not only were such important literary works as Ernest Hemingway's *In Our Time,* Fitzgerald's *The Great Gatsby,* and Dreiser's *An American Tragedy* published, but also Virginia writer Ellen Glasgow's hard-edged novel *Barren Ground.* At the other extreme, the Southern psyche received a new journalistic blow from the coverage by the national press of the famous Scopes "Monkey Trial" in Dayton, Tennessee. Fundamentalism battled against modern science (and won, locally) in a highly publicized legal action that pitted the flamboyant, liberal Chicago attorney Clarence Darrow against the aging Midwestern populist and fundamentalist William Jennings Bryan. The issue was whether to convict a young high-school science teacher who had presented the concept of evolution in his classes, though doing so was against state law. John Scopes had taught evolution in order to test the Tennessee law, but the journalistic focus during the circus-like atmosphere of the lengthy trial was the benighted South. Ironically, almost at the same moment the Scopes trial was drawing attention to hillbilly Tennessee, the young Faulkner, already a poet who imitated both the Edwardian A. E. Housman and the French Symbolists, was establishing himself in the rich culture of New Orleans, where the Midwestern modernist Sherwood Anderson encouraged him in the writing of fiction and thus helped to launch one of the most sophisticated literary careers in the South, America, or the world.

Though Tate continued to have difficulty accepting the importance of the movement he had helped to foster, Faulkner's preeminent position in it would not escape him. Near the end of World War II, when the first phase of the Renaissance was definitely over, Tate looked back once more on a region he had more or less permanently abandoned and remarked,

> The brilliant and unexpected renascence of Southern writing between the two world wars is perhaps not of the first importance in the literature of the modern world; yet for the first time the South had a literature of considerable maturity which was distinctive enough to call for a special criticism which it failed to get. The provincial ideas of the critics of the North and East (there was no Southern criticism: merely a few Southern critics)—the provincial [northeastern] views of Southern writing of the recent renascence, followed a direction somewhat as follows: The South, backward and illiberal, and controlled by white men who cherish a unique moral perversity, does not offer in itself a worthy subject to the novelist or the poet; it follows that the only acceptable literature that the South can produce must be a literature of social agitation, through which the need of reform may be publicized.

The literature being called for by such critics existed in the South, Tate noted, although those who wrote it had produced "not one distinguished novel . . . in or about the South. . . ." It was "the traditionalists whose work I believe will last," he claimed, naming "Stark Young, Elizabeth Madox Roberts, Katherine Anne Porter, Robert Penn Warren, Caroline Gordon, Ellen Glasgow (especially in *The Sheltered Life*), and William Faulkner, who is the most powerful and original novelist in the United States and one of the best in the modern world."[27]

In defining what he meant by traditionalist, Tate provided a key to what has characterized Faulkner's greatness and that of the best writing of the Southern Renaissance: "I do not mean a writer who either accepts or rejects the conventional picture of Southern life in the past," Tate wrote. "I mean the writer who takes the South as he knows it today or can find out about it in the past, and who sees it as a region with some special characteristics, but otherwise offering as an imaginative subject the plight of human beings as it has been and will doubtless continue to be, here and in other parts of the world."[28] In 1959, admitting that the Southern Renaissance had turned out to create "a literature which, I have been told often enough to authorize the presumption, is now the center of American literature," Tate wrote that the reason for this renaissance was that the Southern legend of "defeat and heroic frustration was taken over by a dozen or more first-rate writers and converted into a universal myth of the human condition." "The Southern fictional dialectic of our time," he explained,

> is still close to the traditional subject matter of the old informal rhetoric—the tall tale, the anecdote, the archetypal story . . . [and] is being resolved, as in the novels of William Faulkner, in action. The short answer to our question: How did this change come about? Is that the South not only reentered the world with the first World War; it looked round and saw for the first time since about 1830 that the Yankees were not to blame for everything. It looks like a simple discovery, and it was; that is why it was difficult to make. . . . W. B. Yeats's great epigram points to the nature of the shift from melodramatic rhetoric to the dialectic of tragedy: "Out of the quarrel with others we make rhetoric; out of the quarrel with ourselves, poetry."[29]

One hallmark of writing in the Southern Renaissance, Tate also might have observed, is that many of the writers—or their characters—were indeed fugitives from an imagined South in one way or another, from Quentin in *The Sound and the Fury* and Eugene Gant in *Look Homeward, Angel* to central figures in novels by Flannery O'Connor, Ralph Ellison, and William Styron in the era after World War II.

RICHMOND: Though Tate said that one of the South's problems in becoming a home to great literature was the absence of cities as a locus for literary coteries, apprenticeship, publication, and audience development, the South did of course have cities—some of them modest, sleepy state capitals where life slowed painfully during the long, hot summers in the days before air conditioning. But several of these cities, such as Nashville (home to Vanderbilt and the Fugitives), did provide an environment that fostered the literary renaissance of the 1920s and thereafter. First among these cities in time were Richmond, Virginia, and Charleston, South Carolina, where widely published writers and distinguished, if modest, literary magazines preceded the often-heralded phenomenon of the Fugi-

tives in Nashville. Virginia and South Carolina—which the less aristocratic North
Carolinians sometimes referred to as mountains of arrogance flanking the Tar Heel State's
valley of humility—are both closely associated
with Cavalier myths and plantation culture.
Richmond was of course the capital of the
Confederacy, and South Carolina was the state
in which military action against Fort Sumter
initiated the Civil War. But Richmond produced, long before the Nashville group gathered, a one-woman renaissance in Southern
writing in the person of Glasgow and a later
coterie of writers of high merit and interest, as
well as a regional literary magazine.

Ellen Glasgow in 1902

Glasgow's career as a careful, observant,
unsentimental, and philosophical writer began
at an early age. The brief entry on her life by
scholar Julius Raper in the admirable *Southern
Writers: A Biographical Dictionary* (1979) is a
cogent and hard-edged statement of her
achievement and background such as she might
have written herself. Glasgow was one of eight
surviving children of a well-to-do father who
was manager of the great Tredegar Iron works in Richmond, with Scotch
Presbyterian and Shenandoah Valley roots and a Tidewater mother. She
"received almost no formal education, but relatives and tutors taught her to
read and write," and by the time she was in her teens she had begun to
write novels. Her sister's fiancé "directed her attention to Charles Darwin
and to other thinkers who shaped her views of man and society," and her
"interest in critical realism hardened to pessimism" when a series of family
and personal tragedies affected her life. After two philosophical novels
about bohemian life in turn-of-the-century New York, Glasgow turned to
her own locale and began a series of tough-minded novels that constitute a
social history of Virginia, of which *The Voice of the People* (1900) was the
first.[30] In 1925, in the wake of another set of disastrous personal losses and
disappointments, Glasgow recovered her dedication to an art that univer-
salized the local scene with *Barren Ground*. When a New York critic
observed in a review that, in *Barren Ground*, at last realism had crossed the
Potomac, a reader of Glasgow's earlier work said that actually realism had
crossed the Potomac twenty-five years before, headed north.

ELLEN GLASGOW ON THE SOUTH

"After the Civil War, pursued by the dark furies of Reconstruction, the mind of the South was afflicted with a bitter nostalgia. From this homesickness for the past there flowered . . . a mournful literature of commemoration. . . . That benevolent hardness of heart so necessary to the creative artist dissolved— if it had ever existed—into the simple faith which makes novels even less successfully than it moves mountains. To defend the lost became the solitary purpose and the supreme obligation of the Southern novelist, while a living tradition decayed with the passage of years into a sentimental infirmity. Graceful, delicate, and tenderly reminiscent, the novels of this period possess that unusual merit, the virtue of quality. Yet charming as they are in manner, they lack creative passion and the courage to offend which is the essential note of great fiction. The emotions with which they deal are formal, trite, deficient in blood and irony and as untrue to experience as they are true to an attitude of evasive idealism. In the end this writing failed to survive because, though faithful to a moment in history, it was false to human behavior."

Ellen Glasgow

From "The Novel in the South," *Harper's Monthly*, 143 (December 1928); reprinted in *Defining Southern Literature: Perspectives and Assessments, 1831-1952*, edited by John E. Bassett (Madison & Teaneck, N.J.: Fairleigh Dickinson University Press / London: Associated University Presses, 1997), p. 298.

Glasgow's *The Sheltered Life* (1932), *Vein of Iron* (1935), and her autobiography *The Woman Within* (1954) are proof that she is as good as anyone who has ever written in and about the South and as culturally and philosophically informed. Her circle of literary friends in Richmond, which included Cabell and the poet Emily Clark, was also productive, but they were not as revealing about Southern culture as was Glasgow. From 1921 to 1925 Clark and others published a little magazine of their own, *The Reviewer*. The editors felt no obligation to restrict the magazine to the work of Southern authors, but they did offer opportunity to writers such as Frances Newman of Atlanta, Julia Peterkin and DuBose Heyward of South Carolina, and Paul Green of North Carolina. Thus, not only did such Richmond writers as Glasgow and Cabell precede the Vanderbilt group into literary fame of their own, their literary magazine predated *The Fugitive* by a year.

CHARLESTON, SOUTH CAROLINA: South Carolina's literary renaissance took an even more indigenous form than the one in Nashville, possibly because the state—especially the region around Charleston—had a rich and visible African American culture. Peterkin, who knew low-country plantation life from experiencing it on her large farm, wrote stories and novels about the lives of African Americans in the Gullah-speaking plantation communities of coastal South Carolina. Unlike Faulkner, who later concentrated on the fierce and complicated dynamics of relationships between the races, Peterkin examined the inner dynamics of local black culture. In *Green Thursday* (1924) she attempted to accomplish with objectivity and in accord with the language and beliefs of black culture something of what Anderson had accomplished in *Winesburg, Ohio* (1919). Anderson's novel is a cycle of sketches that give psychological depth and human dignity to ordinary people in a small Midwestern town. Peterkin's *Black April* (1927) and *Scarlet Sister Mary* (1928) make her a pioneer in white Southern writers' attempts to acknowledge and meditate upon the stereotyped life of ethnic cultures set apart by the South's written and unwritten racial codes. Her contemporary and friend Heyward grappled with urban aspects of the same coastal African American culture in the novel *Porgy* (1925), aiming specifically to write a folk novel expressive of a subculture near the Charleston wharfs. His story was adapted as a successful play in 1927 and as the landmark jazz opera composed by George and Ira Gershwin, *Porgy and Bess* (1935). Heyward had been provoked, it is said, by Mencken's "Sahara of the Bozart" to propose a South Carolina Poetry Society in 1920, and he edited its yearbook, the equivalent of a "little" magazine, for four years. Heyward's other writing did not have the success of *Porgy*, but the work he did, like that of Peterkin, created a tradition of writing that inspired others to attempt folk novels and plays and pushed people of intelligence and sensitivity to pay more attention to the humanity of the sometimes officially "invisible" black cultures of the South.

NORTH CAROLINA: A self-conscious—and thus in a sense false—folk art had spread to North Carolina, as well. It showed up in Chapel Hill, no city at all but a vibrant university village like many in the South. The Southern—and indeed the American—college town is often said to have originated as the antithesis to the city. Colleges were placed away from cities because of the Protestant fear that cities were harbors of temptation, not centers of culture. Intellectually, at least, however, even Southern college and university towns grew sufficiently large, diverse, and free in their ideas to offer a reasonable substitute for those things associated with life in great cities: an intellectual and artistic leisure class, a substantial library, venues for publication, forums for debate, and impressionable youth hungry for experiences different from what they had at home. Even in conservative university communities a diversity of points of view existed, and new ideas came in on a regular basis from scholarship and reading. Such new entertainments as those offered by experimental "little" theaters came early to college towns, and in the South especially, college parties were venues for the new music of the 1920s, jazz.

Chapel Hill was a stimulating environment for the young Thomas Wolfe, for example, who responded not only to courses in modern philosophy but also to the instruction of Frederick Koch, a Midwesterner who came to the University of North Carolina to teach theater and founded the Carolina Playmakers as an educational "little" theater. Koch appreciated regionalism, and he taught the importance of writing regional literature for the stage. Wolfe turned Koch's instruction to other ends, though studies in drama did send the gangly and energetic Asheville native to Harvard to study in a theater workshop and on to the alluring metropolis, New York, where he found his voice as a novelist. Paul Green, another native North Carolinian, produced Pulitzer Prize-winning work—as had Peterkin—from observations of African American life. His folk play *In Abraham's Bosom* (1924) was produced in 1926 and won the Pulitzer Prize in drama in 1927. Green's play outspokenly depicted the tragedy of racial discrimination in the South, and he went on to adapt to American idioms the concept of an outdoor, public theater—a modern revival of what Greek drama had been—though the movement turned into something less than what he hoped for: bland, tourist-oriented spectacles at historical sites. Like Peterkin and Heyward, however, Green inspired other Southern writers to tackle the harsher subjects within their culture and made way for performance roles and writing opportunities by African Americans in theater.

ATLANTA: Similar examples of a renaissance during the 1920s in other Southern cities are, by and large, forgotten, consigned to footnotes because the writers involved did not achieve lasting fame or become nationally and internationally known. Atlanta, for example, had many writers besides Margaret Mitchell. Among them was Frances Newman, a librarian who wrote tough-minded modern books with intriguing titles: *Hard-Boiled Virgin* (1926) and *Dead Lovers are Faithful Lovers* (1928). Like the Richmond of Glasgow, however, Atlanta had its own one-woman renaissance, in this instance the result of a single book by a young debutante newspaperwoman known to friends as Peggy Mitchell. *Gone with the Wind* appears to have been read internationally more than any American novel ever written, and it was adapted as a movie that—far more than the novel—boosted the Southern legend and still attracts hordes of viewers.[31] During the period identified with the rise of the Southern Renaissance writers, Georgia also had Corra Harris, whose *A Circuit Rider's Wife* (1910) belonged to a tradition of realism similar to that employed by Glasgow, and Harry Stilwell Edwards of Macon. Edwards was a white writer of black-dialect stories whose masterwork, *Eneas Africanus* (1919), inspired a section of Faulkner's *A Fable* (1954) and ranks with the better-known dialect stories of Roark Bradford, a Tennessee newspaperman who achieved fame with similar material while writing in New Orleans.

By the end of the 1920s Georgia writers had duplicated interest in the subjects and concerns of Southern writers elsewhere, including what the 1940 WPA guide to Georgia's towns and countryside called the "drabness in dignity" of mountain folk in novels by John Fort, Tarleton Fisewood, and Evelyn Hanna that "lay the mantle of sympathy over people almost savagely near to the earth."[32] Caroline Miller, whose *Lamb in His Bosom* (1933) was then recently republished, won the Pulitzer Prize in fiction in 1934, three years before Mitchell won it for *Gone with the Wind*. Erskine Caldwell, who like Mitchell served an apprenticeship working on *The Atlanta Journal*, was writing about Georgia "crackers"— poor rural whites—as early as 1926 and achieved lasting fame with *Tobacco Road* (1932) and *God's Little Acre* (1933).

NEW ORLEANS: If Atlanta has been overshadowed by Mitchell, its place in the origins of the Southern Renaissance has been overshadowed by New Orleans, which, like Richmond and Charleston, had a coterie of writers and an important magazine of its own, though its local writers did not achieve the same success or enduring attention as the so-called Fugitives. As in Richmond, New Orleans writers launched a "little" magazine before the group at Vanderbilt did. *The Double Dealer* was founded in 1921 by a group not too different from the Fugitives, though many of those involved with the magazine worked, like the Atlanta writers Mitchell, Newman, and Caldwell, at newspapers instead of a university. As in Nashville, stimulus and support came from intellectuals in the Jewish community, college faculty, and students, in this case from Tulane University. The title of the New Orleans journal came from the English Restoration-era dramatist William Congreve's comedy *The Double Dealer* (1693), and the first issue stated that its appeal was to "that select audience for whom romance and irony lie not so many leagues apart." *The Double Dealer* would, its editors announced, concern itself with "this human nature, the raw stuff, cleared of the myths of glamor-throwers and Utopia-weavers, casting off the spell of 'all the drowsy syrups of the world,'" and conceived its ideal reader as one who "can agree with Schopenhauer that when man was made, the Creator did not use both hands; scoff with Voltaire at the idea of this best of all possible worlds; touch hands with Mark Twain in his aphorism as to a sense of humor being man's only adequate weapon."[33] The invocation of irony and modern pessimism, along with the rejection of syrupy myths, is in perfect accord with the editorial credo with which *The Fugitive* in Nashville was launched one year later. New Orleans, however, in the heart of old plantation country at the tropical edge of the Deep South, was far different from provincial Nashville. A seaport city and river town, it supported a thriving demimonde into which a genuinely bohemian crowd of artists fitted comfortably. The city, its French Quarter, and *The Double Dealer* had the distinction of attracting the attention and support of one of the most famous modernist writers in America, Anderson, who had moved to the city because, in his view, it was the best place in America for the artist's life.

To young people who came to New Orleans to attend Tulane, to work on one of the city's three newspapers, or, like Faulkner in 1925, to seek greater immersion in the newest forms of the arts, the cosmopolitan culture of the French Quarter differed considerably not only from the small-town South of their childhoods but also from other cities of the South. The old-world charm of the narrow streets, the galleried architecture, and the inhabitants' penchant for leisure made it, in Anderson's view, exactly the kind of place an artist required, a place where the joy of living predominated over the "stupid joy of growth and achievement" and becoming rich. He wondered in print "why it isn't the winter home of every sensitive artist in America, who can earn money to get here."[34] If one were looking for an antithesis to the factory system, New Orleans was undoubtedly the better choice than the family plantation.

The French Quarter centered on the handsome St. Louis Cathedral and Jackson Square, where idlers could talk and observe the rich passing scene nourished by a varied population and the shipping activities on the Mississippi riverfront. The old buildings, the rich but faded history, the mysterious courtyards and gardens, and the looseness of a seaport reflected not only the exotica of international commerce but also the romance of steamboat life on the Mississippi that Faulkner, for example, had singled out in an early essay as one of the two richest funds of dramatic materials for American writing.[35] This colorful setting supported a varied bohemian life. As Anderson wrote in 1922, "the crowds have a more leisurely stride, the negro life issues a perpetual challenge to the artists, sailors from many lands come up from the water's edge and idle on the street corners, in the evening soft voices, speaking strange tongues, come drifting up to you out of the street."[36] The food was good and inexpensive, drink was plentiful even after the enactment of Prohibition, and both sex and art were not merely condoned but granted a certain linked necessity (as the developing musical genre of jazz emphasized). This linkage of sex and art was compatible with the increasingly popular psychoanalytical theories of Sigmund Freud.

The working writers and artists of New Orleans were, like Faulkner when he came among them, mostly in their late twenties, a few just a bit older. Some made a living on newspapers while simultaneously pursuing other literary and artistic interests. Some taught, had family money, or were students. Several had genuine talent and ambition and pursued real, not vicarious, lives in the arts. More than a few of them achieved fame.[37] Of the city newspapers on which some of

Photograph by Walker Evans of a house in the French Quarter of
New Orleans, 1935

Faulkner's new friends worked, one had a fine Sunday book section run
by a poet who also was a founding member of the editorial board for
The Double Dealer, John McClure. Like the Fugitives in Nashville, the
New Orleans literati included both homespun talent and exotic patrons
and benefited from a nearby private university. Like the Fugitives, they
responded concretely to Mencken's satire of the South as a cultural
wasteland, voicing their own displeasure with the "magnolia school" of
writing. "The Old Southern pot-boiler must go out—the lynching bee,
Little Eva, Kentucky Colonel, beautiful Quadroon stuff—a surer, saner
more virile, less sentimental literature must come in," the editors of *The
Double Dealer* declared in the issue of April 1924, shortly before
Faulkner made his first visit to the city.[38]

If New Orleans had helped only one writer of the Southern
Renaissance, Faulkner, to find his vocation, doubtless the city would be
important to the subject, but at this time Anderson's circle also included
Bradford, who achieved great fame when the playwright Marc Connelly

adapted his *Ol' Man Adam an' His Chillun* (1928) into the stage piece *Green Pastures* (1930), a landmark drama of black culture like Gershwin's adaptation of Heyward's *Porgy*. Louisiana writers such as Lyle Saxon, author of *Father Mississippi* (1927) and other nonfiction that recalled the traditions of his childhood, and Hamilton Basso, who wrote successful fiction that challenged aspects of Southern political ideology, developed significant careers not only through their books but also through national magazine journalism, a medium in which they occasionally helped other writers of the Southern Renaissance. Oliver La Farge was a Harvard graduate who wrote fiction based on his investigations of the archaeological record of Mexico, Guatemala, and the American Southwest. One of his novels, *Laughing Boy* (1929), won a Pulitzer Prize. The artist and architecture teacher William Spratling, with whom Faulkner roomed and traveled to Europe, eventually left New Orleans for Mexico, where he became a national hero for spurring the restoration of the country's craft tradition in silver.

Given the variety of intellect and genius represented in the literary coteries of New Orleans in the 1920s and thereafter, and the energy of even those artists who did not enter the stream of history, both the city and *The Double Dealer* were an important source of influence, ideas, and hope for new writers throughout the South. In addition to local writers, *The Double Dealer* published Warren, Davidson, and Tate during its short life, as well as Faulkner and Hemingway. As with *The Fugitive*, the discontinuation of the magazine in 1926 by no means meant the end of literary activity or stimulus in what some locals like to call "the city that time forgot."[39]

MISSISSIPPI: Faulkner belongs, of course, not to New Orleans but to Oxford, Mississippi, the university town in the north of the state where he was raised, as were both of his parents. From Oxford, in Lafayette County, and from surrounding counties, his knowledge of the north-central hills region of Mississippi is demonstrated in a body of work unequaled by any Southern writer. Faulkner's literary career began in his hometown; this was doubtless possible because Oxford, like Nashville and Chapel Hill, was a university town. He explored life in New Orleans and spent a few months in Europe but returned to Oxford more or less permanently. There, despite mostly unwanted but financially necessary trips to Hollywood for screenwriting jobs, Faulkner made his literary life and wrote most of his greatest works about the South. To repeat the judgment of Tate, Faulkner became, in the view of other Southern writers, "the most powerful and original novelist in the United States and one of the best in the modern world," or, as Welty put it, "poetically, the most accurate man alive."[40]

Without Faulkner's commanding achievement, it is likely that Oxford would be known mainly for what has happened at the University of Mississippi over the years, such as the tragic events following the forced admission of James Meredith, the university's first African American student, in the fall of 1962, when riots and shooting broke out that required imposition of martial law on the beautiful old campus. But in the 1920s, like the University of North Carolina, Vanderbilt, and Tulane, the "Ole Miss" campus was as likely a place as any in the South to stimulate at least a small number of students, faculty, and townspeople to become figures in a literary revolution.

Ole Miss had already watched one native son, Stark Young, begin to achieve literary fame in New York as a poet, dramatist, drama critic, and novelist. He had lived in Oxford and attended the university, and it must have excited the young Faulkner to see a local person's name in the prestigious magazines that came to the university's library and its professors. Young, though now a confirmed New Yorker, contributed to a volume of essays on agrarianism instigated by those Fugitives who sought to promote an alternative to either capitalism or communism, *I'll Take My Stand*. In Greenville, in the Mississippi Delta, there was a small-town renaissance under the sympathetic inspiration of William Alexander Percy, a lawyer, planter, poet, and man of the world who was open to the excitement of changing times. Greenville was also the home of David Cohn, who wrote a reminiscence of the Mississippi Delta, *God Shakes Creation* (1935). Percy encouraged the liberal journalist Hodding Carter and stimulated a second generation of Southern writers that included novelist and historian Shelby Foote and fiction writers Ellen Douglas and Walker Percy, one of three young cousins whom Percy raised in his Greenville home after the death of the boys' parents. Ben Wasson of Greenville, whom William Alexander Percy also befriended, went to the University of Mississippi and became Faulkner's

Contents page from the first issue of the influential New Orleans literary magazine friend there. Wasson later worked in New York and Hollywood as a literary agent.

Like that of Young, William Alexander Percy's poetry was out of step with the new American verse. But the work of both men appeared with some regularity in national and regional magazines while Faulkner was developing his own poetic ambition. As an amateur man of letters, Percy concluded his career with an influential Southern memoir, *Lanterns on the Levee* (1941), and for years he kept a literary salon to which regional and national writers came, enriching his literary neighbors' lives in ways similar to what happened in university towns such as Nashville and Oxford.

Though not much of a student and most frequently a hanger-on at the university campus, Faulkner nonetheless developed important friendships with faculty members, just as Warren and Tate did with Vanderbilt's faculty. Ole Miss was a small, provincial university, but its entire focus was on the liberal arts and training for the law; it had faculty who had studied abroad or at great American universities. When for three years Faulkner worked as manager of the university's fourth-class post office, he was trapped into long days on the campus, but he relieved his displeasure by reading patrons' magazines and doubtless also books from the library, which was close by. This reading certainly brought a whiff of international modernism to him before he ever left Oxford to explore the world for himself. An earlier force in Faulkner's modernist education was his continuing friendship with the young Yale-educated lawyer Phil Stone of Oxford. In the mid 1920s Stone ordered books and little magazines for Faulkner to read. Faulkner also participated with like-minded university students in the formation of a drama club, The Marionettes. In 1920 he wrote a modern dream play for them with the club name as title, illustrating six handmade copies in the decadent style of the English artist Aubrey Beardsley. Though no noteworthy literary magazine was started at Ole Miss, Faulkner's frequent contributions to student publications were unique in that collegiate environment: reviews of unusual books, drawings in the style of decadence as well as of the Jazz Age, and poems imitating the French Symbolists. Faulkner had the youthful pleasure of outraging many of his contemporaries, who hooted at his poetry and gave him the epithet "Count No 'Count" for his aristocratic manner, his poses, and costumes (including an unearned Royal Air Force flight lieutenant's uniform, formal evening wear on ordinary days, and British tweeds), and his obscure verse. But his like-minded coterie of literary friends at Ole Miss was as adventurous in some respects as the Fugitives in Nashville.

THE LEGACY OF THE SOUTHERN RENAISSANCE

If almost none of Faulkner's college friends reached the heights attained by four or five of the Nashville Fugitives, one should not be surprised. Art, like nature, is wasteful; and for all the seeds of interest or early talent that spring up in youth, only a few mature, and it is the rare person who produces something majestic and enduring. Throughout the South young people interested in the arts made attempts in various media; some succeeded briefly though they did not have sustained careers. *The American Guide: The South, The Southwest* lists the "important" writers of the Southern "renascence" by state; among the names cited are several never heard of anymore. In all, and counting a few historians and journalists among the crowd, *The American Guide* lists thirty-five Southern writers of the Renaissance, with Faulkner and Wolfe at the top of the list. Tennessee has five listed; Virginia, Georgia, Mississippi, and Louisiana have four each; North Carolina, South Carolina, and Kentucky have three; Florida and Alabama have two; and Arkansas has only one, John Gould Fletcher, a somewhat limited poet who, like Young, is represented in the Agrarian manifesto *I'll Take My Stand*. *The American Guide* includes in its list a few writers who had more recently achieved prominence: Katherine Anne Porter (Texas and Louisiana could claim her); Warren (the Kentuckian who was a member of the Fugitive group in Tennessee); Welty of Mississippi; Carson McCullers, the child prodigy of Georgia; Lillian Smith, also of Georgia, an outspoken and courageous writer on race in Southern society; and Truman Capote, another prodigy who is now claimed by both Alabama and Louisiana.

Such lists are instructive. Jay B. Hubbell, who wrote the first attempt at a real history of Southern literature, *The South in American Lit-*

THE SOUTHERN RENAISSANCE AND THE TRAGIC SENSE

"I am particularly interested in the continuity—or lack of continuity—between certain attitudes, assumptions, and even values that informed southern literature during its first great flowering, the Southern Renascence of the 1920s, 1930s, 1940s, and, we might add, 1950s. During the years of the Renascence it was assumed—and accepted by all, friend and foe—that the South was the defeated, failed, poor, unprogressive part of the United States. But an irony of southern literary history, to go along with all the other southern ironies, is that this legacy of defeat and failure served well the writer in the South. Like Quentin Compson at Harvard, the southern writer wore his heritage of failure and defeat—and often guilt—as his badge of honor. It provided him or her something that no other American writer, or at least American novelist, of the twentieth century had in any abundance—that is, a tragic sense. The Southerner alone among Americans, as C. Vann Woodward has pointed out, had known defeat, had known what it was not to succeed, not to prosper."

Fred Hobson

From *The Southern Writer in the Postmodern World,* Mercer University Lamar Memorial Lectures, no. 33 (Athens: University of Georgia Press, 1991), pp. 1-2.

A reunion of the Fugitives held in 1956: first row, Allen Tate, John Crowe Ransom, Donald Davidson; second row, Alfred Starr, Alec Stevenson, Robert Penn Warren; third row, William Yandell Elliott, Merrill Moore, Jesse Wills, Sidney M. Hirsch

erature (1954), later wrote a book in which he researched the lists of best-sellers, prize winners, and anthologized writers in order to answer the question posed by his title, *Who Are the Major American Writers?* (1972). The results of his research revealed the uncertainty of reputation. Books and authors sometimes rise and fall on popularity lists like questionable offerings on the stock exchange. Some disappear from literary histories, never to reappear.

A measure of how many writers from the first wave of the Southern Renaissance have sustained or regained their reputations may be formed from consulting recent annual lists of scholarship on Southern literature published by *Mississippi Quarterly: The Journal of Southern Culture*. One recent list accounts for thirty-two authors of the 1919–1941 era who have received scholarly or critical attention. In terms of the quantity of published scholarship and criticism, Faulkner is hands down the most frequently written about. Whereas Wolfe was ranked as the second most important Southern writer in the *American Guide* list of 1949, Ellen Glasgow and Tennessee Williams now rank second in terms of published scholarship, according to the *Mississippi Quarterly* bibliography.

In 1984 Lewis Lawson of the University of Maryland counted up the next generation of Southern Renaissance authors in *Another Generation: Southern Fiction Since World War II*. The book concludes with a list of Southern writers who published novels between 1940 and 1983. There are more than 450 names on Lawson's list,[41] and in the years since the book was published scores of new Southern fiction writers have published their work. As for Southern poets, there may be as many, but no one has made an exact count. If one considers Southern dramatists who have worked regionally as well as nationally, more names would be added to the list of writers who have inherited the traditions of the first phase of the Southern Renaissance and strongly identify with the South as a place where literature now seems to challenge King Cotton.

Though the Vanderbilt critic and novelist Walter Sullivan once wrote a "requiem" for the Southern Renaissance, he has since recanted.[42] Much in the South remains unsung and unused for serious fiction and drama. Though the Southern Renaissance of 1919–1941 is gone, recoverable only in the solid monuments left by the writers of the period, the shock waves and ripples from it continue to disturb the waters where new poets, novelists, dramatists, and essayists drink to the degree that they distort comfortable self-images. Thus, the opportunity to carry on is always there. As Flannery O'Connor once said, anyone who has survived childhood is unlikely to run out of material to write about.

NOTES

1. Hershel Brickell, "The Literary Awakening in the South," *The Bookman,* 76 (October 1927); reprinted in *Defining Southern Literature: Perspectives and Assessments, 1831–1952,* edited by John E. Bassett (Madison & Teaneck, N.J.: Fairleigh Dickinson University Press / London: Associated University Presses, 1997), p. 292. Brickell's essay includes many references to H. L. Mencken's 1917 attack on Southern culture, "The Sahara of the Bozart."

2. Howard Mumford Jones, "Is There a Southern Renaissance?" *Virginia Quarterly Review,* 6 (April 1930); reprinted in *Defining Southern Literature,* p. 307.

3. Ibid., p. 308.

4. Ibid., p. 315.

5. Allen Tate, "The New Provincialism" (1945), in his *Essays of Four Decades* (Chicago: Swallow Press, 1968), p. 543; italics added.

6. Henry G. Alsberg and others, eds., *The American Guide: The South, The Southwest* (New York: Hastings House, 1949), p. 729.

7. Louis D. Rubin Jr. and Robert D. Jacobs, eds., *Southern Renascence: The Literature of the Modern South* (Baltimore: Johns Hopkins University Press, 1953).

8. F. O. Matthiessen, *American Renaissance: Art and Expression in the Age of Emerson and Whitman* (New York: Oxford University Press, 1941); Dale Kramer, *Chicago Renaissance: The Literary Life in the Midwest, 1900–1930* (New York: Appleton-Century, 1966); and Nathan I. Huggins, *Harlem Renaissance* (New York: Oxford University Press, 1971).

9. William Faulkner, *Requiem for a Nun* (New York: Random House, 1951), p. 92.

10. Charles Reagan Wilson and others, eds., *Encyclopedia of Southern Culture* (Chapel Hill: University of North Carolina Press, 1989), p. xv.

11. Eudora Welty, preface to *One Time, One Place: Mississippi in the Depression, a Snapshot Album,* revised edition (Jackson: University Press of Mississippi, 1996), pp. 3–5.

12. Federal Writers' Project of the Works Progress Administration, *Arkansas: A Guide to the State* (New York: Hastings House, 1941), p. 257.

13. Federal Writers' Project of the Works Progress Administration, *Mississippi: A Guide to the Magnolia State* (New York: Viking, 1938), pp. 446–447.

14. Faulkner, *Absalom, Absalom!: The Corrected Text* (New York: Vintage, 1990), p. 5.

15. M. Thomas Inge, "Southern Literary Renaissance," in *Encyclopedia of Southern Culture,* p. 841.

16. Ibid.

17. C. Vann Woodward, *The Burden of Southern History* (Baton Rouge: Louisiana State University Press, 1960), pp. 15–25.

18. A survey of resources for investigating revisionist accounts of Reconstruction is found in the text and especially the notes to Edward L. Ayers's *The Promise of the New South: Life After Reconstruction* (New York & Oxford: Oxford University Press, 1992).

19. George B. Tindall, "The Mythic South," in *Encyclopedia of Southern Culture,* p. 1098.

20. Fred Hobson, "Mencken's South," in *Encyclopedia of Southern Culture,* p. 1136. See also Hobson's *Serpent in Eden: H. L. Mencken and the South* (Chapel Hill: University of North Carolina Press, 1974).

21. H. L. Mencken, quoted in Hobson, *Serpent in Eden: H. L. Mencken and the South,* p. 21.

22. Ibid., p. 23.

23. Foreword to *The Fugitive,* 1, no. 1 (1922), p. 1.

24. Tate, "The Profession of Letters in the South," in *Essays of Four Decades,* pp. 530, 531.

25. Ibid., p. 531.

26. Ibid., p. 533.

27. Tate, "The New Provincialism," pp. 543, 544, 545.

28. Ibid., p. 545.

29. Tate, "A Southern Mode of the Imagination," in *Essays of Four Decades,* p. 592.

30. Robert Bain, Joseph M. Flora, and Rubin, eds., *Southern Writers: A Biographical Dictionary* (Baton Rouge: Louisiana State University Press, 1979), p. 181.

31. Mitchell's novel, for example, wiped Faulkner off the charts the year it was published, although he had expressed high hopes for his own complex 1936 epic about the

period of slavery and the Civil War, *Absalom, Absalom!* Specific references to Mitchell's novel or the movie adaptation are curiously absent from Faulkner's published correspondence. Interestingly, Mitchell, working as a journalist a decade earlier, had reviewed Faulkner's first novel with great appreciation and was, perhaps, the first reviewer of *Soldiers' Pay* (1926). See Erik Bledsoe, "Margaret Mitchell's Review of *Soldiers' Pay*," *Mississippi Quarterly*, 49 (Summer 1996): 591–594; the review is reprinted in *Margaret Mitchell, Reporter: Journalism by the Author of Gone with the Wind*, edited by Patrick Allen (Athens, Ga.: Hill Street Press, 2000), pp. 325–326.

32. Federal Writers' Project of the Works Progress Administration, *Georgia: The WPA Guide to its Towns and Countryside*, introduction and appendix by Phinizy Spalding (Columbia: University of South Carolina Press, 1990), pp. 121–122.

33. "The Double Dealer," *Double Dealer*, 1 (January 1921): 2–3.

34. Sherwood Anderson, "New Orleans, The Double Dealer, and the Modern Movement in America," *Double Dealer*, 3 (March 1922): 125.

35. The other source of dramatic material for American writing was railroading. Faulkner's "American Drama: Inhibitions" was first published in the University of Mississippi student newspaper, *The Mississippian* (17 and 24 March 1922) and republished in *William Faulkner: Early Prose and Poetry*, edited by Carvel Collins (Boston: Little, Brown, 1962), pp. 93–97.

36. Anderson, "New Orleans, The Double Dealer, and the Modern Movement in America," p. 126.

37. See W. Kenneth Holditch, "The Brooding Air of the Past," in *Literary New Orleans*, edited by Richard S. Kennedy (Baton Rouge: Louisiana State University Press, 1992).

38. "Southern Letters," *Double Dealer*, 6 (April 1924): 84–85.

39. In addition to *Literary New Orleans*, another collection, *Literary New Orleans in the Modern World*, edited by Kennedy (Baton Rouge: Louisiana State University Press, 1998), features essays that touch upon the Southern Renaissance, including one on Anderson and one on *The Double Dealer*. The book also has essays on Hamilton Basso, Zora Neale Hurston, and the playwright Lillian Hellman.

40. Welty (unsigned essay), "Place and Time: The Southern Writer's Inheritance," *Times Literary Supplement*, 17 September 1954, p. xlviii.

41. Lewis Lawson, *Another Generation: Southern Fiction Since World War II* (Jackson: University Press of Mississippi, 1984), pp. 145–151.

42. Walter Sullivan, *Requiem for the Renaissance*, Mercer University Lamar Memorial Lectures, no. 18 (Athens: University of Georgia Press, 1976).

REPRESENTATIVE WRITERS

INTRODUCTION

Each Southern state was (and in many respects still is) a unique historical and cultural realm, despite some common experiences. Even subregions of these states are so distinct as to produce a unique literary response and a distinct individual writer or a cadre of literary-minded people. Although the renaissance of the literary arts that began after World War I drew attention to itself in several different states, a limited number of specific places and people were involved, and not every Southern state actually produced a truly representative writer of the Southern Renaissance.

An exhaustive list of Southerners who wrote seriously in the period under discussion, 1919–1941, would contain scores of names, for during this period each of the former slave states was home to many serious and initially well-received writers—including journalists and historians as well as writers of fiction, poetry, or drama. In retrospect, all states have had the tendency to claim famous writers who were born within their borders but grew up and wrote elsewhere, as well as writers who were born elsewhere and came to live and write in a particular state. But the test of time and more than a half century of interpretation by scholars, literary historians, and even creative writers have lifted a few groups or individuals to consideration as the most representative figures of the Southern Renaissance.

Readers looking for more exhaustive lists of each state's writers should consult the appendix to John M. Bradbury's *Renaissance in the South: A Critical History of the Literature, 1920–1960* (1963), in which writers are listed by state affiliation; the arts and letters sections of the WPA guides to the Southern states; and the narrative accounts of Southern writing, state by state, in David James Harkness's *Literary Profiles of the Southern States* (1953). Lewis A. Lawson's *Another Generation: Southern Fiction Since World War II* includes an appendix that lists, without state affiliations, some four hundred Southern writers who have pub-

James Branch Cabell with Julia Peterkin

lished novels since 1940. Biographical accounts of the careers of Southern writers can be found in the *Dictionary of Literary Biography*, as well as
in such useful regional reference books as *Southern Writers: A Biographical Dictionary* and the *Encyclopedia of Southern Culture*.

The following brief biographies are organized by the chronology
of state movements in the arts that are now acknowledged as flashpoints
in the development of the Southern Renaissance.

RICHMOND

James Branch Cabell (1879–1958). By virtue of being a little
older, Cabell preceded most of the now well-known writers of the Southern Renaissance of 1919–1941. He also preceded them as an odd early
modernist and a rebel against convention. He poked critically into the
vanities of the Southern aristocracy, explored myth and the occult as
sources of importance for fiction, and preceded William Faulkner by a
decade in shocking middle-class defenders of literary decorum.

Like many of the young Southern gentry, whether of so-called
aristocratic heritage or merely middle class, Cabell was trained in youth

as a classicist, and like many bookish young Southerners after him, he worked for a time in the newspaper business. While still young, his other pursuits included working in a coal mine in West Virginia and setting himself up as a professional genealogist for heritage-obsessed Virginians. All of these striking experiences helped Cabell in his later career as a writer of fiction, for he used both classical references and the common characters and depicted both the proletarian and the aristocratic in his most characteristic works.

After marrying a young widow with five children when he was in his mid thirties, Cabell worked at various occupations, as well as at the vocation of writing. In 1919, already the author of more than a dozen books, he surprised himself by publishing one that became both famous and notorious, *Jurgen*. His publisher was prosecuted for violating the obscenity laws of the state of New York, but the book fell into the hands of a new generation of readers who received it warmly. Ironically, the book was cleared of obscenity charges in 1922, the year James Joyce's *Ulysses* was published. Cabell, however, had by this time become a symbol of the courageous and persecuted American artist, the anti-Puritan. He was even championed by that high-spirited critic of the "booboisie," H. L. Mencken. In the 1920 republication of "The Sahara of the Bozart," Cabell is the only writer whom Mencken mentions as an exception to the South's cultural wasteland.

Cabell's imagination ran not to the realistic but to the fantastic, and his bent was for spiritual autobiography, often masked beneath a cloak of the mythic and mock-ancient. He grappled with Southern subjects and with the story of his own life, which was itself a Southern subject, but most often he wrote in terms of a truly imaginary world, the medieval kingdom of Poictesme, where he set *Jurgen* and other books. It is a realm nothing like the realistically portrayed, though mythical, Mississippi county of Yoknapatawpha that Faulkner later wrote about. Still, many young Southerners of the interwar generation came of age reading *Jurgen*. Faulkner read it and even mildly imitated it in *Mayday* (1926), a handmade allegorical book about a "knyghte" often betrayed by women. In his first novel, *Soldiers' Pay*, the title character of *Jurgen* is cited. Faulkner's chief biographer suggests that when the Mississippi writer read one of Cabell's earlier novels, *The Rivet in Grandfather's Neck* (1915), he would have identified with the artist-hero because of his own spotted family history.[1]

Ellen Glasgow (1873–1945). Like Cabell, Glasgow represented not only a slightly older generation but also was highly productive as a writer before 1920. She worked in the traditions of realism and philosophical fiction but also in that of the novel of manners. Self-educated in a time when Southern girls largely depended on tutors, relatives, and family libraries if they were to develop their intellects at all, Glasgow achieved a remarkable career that she managed with both aesthetic and financial wisdom. Despite personal setbacks on many levels and increasing deafness, about which she was self-conscious, she wrote steadily and with ever increasing artistry. All along, Glasgow used ideas from her reading in the works of such influential thinkers as the evolutionist Charles Darwin, the nineteenth-century German philosophers Arthur Schopenhauer and Friedrich Nietzsche, and the modern French philosopher Henri Bergson, whose reflections on time and memory are mirrored brilliantly in a section of her 1932 novel *The Sheltered Life* titled "The Deep Past." Like her friend and fellow Richmond writer Cabell, Glasgow fused her deep knowledge of local families, local history, and local peculiarities with the radical perspectives of modernist thought. She never shied away from a subject as too daring, even though she never flouted convention as sharply as writers such as Cabell and Faulkner. In fact, Glasgow did not approve of Faulkner's work when it began to achieve notoriety, believing, erroneously, that the Mississippi writer was exploiting violence for the sake of sensation and monetary reward. Her negative opinion was not improved when Faulkner, who had been drinking heavily, passed out more or less at her feet during a festival of Southern writers in Charlottesville, Virginia, in 1931.

The Voice of the People (1900) was Glasgow's first novel to make use of the Virginia settings she knew so well, though it was not her first novel. Thereafter, she composed many different novels that constitute a

ELLEN GLASGOW ON SOUTHERN LITERARY STYLE

"[It] is well to remind ourselves that, if the art of the South is to be independent, not derivative, if it is to be adequate, compact, original, it must absorb heat and light from the central radiance of its own nature. The old South, genial, objective, and a little ridiculous—as the fashions of the past are always a little ridiculous in the present—has vanished from the world of fact to reappear in the permanent realm of fable. This much we have already conceded. What we are in danger of forgetting is that few possessions are more precious than a fable that can no longer be compared with a fact. The race that inherits a heroic legend must have accumulated an inexhaustible resource of joy, beauty, love, laughter, and tragic passion. To discard this rich inheritance in the pursuit of a standard utilitarian style is, for the Southern novelist, pure folly. Never should it be overlooked that the artist in the South will attain his full stature, not by conforming to the accepted American pattern, but by preserving his individual distinction. . . ."

Ellen Glasgow

From "The Novel in the South," *Harper's Monthly,* 143 (December 1928); reprinted in *Defining Southern Literature: Perspectives and Assessments, 1831–1952,* edited by John E. Bassett (Madison & Teaneck, N.J.: Fairleigh Dickinson University Press / London: Associated University Presses, 1997), p. 299.

social history of her place and time but also offer much more. Some of them satirize upper-class Virginia society, as her contemporary Edith Wharton satirized society in New York, but all of them are tough-minded and realistic studies of poignant events stirred up and resolved by the specifically local social situations Glasgow portrayed. *Barren Ground, The Sheltered Life,* and *Vein of Iron* have expressive titles that announce core elements in her fictional universe. These novels are among Glasgow's most successful and now most often discussed works, though modern critics would agree that one cannot discount any of her fiction as "minor" writing.

Glasgow was friend and champion to many writers of the rising generation of the Southern Renaissance and kept up a lively correspondence with many of them. To Allen Tate, who was one of the Fugitives at Vanderbilt University, she wrote in March of 1933:

> Only yesterday I was asking if the time had not come when the South might begin to do its own thinking. Perhaps at last we may abandon the attitude of defense and apology, and refuse to borrow our standards from the Middle West. What I have always resented, with a kind of smothered indignation, is the way we have continued to regard the South as a lost province, to be governed, in a literary sense at least, by superior powers.

The following month, as Tate's magazine venture, *The America Review,* was being planned, Glasgow wrote him,

> I agree with your assertion, "An artist vindicates his tradition not by arguing for it, but by assuming it, and that assumption permits him to take all the world, even when he sees it in terms of a single country, as his province." This expresses, without altering a syllable, what has been my faith from the beginning. I believe, too, that literature must be free to feed in strange pastures, and must remain alive to the world even when it draws inspiration from dying and death.[2]

One of Glasgow's biographers has pointed out that she is most usefully compared with the great European and English realists of the late nineteenth century—Thomas Hardy and George Eliot, for example—but also sits well with such Southerners as Faulkner, Robert Penn Warren, and Eudora Welty, whom she influenced.[3]

NASHVILLE

John Crowe Ransom (1888–1974). Born in Pulaski, Tennessee, Ransom was the child of a Methodist minister who had served in California, Cuba, and Brazil, but the future poet grew up in middle Tennessee, near Nashville, where his father also served. After tutoring at home and some schooling in a private academy similar to the ones many provincial Southerners attended for a classical education, Ransom entered

Vanderbilt in Nashville when he was only fifteen. After two years he withdrew to teach in small towns in Mississippi and Tennessee, earning enough money to finish his studies at Vanderbilt. He graduated in 1909, winning a Rhodes Scholarship to Christ College of Oxford University, where he earned a degree in 1913. Ransom joined the faculty of Vanderbilt in the fall of 1914, left temporarily to serve with the American forces in World War I, and remained an influential professor at the university until he moved to Kenyon College in Ohio in the fall of 1937.

Ransom, along with fellow Vanderbilt professor Donald Davidson, a few other faculty members and townspeople of intellect and imagination, and several remarkable undergraduates (including Tate and Warren), founded *The Fugitive,* a modest literary magazine that was published from 1922 to 1925. Ransom published much of his poetry in the magazine. His biographer, Thomas Daniel Young, has written that his poetry "made *The Fugitive* one of the most important magazines of verse published in modern America," but the regular appearance of the little journal "also aided materially in the development of the literary careers of Allen Tate, Donald Davidson, and Robert Penn Warren," assisting each of the younger poets in finding either a poetic voice or the kind of poetry he wanted to write.[4] Ransom winnowed his poetry over the years, so his *Selected Poems* (1945; revised, 1963, 1969) is a truly modest selection of the poems by which he felt he could stand as he devoted more time to editing and criticism later in life.

John Crowe Ransom

Ransom wrote a book about the decline of religious feeling, *God Without Thunder* (1930), and in the same year he participated as a central contributor to a book of essays by associates and like-minded Southern intellectuals, *I'll Take My Stand.* The book has been called an "Agrarian Manifesto"—in contradistinction to Karl Marx and Friedrich Engels's *Communist Manifesto* (1848)—but it is not a systematic treatise. On the cover is the announcement that the book is "By TWELVE SOUTHERNERS." The contributors—some of whom had been involved with *The Fugitive* and subsequently were referred to as both "Fugitives" and

"Agrarians"—sought by various reflections to offer an alternative to modern industrial materialism, a form of economy that Ransom and his associates saw as no better under the American system than under the Soviet Union's experiment with loosely Marxist practice. *I'll Take My Stand* did not produce a revolution or even launch a program of political activism. Its authors had too many other things to do and learn. Ransom finally came to understand that agrarianism could not restore human innocence, nor, in a scientific world, create for most people the leisure time that allowed for poetry, philosophy, or spiritual thought. In particular, he realized that agrarianism certainly had no answers for the farmer's wife, whose existence was barren, confining, and burdensome.[5]

Ransom's gift for teaching and for commenting on creative work, demonstrated in his book *The New Criticism* (1941), set in motion a revolution in the teaching of literature in America. The teaching of literature was dominated through the first half of the twentieth century by an historical approach characterized by Mencken as the practice of "learned and diligent but essentially ignorant and unimaginative men" who preached that "it is scandalous for an artist—say a dramatist or a novelist—to depict vice as attractive" because it "is not his business to depict the world as it is, but as it ought to be."[6] One popular teaching anthology published during this era, for example, was *Literature and Life* (1922–1924), and the meaning of the title was clear: literature was important only as it reflected "life," not in and for itself. Ransom advocated close reading and aesthetic judgments based on the effectiveness of the language and structure of the literary work, not on the author's life and possible motives. Like Warren and Cleanth Brooks, editors with *The Southern Review* from 1935 to 1942, and Tate, an editor at *The Sewanee Review* from 1944 to 1946, Ransom edited a literary magazine that became justly renowned under his New Critical supervision; his editorship of *The Kenyon Review* ran from 1939 to 1959.

Because Ransom focused on the text of a literary work and was an acute and inspired reader who understood something of the creative process, one of his greatest achievements was as a teacher. By virtue of his ability in that vocation he literally gave a host of fine writers to his region, his country, and the world. Ransom changed the lives of students who took his classes. Later, either because they had studied with him or because they knew his reputation, more than a few students followed him from Vanderbilt just to sit at his feet at Kenyon College—including the poets Robert Lowell and Randall Jarrell and a promising writer of fiction, Peter Taylor. Ransom, like his colleague Davidson, made writers of his students without teaching what is now called creative writing. His passion for communicating the feeling, meaning, and craft of difficult poetry inspired others to learn for themselves how they might accomplish similar feats of writing in their own ways, not only in poetry but also in fiction.

Donald Davidson (1893–1968). Davidson was a Tennessee native whose family was of modest means; his father was a schoolteacher and music teacher. Davidson received a rigorous early education in classics and writing and entered Vanderbilt at age sixteen. Like his father before him (and like Ransom), he dropped out for a while to earn tuition by teaching in small-town schools. Upon finishing his undergraduate degree he joined the army and fought overseas in World War I. Davidson's description of a training incident as he prepared for infantry duty overseas offers special insight into the mixed sensibilities of his generation of Southerners:

HOW AGRARIAN WERE THE AGRARIANS?

"[T]he Agrarians derived from a remarkably uniform background of established, though modest, social advantage. While they did not live so far from the realities of farm life as Thomas Wolfe would suggest, they did experience them vicariously. For example, John Crowe Ransom's claim to agricultural expertise rested partially on the fact that he 'had a garden.'"

Michael Grimwood

From *Heart in Conflict: Faulkner's Struggles with Vocation* (Athens: University of Georgia Press, 1987), p. 153.

> One summer evening in 1917 when I was among the trainees . . . at Fort Oglethorpe, Georgia, the fifteen training companies were marched into a grove to hear a guest speaker. He was Federal General John T. Wilder, who had commanded a unit of mounted infantry in Rosecrans' Army of the Tennessee and had waged deadly war against our Confederate forebears . . . on the very field of Chickamauga where we were then encamped. With great pride the old General . . . dwelt long and, it seemed to me, with vicious exultation upon the fact that his mounted infantry were armed with Sharp's repeating rifles, and therefore did bloody execution upon the Johnny Rebs opposite him, who had only single-shooters. It did not seem to matter to General Wilder that the young men before him were descendants of the Confederate soldiers whom he had so gleefully slaughtered in 1863. . . . It was, you might say, a peculiarly awkward moment in American military history. Frigid silence prevailed when the General took his seat . . . but we were of course under military discipline. In fact, we had joined the Federal army.[7]

More than any other member of the Nashville group, Davidson remained bitter about what he saw, in Northern criticism of Southern culture, politics, and daily life, as a "cold Civil War" to rival the Cold War between the Western powers and the Soviet Union.

As a poet, Davidson early fell into the trap he later identified in his 1957 Lamar Lecture at Mercer University, resisting modernist verse by writing imitations of late-nineteenth-century lyrics, just as Faulkner did during the same period on the campus of the University of Mississippi (their poems even have similar titles and an equal profusion of water- and tree-nymphs). Faulkner eventually broke out into fiction that magnified his own experience and surroundings; Davidson broke out of his weak imitations into narrative poems in blank verse that exploited his own experience, blending "his personal past with his region," in *The Tall Men* (1925).[8]

Like Ransom, Davidson was a demanding but highly effective teacher of literature who, without practicing the creative-writing teaching method popular today, turned bright but unsuspecting students into creative writers. His continued influence at Vanderbilt helped sustain for quite a long time some of the excitement and creativity that had characterized the early 1920s, when the likes of Warren, Tate, Brooks, and many others were transformed from bright, small-town Southerners into men of letters in the modern world.

Allen Tate (1899–1979). Like his friend and fellow Vanderbilt graduate Warren, Tate was born in Kentucky, but his two older brothers had also attended Vanderbilt, and Tennessee claims him by virtue of his lifelong association with the Fugitives and his frequent returns to Tennessee for reunions and lectures. He also held a post in the 1940s at the University of the South near Chattanooga, where he edited *The Sewanee Review,* and retired to the state a decade before his death. Like Warren, but to a greater extent, Tate built a career as a professional man of letters that was national and international in scope. It was obvious from the first to Ransom, his English teacher at Vanderbilt, that Tate was already familiar with literary traditions and styles that he himself did not know.[9] Ransom and Tate maintained a lifelong correspondence that expressed their differences as poets and critics, but there was mostly pleasure in their passionate exchanges of ideas. In the process each writer honed, without abandoning altogether, his own perspectives.

As a professional writer of reviews, biographies (*Stonewall Jackson, The Good Soldier,* 1928; and *Jefferson Davis, His Rise and Fall,* 1929), and brilliant essays, and as guest lecturer at many different educational institutions, Tate rarely settled in one place for long, but his career as a writer maintained a consistency even as his intellectual, theoretical, and ethical interests developed. In an early essay about the "renascence" in the South that journalists were beginning to perceive, he lamented that it would doubtless be short-lived because the region had no intellectual, artistic, or publishing centers that could foster and support a specifically "Southern" literature.[10] Yet, like many other Southerners, Tate did in fact have a literary career, much of it in cities or university towns of the Northeast and even abroad, without ever abandoning his roots, memories, and feel for fading things in the South or losing his ability to write fine poetry about such things. Doubtless for Tate, and for others from the Nashville group, the possibility of keeping a foot in Southern experience was helped by their continued close relationships. Among these friends was Davidson, who obdurately remained a kind of rebel and lived his career in the South; the others came home frequently from their positions elsewhere. All of them, Tate included, were observers of the South as well, looking for new talents that came along and praising them when praise was merited.

Tate's best-known, if not his best, poem is "Ode to the Confederate Dead," which he composed in 1925–1926, after *The Fugitive* was shut down so that the editors and writers could work on other projects. As Young explains, "Although the poem carries the word 'Ode' in its title, it is not an ode—a kind of poem which in the Greek poet Pindar's time was composed to celebrate an important state occasion," and "Tate informed Davidson that he really wrote the poem to demonstrate that the form was inaccessible to the modern poet" because modernist fragmentary chaos had supplanted the program of faith that characterized traditional myth-based or religious societies.[11] Tate was not, of course, the only American writer to feel the breach in tradition, as the South was not the only region in which young people had a similar experience, under the pall of materialism, acquisition, and regimented work. One of his responses was to convert to Catholicism; another was to continue to write philosophical poems charting his spiritual movement, such as "Seasons of the Soul" (1944).

Tate published one novel, *The Fathers* (1938), which is still highly regarded by many who teach and study Southern literature, many volumes of poems, and many essays collected into several volumes, including the final *Essays of Four Decades* (1968). His correspondence with his literary friends, including Davidson, Ransom, and Warren, is invariably a glimpse into minds engaged eloquently with the literary, the historical, the philosophical, and the personal.

Robert Penn Warren (1905–1989). The term *man of letters* is now considered outmoded on several grounds, but, gender aside, the concept identified gifted public intellectuals. A man of letters might write biography, fiction, poetry, critical essays and reviews, memoirs, and cultural history, while also lecturing widely, editing journals devoted to literature and ideas, teaching at a variety of colleges and universities, and carrying on a lively correspondence and debate with those who possessed similar interests. Though other writers may have surpassed his achievement in an individual writing genre, Warren was perhaps the most accomplished man of letters the South produced during the Southern Renaissance.

Warren was born in the upper-South town of Guthrie, Kentucky, and educated in public schools. In the fall of 1921 he entered Vanderbilt, where he planned to study science, but the influence of two of his English professors, Davidson and Ransom, helped him to refine his talent as a writer. By the time of his graduation from Vanderbilt in 1925, Warren was listed on the masthead of *The Fugitive*. Though a member of the magazine staff and later a contributor to the Agrarian manifesto *I'll Take My Stand*, he was rarely in total agreement with his fellow Southerners or, for that matter, with the poetic critiques the Fugitives engaged in.

After earning a master's degree in English from the University of California and studying at Oxford on a Rhodes Scholarship, Warren began the writing career that brought him Pulitzer Prizes in both fiction and poetry and a commanding place in the history not just of Southern but of American letters. He taught English at Southwestern University (now Rhodes College) in Memphis, at Vanderbilt, and at Louisiana State University in Baton Rouge during the Huey Long era in Louisiana politics. At Louisiana State, Warren was reunited with another brilliant Vanderbilt graduate and fellow Rhodes Scholar, Brooks, with whom he edited *The Southern Review*, which they made into an influential literary quarterly.

Warren's first book was a biography, *John Brown: The Making of a Martyr* (1929). His fiction began to appear soon thereafter, and his first volume of poetry, *Thirty-Six Poems*, was published in 1935. Warren and Brooks coedited several influential literary textbooks, beginning with *Understanding Poetry* (1938) and *Understanding Fiction* (1943), which substituted close reading of poems and stories for the historicist approaches to "literature and life" then current in America. Eventually they taught together at Yale, though in different departments, sustaining one of the many lifelong friendships Warren developed with the literary friends of Vanderbilt days. His first novel, *Night Rider* (1939), concerns the so-called tobacco wars in Kentucky at the turn of the century when manufacturers of tobacco products attempted to gain monopolistic control over crop prices.

Though described early on, as well as later, by all of his brilliant associates as the most promising mind among them, Warren went through many periods of doubt, perhaps because he frequently questioned himself, his culture, even his art, a habit that allowed him to achieve the high place he holds in American letters. *All the King's Men* (1946) remains his most highly regarded novel, a book that takes on changing values in the Deep South through juxtaposing the "redneck" politician as derived from Long; the modern, alienated intellectual's search for meaning in the appropriately named character Jack Burden; and the Southern past as Faulkner might have conceived it in the background story of Cass Mastern, a nineteenth-century planter.

Throughout his long life, Warren sustained a phenomenal creative energy and a lively interest in ideas and the literary arts. His essays on American writers in a variety of ambitious textbooks and anthologies of criticism remain useful guides to their subjects. On Faulkner, especially, he wrote detailed and elegant criticism, including landmark essays that appeared when almost no other American critic was pointing out Faulkner's morality, his humor, or his mastery of the novel form. At the height of his own career, Warren eloquently

Robert Penn Warren while a student at Vanderbilt University

recalled the ways in which Faulkner's writing—even the "images of degradation and violence" that offended the pride of so many ordinary Southerners— had given him and other Southern writers "the thrill of seeing how a life that you yourself observed and were part of might move into the dimension of art" and "the thrill of discovering your own relation to time and place, to life as you were destined to live it."[12] Warren's receptivity to Faulkner's writing is cognate with his expressions of social concern in such books as *Segregation: The Inner Conflict in the South* (1956) and *Who Speaks for the Negro?* (1965).

Despite his success in many genres, Warren believed that his poetry would be his chief monument, and modern commentators appear to agree. His highly developed gifts in the use of language, his prodigious memory of place and feeling, his willingness to explore the moral ambiguities of human experience, and his expressive use of narrative make his poetry both readable and powerfully affecting.

Individual poems in his many collections and such poetic sequences as *Brother to Dragons* (1953), *Audubon: A Vision* (1969), and *Chief Joseph of the Nez Perce* (1983) have earned Warren a reputation as one of the most highly regarded and influential poets of the second half of the twentieth century.

Andrew Lytle (1902–1995). Andrew Lytle came to Vanderbilt in Nashville from nearby Murphreesboro in central Tennessee, where his parents on both sides were descendants of prominent farmers who had settled the area before the Revolutionary War. He was privately educated and studied a year in France before he entered Vanderbilt, studying there with Warren, Tate, Brooks, and other students who benefited from the instruction, manuscript evaluation, and literary interests of Ransom and Davidson. Lytle's friendships with these men were lifelong, but at that time his literary interests focused on drama and the stage; thus, like Thomas Wolfe, he sought out George Pierce Baker's playwriting workshop at Harvard and then made an attempt at an acting career in New York.

Like Tate, Warren, and Brooks, Lytle fashioned a peripatetic academic career, teaching history and editing *The Sewanee Review* at the University of the South for a year during World War II and then holding longer appointments at the University of Iowa and the University of Florida. He returned to the University of the South in 1961, where he edited *The Sewanee Review* for a dozen more years with great distinction. Like some of his friends with whom he had collaborated on *I'll Take My Stand,* Lytle began his career in narrative with a Civil War–related biography, *Bedford Forrest and His Critter Company* (1931). Two of his four novels, *The Long Night* (1936) and *The Velvet Horn* (1957), are still highly regarded, as are a book of essays, *The Hero with the Private Parts* (1966), a chronicle of his family titled *A Wake for the Living* (1975), and short stories such as "Jericho, Jericho" (1936).

Lytle is given credit for being the only one of the "Agrarians" who was actually a farmer, but like the rest of the authors who contributed to *I'll Take My Stand,* he was a modernist intellectual whose backwoods bravado was the deliberately poetic yawp of a man who had studied popular playwriting at Harvard, tried a theater career in New York, edited a major American literary journal, and taught for years in American universities.

Caroline Gordon (1895–1981). Although a Kentuckian like Warren and Tate and never a Vanderbilt student, Gordon is associated with the Vanderbilt group because of her marriage in 1924 to Tate. Her literary career was, in fact, much like the careers of her husband and his friends. Gordon's father was a schoolmaster, and her mother's family descended from early settlers in Kentucky. Mostly at home, without receiving formal instruction until she was fourteen, Gordon received a classical education. She later went to a small college not far from home and, after graduation, taught school and worked as a journalist in Chattanooga. Warren, who introduced her to Tate, was from the same Kentucky county as Gordon and had attended her father's school in nearby Clarksville, Tennessee.

After their marriage Gordon and Tate lived for several years in New York as full participants in the new literary scene. They then moved to an old house in rural Tennessee—a period fictionalized in *The Strange Children* (1951)—where they lived a semblance of an agrarian life, though tenants struggled with the actual farming and literary friends from the East and Nashville visited them often. Later, Gordon, like Tate, held appointments at various academic institutions, including what was then called the Woman's College of the University of North Carolina (now the University of North Carolina at Greensboro), Emory University in Atlanta, and the University of Dallas. She and Tate were divorced in 1959.

Caroline Gordon in 1938

Gordon's teaching anthology, *The House of Fiction: An Anthology of the Short Story* (1950), coedited with Tate, and her *How to Read a Novel* (1957), like Brooks and Warren's *Understanding Fiction*, instructed a generation of students not only how to read fiction but also how to write it. Though she moved around during her marriage to Tate, much of her work was accomplished in the South, and the Kentucky of her youth was the setting for most of her excellent fiction. Gordon is highly regarded for her novels and short stories. She was also known as an exacting teacher of the craft of fiction who required students to read great stories closely, sentence by sentence, in order to explain what the authors were accomplishing.

Gordon's short-story-writing career is represented in *The Forest of the South* (1945), *Old Red* (1963), and *The Collected Stories of Caroline Gordon* (1981). Among her novels, *Aleck Maury, Sportsman* (1934), *None Shall Look Back* (1937), *The Women on the Porch* (1944), and *The Strange Children* continue to engage readers.

NORTH CAROLINA

Paul Green (1894–1981). Green won a Pulitzer Prize in 1927 for the 1924 "folk play" *In Abraham's Bosom*. The subject of the play is African American life, making Green one of several white writers in the South who had the vision to portray a culture both local and regional that others ignored, treated with condescension, or misperceived. He came to the subject in some degree through the influence of Frederick Koch, who taught drama and founded the Carolina Playmakers little-theater group at the University of North Carolina in Chapel Hill. Koch, a Midwesterner, urged his students to write out of their own regional experience and promoted the folk play as a logical outcome of paying attention to the language and folk life of small Southern places. Another of Koch's prize pupils, Wolfe, later said that a folk play was one in which some of the characters said "hit ain't." The most successful student play that Wolfe wrote under Koch's tutelage was derived from an incident recorded in North Dakota that he read in the newspaper.

Green, however, took the folk play as a medium seriously, even though the experiences he drew upon were not his own but those then buried beneath the prejudices of Southern culture. He infused his plays about African American life with his own liberal humanism, but he did not turn them into tracts. Eventually, Green also tried to create a broadly based American public theater, focusing on historical themes and performed in outdoor settings, seeking to emulate the rise of indigenous theater in ancient Greece and such examples of early outdoor drama as the Corpus Christi cycles of medieval Europe. As the editor of his letters points out, "Green's symphonic dramas"—as he preferred to call his outdoor theater—are experimental in technique, using music, dance, and special lighting effects, while also seeking to "dramatize themes central to their culture with the aim of revivifying communal beliefs."[13]

African American life was a subject Green returned to many times, always with sympathy and usually with the attempt to raise white consciousness about the pressures and social wrongs heaped upon this large portion of the South's population. He published a volume of short plays that he hoped would help to create an African American theater, *Lonesome Road: Six Plays for the Negro Theatre* (1926), and in Chapel Hill he worked with the black author Richard Wright—an unprecedented collaboration in the segregated South—on a stage adaptation of Wright's powerful novel of black life, *Native Son* (1940). This collaboration took place at a time when a Chapel Hill social scientist was arrested in Georgia for saying "Sir" to an African American man.[14]

Though Green is remembered less for his prose fiction, his collected stories fill four volumes and his essays, three. He remains a writer worth consideration by contemporary students, for he was the first Southern dramatist to attract national attention. Green anticipated even Faulkner with his 1926 drama *The House of Connelly*, which, according to Laurence G. Avery, "is among the early works of imaginative literature to forge the picture of the South later used in one version or another" by other Southern writers: "a South whose aristocrats go back in memory to a time when social power and enlightened values coincided in their families but who in the present lack the will or character to act and find themselves threatened with extinction."[15] Green's dream of a public theater inspired by American places and played to large outdoor audiences awaits realization in the hands of dramatists as serious-minded as the crusading author himself. As a presence in Chapel Hill, where he lived most of his life, he was a generous and liberal example to the many young writers who had the chance to meet him.

Thomas Wolfe (1900–1938). Wolfe wrote what is perhaps still the most compelling legend of Southern adolescence, the 1929 novel *Look Homeward, Angel*. The message of the book, in part, is that from the moment he could crawl, its hero, Eugene Gant, was crawling toward the door. The door reflects escape from the constraints that a large and eccentric family impose on the gangling young protagonist. For many readers in Wolfe's lifetime and afterward, the story of Eugene's escape holds up both as the archetype of adolescent rebellion from family and an allegory of the modernist Southerner's relationship to the South itself.

Wolfe was a titan—a large man with great appetites, great hunger for experience, and an incredible capacity for headlong invention in rhapsodic prose. It is said condescendingly that the best time to read Wolfe is when one is under the age of twenty, but in 1947, when Faulkner was fifty years old, he ranked Wolfe first among his contempo-

Thomas Wolfe in 1935

rary fellow novelists, because Wolfe had a daring vision for an encompassing fictional work. He had sustained the imagination and energy to believe that his whole world—not just the South but America—could be captured in one great multivolume work.

Born in Asheville, North Carolina, the setting of major portions of his most popular books, Wolfe became a student of the drama professor Frederick Koch at the University of North Carolina in Chapel Hill. Wolfe's studies were concentrated on classics and literature—the common curriculum for well-prepared young Southerners—but under "Prof Koch" he developed a passion for writing drama. As an undergraduate, Wolfe wrote and starred in "The Return of Buck Gavin," a folk play he had dashed off after reading a newspaper account of something that happened in North Dakota. The dramatic training he received in Chapel Hill sent him off to Harvard to George Pierce Baker's famous dramatic workshop. Baker aimed to make popular and financially successful playwrights out of his students, but Wolfe's gifts, unlike like those of Green, were not easily adapted to the rigors of play construction. He wrote plays that had too many characters and themes and ultimately found himself turning to fiction, which seemed to be his natural medium. Even in the genre of the novel Wolfe wrote superfluous lyrical passages. When asked by his editor, Maxwell Perkins, to remove some of them and write a short bridge between scenes, he sometimes returned even longer sections to replace what he had removed.

Wolfe called *Look Homeward, Angel* "a story of the buried life," a statement that speaks of the psychological and philosophical underpinnings of the novel. Whether he ever excavated or even fully accounted for that buried life is matter for debate. But even in a prosaic age he has become a legendary writer—bardic, larger than life, and tragic because of his early death, at the age of thirty-eight, from a tuberculosis infection that modern antibiotics could have halted. Because of editorial intervention in what became Wolfe's grandiose plan to capture all of American life in a single work of fiction, his large works published in his lifetime are nearly as problematical as those works assembled from the vast hoard of manuscripts left after his death. His reputation appears to have dwindled in American classrooms, in part because his clear-cut identity as the individual author in all his work is problematical. What Faulkner understood about Wolfe—his ambition to fashion a multivolume epic of American restlessness and variety—was thwarted by editors, such as Perkins and, later, Edward Aswell, who attempted to fashion more or less conventional novels from his writing and was conclusively stopped by his early death.

In 1936, escaping the tensions of a libel lawsuit against his fiction in New York, Wolfe stopped off in Richmond, Virginia, at a Modern Language Association convention—an annual gathering of college teachers of English and other modern literatures—and had a pleasant evening with members of the Nashville group, who were now all college professors: Ransom, Warren, Tate, and Brooks. Whether Wolfe met any of the Virginia literary luminaries is not recorded; from Richmond he went to New Orleans, meeting with the remnant of the old French Quarter crowd who had founded *The Double Dealer*.[16] Thus, though his search for America made him a kind of rootless wanderer based in New York, he connected with the major flashpoints of the first flowering of the Southern Renaissance.

SOUTH CAROLINA

DuBose Heyward (1885–1940). As Southern pedigrees go, Heyward's was good in a city—Charleston, South Carolina—where such things mattered a great deal. (One of his ancestors had signed the Declaration of Independence.) The early death of Heyward's father in an accident, however, had the result of turning him, financially, into a self-made man, and his résumé before he succeeded in the insurance and real-estate business reads a little like Cabell's: work in a hardware store and on the Charleston wharf checking cotton shipments constituted a large part of his early education. Later success nevertheless opened opportunities for Heyward to test his mettle in the arts. By 1924, when he retired from business just short of the age of forty, he was able to devote himself to writing full-time.

Heyward was one of those Southerners who responded directly to Mencken's description of the South as a cultural desert. In 1920 he proposed to several talented friends the organization of the Poetry Society of South Carolina in Charleston. Like the members of the Nashville group, who launched *The Fugitive* after critiquing one another's poetry, those in Heyward's group, which included several already published writers, discussed their writing together. They published their own work and that of others in the *Year Book of the Poetry Society of South Carolina,* which Heyward himself edited for the first four years.

Heyward published several volumes of unremarkable poetry and then had remarkable success when he turned to fiction, writing novels of the trials and triumphs of the African Americans who built lives and cultures in the old port city of Charleston. His most notable success was the 1925 novel *Porgy,* which he dramatized in 1927 with the collaboration of his wife, Dorothy, an experienced playwright whom he had met at a writers' colony. The white writer Heyward's depiction of African American life coincided with similar works by other white Southerners published at about the same time. These works included New Orleans newspaperman Roark Bradford's black dialect stories collected as *Ol' Man Adam an' His Chillun,* Green's *Lonesome Road: Six Plays for the Negro Theater* and *In Abraham's Bosom,* and fellow South Carolinian Julia Peterkin's *Black April* and *Scarlet Sister Mary.*[17] Heyward's *Mamba's Daughters* (1929), written with his wife, was another novel exploring urban African American life in Charleston. His continued reputation rests, however, on the further adaptation of *Porgy* as an American jazz opera, the 1935 hit *Porgy and Bess,* with music by George Gershwin and lyrics by Ira Gershwin and Heyward.

Heyward's poems about the South Carolina low country do not have the bite of what the best of the Fugitives accomplished in verse written about their backcountry heritage, nor does his fiction have the tragic meditations on racsim and its consequences found in Faulkner. Still, he opened a window into the black experience that remains of interest.

Julia Peterkin (1880–1961). Born to wealth and social position in the old plantation country not far from Charleston, Peterkin published her first book about African American life, *Green Thursday,* in 1924. At her best, as her biographer declares, she brought to her perennial subject "Chekovian detachment, her gift for capturing character in a few words of dialogue, her deadpan humor, her spare lyrical prose." Peterkin achieved a fame that in just a few years brought her stories about the "dangerous and difficult" lives of blacks to national prominence, including the high praise, early on, of Mencken, who saw her as a bright exception to the "Sahara of the Bozart" he had perceived in the Deep South.[18] *Green Thursday* was welcomed in the literary magazine of the Richmond branch of the Southern Renaissance, *The Reviewer,* and it was reviewed with admiration by Davidson, who called it "the first genuine novel in English of the Negro as a human being."[19]

Peterkin teamed with a noted female photographer, Doris Ulmann, for *Roll, Jordan, Roll* (1933), a book of Deep South photographs for which

Peterkin wrote the text. Sentimentalized like many Depression-era photography books, it represented, as one study of the era argues, an "ecstatic preindustrial vision," especially in Ulmann's celebratory approach to African American farmworkers, soft-focus portraits of a hardworking people. This project anticipated Georgia writer Erskine Caldwell's and photographer Margaret Bourke-White's more "radically inclined"[20] book on farm conditions in the South, *You Have Seen Their Faces* (1937); Tennessee writer James Agee's and photographer Walker Evans's portraits in words and pictures of Alabama sharecroppers, *Let Us Now Praise Famous Men* (1941); and Wright's collaboration with photographer Edwin Rosskam, *12 Million Black Voices: A Folk History of the Negro in the United States* (1941).[21]

Domestic worker in the South, photographed by Doris Ulmann for *Roll, Jordan, Roll* (1933); Peterkin wrote the text

For all that was revolutionary in her art—and in her life (she had an extended affair with a young Jewish intellectual and writer, Irving Fineman)—Peterkin, like Glasgow, could not see in Faulkner's writing a form of the same daring she herself first exhibited. Faulkner, she confessed to Georgia-born novelist and screenwriter Laurence Stallings, gave her the "creeps," and she considered his novels—which included *The Sound and the Fury* and *As I Lay Dying* (1930) at the time of her comments—"degenerate." Stallings correctly predicted that Faulkner would "eclipse" Peterkin's own fame.[22] Nonetheless, her biographer and others have argued, she deserves a much higher reputation than the one she has, and a study of her career provides valuable insight into those of her contemporaries, men and women, famous and obscure, in the prime of the Southern Renaissance.

GEORGIA

Jean Toomer (1894–1967). Grandson of a Georgian who had served as a lieutenant governor of Louisiana during Reconstruction, Toomer was raised in Washington, D.C., in his grandfather's house. His heritage was African American, but in appearance he could have "passed" in those days of racial absolutes. Modern commentators on Toomer's life have suggested that the uncertainty of his racial identity affected many aspects of his development, but his unwillingness to stick to any of the paths of opportunity available to him appears, in a different light, to have been a common trait of many bright young people who came of age during the extreme cultural changes that followed World War I. His poses, his dabbling in various academic fields at several colleges without taking a degree, his somewhat uncertain literary interests—all of this is not greatly different from the early career of Faulkner, except, of course, for the trump card of race that made Toomer's life more problematic in a racially divided culture.

Like some of the Fugitives, Toomer tried teaching in a small school, but for him, teaching was a more revolutionary experiment. He went to Sparta, Georgia, a town described in the WPA guide to the state as located in an area "so remote from the main thoroughfares and railroad centers that it has retained much of its old-fashioned atmosphere" of large farms "worked by sharecroppers among whom Negroes predominate."[23] Toomer's interest in rural African American life stirred a sense of heritage, and his identity as an "outsider" was not the same, obviously, as that of such white contemporaries as Bradford, Green, Peterkin, Faulkner, and the Midwesterner Sherwood Anderson, all of whom attempted with varying degrees of engagement and success to depict cultures similar to the one that Toomer entered and wrote about himself. At about the same time that Faulkner was making an unsuccessful assault on life in New York, Toomer spent three months in Sparta in 1921. Afterward, he wrote *Cane* (1923), an experimental "novel" similar to Anderson's *Winesburg, Ohio*. *Cane* is composed of narrative episodes—in effect, modern, lyrical short stories—alternating with poems, the whole held in suspension by a common narrative voice and the repetition and variation of themes. The book touches on racial themes, but also—in keeping with the thematic obsessions of much writing in the 1920s, from the Fugitives' poetry to Faulkner's fiction—Freud's themes of sex and death, the Lost Generation's themes of alienation and disillusionment, and the Southerner's themes of disappearing community and flight to the city. Toomer's book is a kind of triptych, presenting the life of rural African Americans, the life of African Americans displaced to Washington, D.C., and the life of a man like himself who is unable to participate fully in the vitality of his country cousins.

For reasons that are unclear, Toomer was a one-book author, though after *Cane* he published a few occasional pieces in magazines and privately published a play and a collection of personal philosophical writings. Among his papers at Fisk University in Nashville are several unpublished works in different genres that he left after a lifetime of writing. *Cane* has enjoyed a successful revival and is taught frequently in school and university courses, where it blends in interesting ways with such works as Anderson's *Winesburg, Ohio* and *Dark Laughter* (1925), Ernest Hemingway's *In Our Time* (1925), John Dos Passos's *USA* trilogy (1930, 1932, 1936), Zora Neale Hurston's *Their Eyes Were Watching God* and *Mules and Men* (1935), and Faulkner's *Go Down, Moses*.

Caroline Miller (1903–1987). Caroline Miller is one of many writers of the Southern Renaissance who rose out of obscurity with a surprising achievement in one book and then, for one reason or another, became forgotten. Born in Waycross, Georgia, in a farming and timber region not far from Savannah, Miller was married and raising children when, in her spare time from housekeeping, she wrote a novel that touchingly but realistically chronicled life in rural Georgia from the Revolutionary War period to the mid nineteenth century. Published in 1933, *Lamb in His Bosom* won the Pulitzer Prize in fiction in 1934 and became a critical and financial success. Though Miller continued to write for popular magazines and published a second novel, *Lebanon* (1944), *Lamb in His Bosom* remained her only real success. It was republished by a Georgia publisher in 1993.

"MORE THAN 'JUST' A LITERARY MOVEMENT"

"[T]he Southern Renaissance was more than 'just' a literary movement. It was certainly that, but it also represented an outpouring of history, sociology, political analysis, autobiography, and innovative forms of journalism. W. J. Cash, James Agee, Lillian Smith, Howard Odum, and William Alexander Percy were as central to the Southern Renaissance as William Faulkner, Robert Penn Warren, Allen Tate, and John Crowe Ransom. To be specific, [C. Vann] Woodward's biography of the Georgia Populist leader Tom Watson, which appeared in 1938, deserved the kind of attention which Warren's novel about a Huey Long-like figure, *All the King's Men* (1946), attracted. This is not to say that *Tom Watson* and *All the King's Men* are the same kind of book. They are, however, embedded in the same historical context and informed by a 'structure of feeling and experience' . . . common to the writers and intellectuals of the Renaissance."

Richard King

From *A Southern Renaissance: The Cultural Awakening of the American South 1930-1955* (New York & Oxford: Oxford University Press, 1980), p. 5.

Frances Newman (1883–1928). Newman, like Miller, is a writer whose reputation has vanished, but in Newman's case it was her early death that cut short a promising career. Born in Atlanta of well-to-do parents, she began a career in librarianship, wrote book reviews for the Atlanta newspapers, and turned to fiction with short stories and then novels. Her two novels had striking titles, especially for a socially well-placed Southern woman writer of the 1920s in the mildly progressive Georgia capital. *The Hard-Boiled Virgin,* published in 1926, and *Dead Lovers Are Faithful Lovers,* published in 1928, proved in both title and content that the "new" woman of the 1920s had found a place in the genteel South.

Erskine Caldwell (1903–1987). Set against the careers of his fellow Georgians Miller and Newman, Caldwell perhaps demonstrates the greater latitude that male writers of the Southern Renaissance era were afforded by the values and conventions of the day. A preacher's son born in a small community not far from Atlanta, Caldwell exploited some of the more lurid aspects of rural life and sexuality in a long and checkered life as wanderer and professional writer. Some of his subject matter and point of view may give the impression that he was himself of the poor white class he so often portrayed, but he was in effect middle class and had some college education. While he tried to get his writing career off the ground, he worked at middle-class jobs, including a stint at the same Atlanta newspaper where Newman published reviews and Margaret Mitchell apprenticed as a reporter, and spent several years in Maine. Later, like Faulkner and some lesser Georgia writers (Stallings and Nunnally Johnson, for example) Caldwell wrote for the movie industry. He adopted proletarian politics, championed the rural poor, and acted as a correspondent in Eastern Europe and Mexico and in Spain during the Spanish Civil War.

Tobacco Road, published in 1932, and *God's Little Acre,* published the following year, created enough scandal and fame to fuel Caldwell's career for most of his life. Both novels had an incredible run as popular lurid paperbacks and inspired a host of imitations, including novels by Faulkner's brother John that were similarly marketed. The 1933 stage adaptation of *Tobacco Road* had a long run on Broadway. The quantity of Caldwell's writing never seemed to flag, allowing him to complete and publish more than fifty books in various genres. As she had with Faulkner, the tough realist Glasgow thought that Caldwell exploited extremes for sensation and popularity and that his portrayal of the monstrous in rural affairs was romantic excess.[24] Such a view, however, missed what the Southern critic Richard M. Weaver has observed in the best of Southern writing: that both the monstrous and the comic are allowed to coexist because in fact they rise up so often in human affairs.[25]

Caldwell had the itch to write, one of the scholars of his work has observed, rising—as did Tennessee Williams—each day to do a stint of work whether he felt like it or not, or even whether he had anything to say, but believing always that the act of writing was worth doing. In his most acute and honest work, Caldwell shows just how far to the edge of desperation that poverty, ignorance, and exploitation can drive a family. Often, and in a time when such a position was doubtless needed, he came to rural subjects with a reformer's agenda and zeal—as did several Southern writers now less well remembered, such as Grace Limpkin, also from Georgia. One study of the fictional presentation of poor Southern whites has pointed out a difference between Caldwell's and Faulkner's approach to the subject: "Faulkner's treatment of the southern poor white leaves no doubt that his sympathies were not with mass movements that based their reform ideology on a rational analysis of man's role in an economically determined society" but were an expression of his view that human folly, absurdity, avarice, and monstrousness could rise up in anyone, regardless of whether they were also to be pitied for being exploited. Faulkner, in this interpretation, ultimately seems more optimistic because he has hope for human community, whereas in Caldwell "the myth [of the land] is empty and destructive . . . the land itself is exhausted and barren," and "physical and moral depravity" have encroached on "spiritual integrity."[26]

Margaret Mitchell (1900–1949). Born the same year as Wolfe, Mitchell had a quite different life from the North Carolinian, accepting reluctantly some of the roles expected of young women of her class and time in her hometown, Atlanta, including a debutante's coming out and marriage to an appropriate partner at an appropriate age. The debut and the 1922 marriage did not take—she and her first husband were divorced in 1924—and in many respects, like Newman and the South Carolina novelist and poet Josephine Pinckney, Mitchell assumed the role of the new, independent woman of the 1920s. She worked for the same Atlanta newspaper where Caldwell worked later, and she began writing fiction. Like Wolfe, she was a great listener, reader, and taker of notes, and like him she created a mythic Southern experience, but her single book, the 1936 novel *Gone with the Wind,* was not about flight or the buried life. It was about nineteenth-century Georgia; the disappointments and fortitude of a headstrong young woman, Scarlett O'Hara; and the impact of the Civil War on the South portrayed in a way that Depression-era America could apparently embrace completely. Mitchell's novel has sold more copies all over the world than even the millions sold of all of Caldwell's books combined. Large in scale and readable, *Gone with the Wind* has a rich and fascinating cast of characters and a love story touched by disasters that made people forget the economic troubles of the 1930s. In 1939

A MYTHICAL ARISTOCRACY

"Ironically, New South thinkers coupled their commitment to modernization with a strong element of nostalgia in the form of an unyielding determination to preserve that vital centerpiece of Old South culture and regional identity, the Cavalier myth. Indeed, this mythology, with its vision of the South as the last remaining home of aristocracy in America, blended perfectly with the Victorian cult of gentility. Just as the rising businessman in England or the North felt the need to acquire the persona of the gentleman, New South promoters and entrepreneurs took upon themselves the mantle of the antebellum planter. In this fashion, they could justify to themselves and their society their acquisitive behavior and, at the same time, assert their identity as southerners."

Daniel J. Singal

From *William Faulkner: The Making of a Modernist* (Chapel Hill: University of North Carolina Press, 1997), p. 6.

it was adapted as one of the most compelling and successful motion pictures of all time. The spell cast by the book and the movie has yet to dissipate.

One interesting side effect of *Gone with the Wind* is that it blew out of contention a Civil War novel about a doomed plantation, a thwarted marriage, and a persistent Southern survivor that was published the same year, Faulkner's *Absalom, Absalom!* The enormous popularity of Mitchell's novel has thus often provoked a contrast with what is said to be greater moral and historical seriousness in the fiction of writers such as Faulkner. The critic Frederick Hoffman has written that "*Gone with the Wind* is . . . the simplest and most superficial of historical equations,"[27] and Weaver has wryly observed that the "tremendous impression which Miss Mitchell's Scarlett O'Hara made upon the Northern audience is owing to the fact that Scarlett is a type of ruthless entrepreneur which Northerners have met in their own life and can therefore understand and credit."[28] Many fine critics regard *Gone with the Wind* quite seriously, however, resisting the temptation to discount it on the basis of its popularity. In fact, some regard this popularity as a factor demanding close study of the novel and its effect when it was published. Contemporary novelist Doris Betts has observed that Scarlett's vaunted optimism is a tough posture that one continues to find in the best work of Southern women writers, "stoicism with its teeth in view."[29]

W. E. B. Du Bois (1868–1963). Though born in Massachusetts, Du Bois entered the "humiliation" of the Southern experience when he was twenty and came to Nashville to study at Fisk. Completing his graduate education in the North with a doctoral dissertation on the slave trade, he returned to the South in 1897, the year Faulkner was born, to teach history and sociology at Atlanta University. Du Bois's sojourn in the South bears comparison to Toomer's, though Du Bois stayed longer and had more impact on the region and its people. His *The Souls of Black*

Folks (1903) also bears comparison to Toomer's *Cane,* though it is not fiction but reflections in essay form on every aspect of African American life in the South, the topic that took most of Du Bois's attention during a long activist and educator's life in a racially divided country. Late in life he wrote a trilogy of novels reflecting his experience, *The Black Flame* (1957–1961), but he is best remembered for his philosophical and cultural opposition to the ideas of Alabama's Booker T. Washington regarding how African Americans should plot their course toward full economic, social, and political equality. Du Bois's teaching and research in the South were interrupted by a long stint as executive director of the National Association for the Advancement of Colored People (NAACP) in New York and editorship of the organization's journal *The Crisis* from 1910 to 1934 and from 1944 to 1948. In 1922 he was regarded as enough of an expert on Georgia to pinch hit for the Georgia planter-professor John Donald Wade in writing an essay about Georgia for *The Nation,* a liberal journal in New York that organized a series of impressions of all the forty-eight states, written primarily by well-known authors (Mencken, for example, wrote on Maryland, and Willa Cather wrote on Nebraska). Du Bois's essay, "Georgia: Invisible Empire State"—which a reader of the time might have expected to speak about the revival of the Ku Klux Klan, since it was known as the "invisible empire"—is lyrical and affectionate:

> Georgia is beautiful. High on the crests of the Great Smoky Mountains some Almighty Hand shook out this wide and silken shawl—shook it and swung it two hundred glistening miles from the Savannah to the Chattahoochee, four hundred miles from the Appalachians to the Southern sea. Red, white, and black is the soil and it rolls by six great rivers and ten wide cities and a thousand towns, thick-throated, straggling, low, busy, and sleepy. It is a land singularly full of lovely things: its vari-colored soil, its mighty oaks and pines, its cotton fields, its fruit, its hills.[30]

Du Bois addressed the "invisible empire" of planters and factory owners who conspired to keep poor whites and blacks in economic bondage by creating an atmosphere of antagonism and terror that distracted the whites and threatened the blacks. The chilling aspects of Georgia were the hypocrisy of its religion and the horrific contradiction that side by side "with that warm human quality called 'Southern' stands the grim fact that right here and beside you, laughing easily with you and shaking your hand cordially, are men who hunt men: who hunt and kill in packs, at odds of a hundred to one under cover of night." Yet, as he rode north in the Jim Crow car to which black travelers were then restricted, Du Bois, north of Atlanta in the Georgia hills, looked out the window at the "dead white faces and drawn, thin forms" of the "remnants of the poor whites" and realized that "here in the Jim Crow car and there in the mountain cabin lies the future of Georgia—in the intelligence and union of these laborers, white and black, on this soil wet with their blood and tears."[31]

Though, like Wright, Du Bois eventually abandoned America (he even renounced his citizenship in order to become an African, settling in Ghana), he came to believe by the 1940s that the hope of the African American—and of the South—did indeed lie in a return to a region that had need of the African American's ideas, labor, and dreams.

MISSISSIPPI

Stark Young (1881–1963) and **William Alexander Percy (1885–1942)**. Neither Young nor Percy is much read now, but each played a role in the prime years of the Southern Renaissance. They developed literary relationships with principal figures of their own generation, wrote typically Southern work considered important in their time, and affected Mississippi writers of subsequent generations. Young had some relationship with the career of Faulkner, and Percy not only raised a young cousin, Walker Percy, who became an important writer, but as the host of literary salons in the Mississippi Delta river town of Greenville, Percy inspired, influenced, and encouraged several writers.

It is instructive to see the reputation of Mississippi's literary lights at the height of the Southern Renaissance. The arts and letters section of the 1938 WPA guide to Mississippi linked Young, Faulkner, and Percy as the state's three major serious authors. Young and Faulkner were seen as "outstanding exponents of both the romantic and realistic schools of regional literature" who have "drawn accurate pictures of Southern life: one, the most charming; the other, the most revolting." Percy was regarded as untypical of Mississippi because his lyrical poetry appeared to reflect ancient rather than present realities, but a few poems were "as persuasive an interpretation of the Delta as any of Stark Young's pronouncements."[32] Such a judgment in effect predicted Percy's nostalgic 1941 memoir of his life in the Delta, *Lanterns on the Levee,* a best-seller.

Like many Southerners of their time and class, Young and Percy received classical schooling in their early years and excellent college training. Percy studied first at the University of the South and then at Harvard Law School. His inheritance of a large Delta plantation precluded his need to pursue assiduously the legal career for which he had studied, but he assumed many demanding local, regional, and national responsibilities during his active life. Percy served in World War I and nearly exhausted himself managing Delta relief work following the great

1927 Mississippi River flood. Young, who grew up in Oxford, Mississippi, as well as in the Delta, studied first at the University of Mississippi and did graduate work at Columbia University.

Both Young and Percy began writing and publishing poetry while in college. Perhaps because they started somewhat prior to the modernist revolution in poetry, neither wrote the kind of ironic poems that came from the Fugitives at Vanderbilt or experimental lyrics like those of the high modernists. Still, each found acceptance with major publishers and created a body of poetical works. In midlife Percy became a general man of letters as well as a sometimes reluctant man of action in state and national affairs. He also took over the upbringing of a first cousin's three young sons, including Walker. Their father had committed suicide, and their mother died soon thereafter in an automobile accident.

Early in his life, like some members of the Fugitive group, Young succeeded admirably in an academic career. At the University of Texas in Austin he founded *The Texas Review,* as well as a successful drama group. After he took a job at Amherst College in Massachusetts, Young turned increasingly to teaching and writing about drama, composing plays himself. Not long after he abandoned his university career for a life in literary journalism, he became the drama critic for *The New Republic* in New York. As with his poetry, his many plays did not attain a reputation to match those of the more successful modernists of the period. Young also wrote several nostalgic Mississippi novels that the editors of the WPA guide to Mississippi describe as "less novels than descriptive essays of Mississippi life hung on the convenient framework of the McGehee family"—Young's forebears.[33]

The work of both Young and Percy appeared in the new literary magazines springing up in the South, as well as in national magazines, and Young contributed an essay to the Agrarians' *I'll Take My Stand* in 1930. In considering the inclusion of Young in the symposium, Davidson wrote Tate that Young "knows the tone of Southern life at its best and writes extremely well; he comes from Mississippi originally, but has wandered widely enough not to be accused of narrow parochialism; we need at least one such eminent Southern writer, outside of our own circle, to strengthen our array; and he would put us in no danger, I think, of being swallowed up by New York."[34] Young's writing career was as expansive as Faulkner's, whom he preceded in publishing his first work and later matched year by year, book by book. The first of Young's four novels about Mississippi, *Heaven Trees,* was published in 1926, the same year as Faulkner's first novel, *Soldiers' Pay.* Young's autobiography, *The Pavilion:*

Of People and Times Remembered, of Stories and Places, was published in 1951, the year after *Collected Stories of William Faulkner* was published.

Percy was not as prolific as Young, but his responsibilities for a model Delta plantation, three growing boys, and a community in transition did not allow him to devote his life to art as much as Young was able to do. Percy's poetry appeared widely in commercial periodicals, however, and was also published in *The Fugitive* and *The Double Dealer.* Reviewing a volume of his poetry in the University of Mississippi student newspaper in 1920, the would-be poet Faulkner wrote, "Mr. Percy—like alas! How many of us—suffered the misfortune of having been born out of his time. He should have lived in Victorian England and gone to Italy with Swinburne, for like Swinburne he is a mixture of passionate adoration of beauty and as passionate a despair and disgust with its manifestations and accessories in the human race."[35] The line describes accurately the ambivalence of many of Faulkner's male characters regarding women (for example, Joe Christmas in *Light in August,* 1932). After the popularity of *Lanterns on the Levee,* Percy's publisher, Alfred A. Knopf, brought out a posthumous volume, *The Collected Poems of William Alexander Percy* (1943), that went through three printings by 1950.

In some sense Young and Percy were also-rans in the Southern Renaissance, but they were beacons and bridges to the future for many other Southern writers. As successes in more than one genre whose work appeared frequently in national magazines, they proved to Faulkner, the Fugitives, and Tennessee Williams, for example, that small-town Southern origins should not prevent their attaining the literary limelight. As even their Mississippi admirers concluded, however, Young and Percy chose not to face all the monstrous realities about Southern culture that Faulkner confronted and struggled with, nor did either of them embrace the ironic and critical postures toward the Southern experience that made writers such as Glasgow, Warren, Ransom, and Faulkner more modern than Victorian. In a time when, as Daniel Singal writes, "the question of southern culture itself, past and present, became the most emotional issue of debate," Young and Percy remained among those "who tried consciously to break with the strictures of Victorianism, but whose underlying loyalty to nineteenth-century values dominated in the end."[36]

William Faulkner (1897–1962). By most standards, today Faulkner is regarded by a worldwide audience, as well as by a remarkable number of significant Southern writers, as the greatest Southern—and American—novelist of his time, a high modernist who peered deeply into the contradictions and dramatic conflicts of a rapidly changing Southern culture. He denied having received the kind of classical and university education that was nearly the norm for most of the male writers of the Southern Renaissance, and often he insisted that he had dropped out of school after the seventh grade, but his upbringing and development as a writer actually resembled that of other writers who developed during the 1920s. In fact, Faulkner had some early advantages many of his contemporaries did not have. Whereas the Fugitives, the North Carolinians Wolfe and Green, several members of the group associated with *The Double Dealer* in New Orleans, and even the Mississippians Young and Percy had to leave their provincial Southern hometowns in order to find a stimulating university setting, Faulkner grew up in a college town. He actively enjoyed and benefited enormously from the University of Mississippi, which was an integral part of his hometown of Oxford. He participated in student life even when he was not a student, published esoteric poems and essays in student publications, wrote an experimental "dream play" for the student theater group, used the university library thoroughly, held conversations and took classes with professors trained at great American and European universities, and for three crucial years read his patrons' magazines while he made a good living as postmaster of the university post office.

Even before his exposure to the university, Faulkner, like Glasgow, received a rich literary education from several good home libraries and through association with bookish family members and friends. His mother read "modern" books, attended lectures and other cultural programs at the university, and taught all of her four boys to read earlier than public school would have. His father and paternal grandfather were readers who signed and dated the books that meant the most to them. So much of what these formative influences admired was passed to Faulkner that he was understandably bored with school. He did not drop out after the seventh grade, as he sometimes implied, but he did lose interest, although he stayed in school into the optional twelfth grade. From about the time he lost interest in secondary school, however, Faulkner came under the influence and tutelage of Phil Stone, a patrician young lawyer a few years his senior, a man of good family more suited to literature than the law he had studied at Ole Miss and at Yale.

Unlike many other writers of this period, Faulkner resisted leaving his parents' house, except for short sojourns away, or sincerely accepting a responsible job, until he was thirty years old. For at least half of these thirty years he read great books—from his father's favorite cowboy stories (Owen Wister's *The Virginian*, 1902) and the humorists

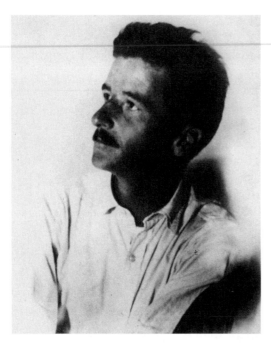
Publicity photo of William Faulkner for his first book, *The Marble Faun* (1924), a poetry collection

of the old Deep South (George Washington Harris's *Sut Lovingood, Yarns Spun by a "Nat'ral Born Durn'd' Fool,"* 1867) to his grandfather's sets of the works of Charles Dickens and Alexandre Dumas *père*. Faulkner's reading with Stone included the Loeb editions of the Greek and Roman classics; the works of Honoré de Balzac and Gustave Flaubert; a 1924 edition of Joyce's *Ulysses;* and the poetry of Algernon Charles Swinburne, A. E. Housman, and T. S. Eliot. As was later the case with the much less advantaged Wright, books were the aspiring writer's Yale and Harvard.

Faulkner also practiced graphic arts and book design; tried on several dandified personas in Oxford and at the university, complete with appropriate wardrobes and hairstyles; and wrote imitative poetry, astute critical essays, and a small amount of fiction for university publications, mostly while he was not a student. Though he read about the South, the Civil War, and Reconstruction, like some of the Fugitives he also heard much about these matters from members of his family. Faulkner prided himself on his paternal great-grandfather, who had written novels and poems while constructing a family legend as a Mexican War soldier, Civil War colonel, and postwar entrepreneur who founded a narrow-gauge railroad. Because this founder of the family's dwindling fortunes was also a murderer (two cases ruled self-defense) and apparently sired a shadow family by a former slave, Faulkner had a good background for comprehending the lower layers of Southern life. He never knew this great-grandfather, who was murdered by a business partner before his birth, but many members of his immediate family told stories of the old man. Even as a child Faulkner had decided he wanted to become an author like his ancestor.

Like many authors of the Southern Renaissance, Faulkner began with poetry. His first published work was a collection of verse, *The Marble Faun* (1924), and he took copies of it with him to New Orleans in 1925. The French Quarter group into which he was immediately accepted included newspaper writers, students and faculty at nearby Tulane University, and Sherwood Anderson. One of the most esteemed modernist writers in America at the time, Anderson regarded the cosmopolitan Louisiana port city as the best place in America for an artist to live. Faulkner, who had come there to book passage for Europe, following in the footsteps of such American writers as Robert Frost, F. Scott Fitzgerald, and Hemingway, concurred. New Orleans represented in some respects a continuation of Faulkner's education in the university town of Oxford, but the city had a richer intellectual and artistic tradition. Faulkner's bohemian postures did not stand out as much, and he had to produce real work to earn the reputation of an artist.

The Double Dealer, the local literary magazine, was much like The Fugitive, with a similar managing body, but it was much above the student publications in which Faulkner had published at Ole Miss. He delayed his planned trip to Europe long enough to learn how to write a novel from Anderson, and in New Orleans he wrote his first novel, Soldiers' Pay, and gathered material for his second, Mosquitoes (1927), before he took passage on a freighter to Europe with the artist and university teacher William Spratling. Other writers of the Southern Renaissance had served in World War I (Ransom, Davidson, and Percy) or studied in England on Rhodes Scholarships (Ransom, Warren, and Brooks). Faulkner missed the war by a few months when the armistice of 11 November 1918 was called before his completion of flight-school training for the Royal Air Force in Toronto. Though he claimed first that he had been in a crash during training and later that he had lost two planes in France during the war as a combat pilot, the only injury he sustained in the Great War was to his expectations. Faulkner's trip to Europe in 1925 was his first; it was also unlike those of most of his contemporaries. He did not stay long, he did not publish or make literary connections, and what he absorbed was minimal compared to the fund of memories derived from growing up in Oxford, Mississippi, among a family of readers and storytellers.

After the publication of Mosquitoes, written about his friends in New Orleans, Faulkner was not as welcome in that city as when he first visited. For this and other reasons, he returned to his parents' home in Oxford. First, he wrote a family-chronicle novel about the heritage of his father's family, putting his imaginary flying experience into a fated twin whose brother died gloriously in combat with the Germans. The Southern past, however, plays as strong a role in "Flags in the Dust," as the work was first called, as the fractured postwar lives of the younger characters in the book. Anderson's publisher, who had published Faulkner's first two novels, turned down "Flags in the Dust." It was finally published in a shortened version in 1929 as *Sartoris* by another publisher, who in turn refused his next novel, the highly modernist chronicle of the Compson family, *The Sound and the Fury.*

Faulkner completely connected the Southern past and its values to the modernist perspective. He also adopted Southern rhetoric—the pompous pedantry of lawyers, the whine of disappointed old ladies, the drunken ramblings of the defeated, and the sensitive uncertainty of the current generation—to the modernist project. In the words of Emily Dickinson, "Tell the Truth, but Tell it Slant."

The Sound and the Fury is told in the first of its four sections by a voice issuing from the mind of a thirty-three-year-old man identified by his family and community as an "idiot" who is always "trying to say." This is not a bad image of the critically minded artist living in a culture that has largely abandoned honor in favor of bragging but has retained a golden myth of the past. That the father and the last "normal" son of the Compson family both bear the name "Jason"—seeker of the Golden Fleece—is as appropriate in the land of cotton as is Faulkner's setting of the novel at the Easter season in what Flannery O'Connor later identified as the "Christ-haunted" South.

The Sound and the Fury confirmed Faulkner's genius and sealed his fate, though the novel was in no way a commercial success. He struggled for years to make a living as a writer. None of his books was like the one before it, so he constantly violated the expectations of busy reviewers, who liked to put a simple handle on things. *As I Lay Dying,* published in 1930, dramatizes another family, this time rural: a marriage between a shiftless, exploitative hill farmer and a country schoolteacher who feels she cannot reach anyone, including herself, produces five strange children who conflict dramatically as they participate in a journey through water, fire, and the smell of corrupting flesh to take their mother's corpse to be buried beside her father. *Sanctuary* (1931) shows Southern womanhood exploring the sexual demimonde and concludes with a man named Lee lynched by the people of a town named Jefferson for a rape someone else committed. Faulkner was briefly a sensation, but the only lasting outcome was increasingly long periods of work in Hollywood as a screenwriter.

Faulkner's 1936 novel *Absalom, Absalom!* yokes the passively fated Compsons together with the aggressively fated Sutpens. *The Unvanquished* (1938) tells the background story of *Sartoris. The Hamlet,* published in 1940, was the first part of a tragicomic trilogy. With *The Town* (1957) and *The Mansion* (1959), it traces the drama created when a clever, pleasureless former sharecropper, Flem Snopes, learns the ropes of county commerce and wages spiritual war with a less acquisitive and more humanistic former sharecropper, a sewing-machine salesman named V. K. Ratliff. *Go Down, Moses,* published in 1942, presents two sets of stories Faulkner conceived for the lucrative popular magazine market; delving deep into the arrogance and hypocrisy of Southern history, he yoked together the hunting grounds and the farm lands in a dystopia of personal failure. A well-meaning young man, with the best but also the last available training in the meaning of tradition, is supposed to inherit and improve upon the South's typical community, the plantation, and its typical spiritual retreat, the annual hunt for bear and deer. Shamed by his grandfather's arrogance, Ike McCaslin demonstrates that he has misread the New Testament and not read the Old Testament, in which the patriarchs became heroes of cultural change despite a range of human faults and sins against their wives, sons, daughters, and religious values.

Faulkner created a recurring scene for most of his stories and novels—the town of Jefferson, Mississippi. It was modeled to a high degree on his native Oxford—though with the university and its influence strictly removed. He placed it within an even more mythological frame, Yoknapatawpha County, of which Jefferson is the county seat and commercial center. Faulkner made Yoknapatawpha as big as four Mississippi counties, gave it a population more than half African American, and once told the critic Malcolm Cowley that it "moved West a little bit every year."[37] Thus, he was able to employ Yoknapatawpha County as a microcosm for more aspects of Mississippi, and of the South as a whole, than if he had stuck strictly with his own Lafayette County in the north-central hills region of the state.

It has been noted in life sketches of writers such as Glasgow and Peterkin that not all authors found Faulkner's fiction to their liking; Cabell admitted to avoiding it. Most of the writers in the 1919–1941 period of the Southern Renaissance, however, including those from far different sections of the South than Faulkner's, found his work increasingly exciting and apt and ultimately even a touchstone for what the committed and observant Southern writer might accomplish.

Noting Davidson's negative review of *Porgy* author Heyward's second novel about African American life, *Mamba's Daughters*—a review in which Davidson wrote that Heyward's book was "without the passionate absorption in the subject that we must demand of a regional novelist"— Heyward biographer William Slavick observes that "Faulkner is a good touchstone for measuring more pervasive faults in Heyward's novel. After

JOHN CROWE RANSOM ON FAULKNER

"Mr. Faulkner, I suppose, is the most exciting figure in our contemporary literature just now; he is original, and he has not been classified. It is my impression that his critics as yet have hardly got beyond the exclamatory stage. It is still being discovered that he is a powerful new genius, with a bias toward horror and the morbid.

"He is adept at the modern techniques, but much too bold to content himself with any safe or consistent craftsmanship. He obtains atmosphere and characterizations with almost a new minimum of machinery; and I suppose this is the consequence not of some particular trick which he has discovered so much as of the speed and strength of his mind. He presents his story preferably from the points of view of a succession of interested characters. These characters will probably be low in their social and literary standing, but it doesn't follow that their reception is not acutely sensitive or their mental associations fairly complex."

John Crowe Ransom

From "Modern with the Southern Accent," *Virginia Quarterly Review,* 11 (April 1935); reprinted in *Defining Southern Literature: Perspectives and Assessments, 1831-1952,* edited by John E. Bassett (Madison & Teaneck, N.J.: Fairleigh Dickinson University Press / London: Associated University Presses, 1997), pp. 342-343.

asserting that true regionalists 'write of their chosen section as if no other region exists,' Donald Davidson's review argues that Heyward does not."[38] Davidson even went so far, on another occasion, as to use Faulkner's greatness to refute the sociological conclusions of the Chapel Hill school of social scientists with which the humanistic Agrarians of Vanderbilt were at war. Howard Odum had certified with statistics the "backwardness" of Mississippi. Davidson argued that either the sociologists' "tables" had to be wrong about Mississippi's backwardness—since the state had produced the South's greatest writer as well as a great number of other writers—or the message was "that the way for a society to produce a William Faulkner is to have him born in a thoroughly backward state like Mississippi."[39] Odum's response was equal in its praise of Faulkner, for Odum had grown up as a rural Mississippian himself. He granted that such genius as Faulkner's transcended sociology, and he observed movingly that as a boy he had himself "been close enough to Faulkner's quicksands to sense something of [their] terrors and . . . often imagined, behind the cedars and columned houses, that anything could happen there."[40]

Regarding Faulkner's achievement, Singal has compared the Mississippi writer's achievement favorably with that of the best and most rigorous students and scholars of the South. Of course, novel-writing, Singal observes,

> is a medium obviously better suited to impressionism than sociology, one in which ambivalence could be turned to aesthetic advantage. . . . To label Faulkner a traditionalist, moralist, nihilist, sensationalist, Christian, Stoic, atheist, or naturalist, as various critics have done, represents a fruitless effort. Partially accurate at best, none of these labels does full justice to Faulkner's awesome complexity. One can comprehend Faulkner only by viewing his work in terms of its ongoing process—as a continuing search to resolve the mysteries that presented themselves as he probed deeper and deeper into the southern con-

sciousness, discovering, as he went, occasional moments of stable insight but more often uncovering a furthering of paradox.

Faulkner, Singal concludes, is best seen as "an immensely gifted intellectual living through an experience of intractable cultural change, a southerner just over the threshold of Modernism."[41]

LATER MISSISSIPPI WRITERS

The first successful efforts of three Mississippi writers, Wright, Welty, and Tennessee Williams, came near the end of the full flowering of Southern letters between 1919 and 1941. But for several reasons they deserve attention in a book on the Southern Renaissance. Important writing by Wright and Welty first appeared in the late 1930s, when Faulkner's career was at its most productive and daring stage. Wright's stories began to appear in magazines at this time, and his collection of short novels, *Uncle Tom's Children,* was published in 1938. Welty placed her first serious short story in a literary magazine in 1936, and her work was accepted by Warren and Brooks at *The Southern Review* in 1937 and 1938. Welty started but abandoned an unsuccessful novel in 1938, the same year Williams finished college and was still writing pieces that were mostly unsuccessful, too.

As transitional voices in the South during the period of changes wrought by World War II, Wright, Welty, and Williams expressed a region at war with itself in somewhat different ways from what had been the case in the 1920s. Each drew on different traditions and excelled in different genres. They not only struggled with the nature of their region but also fought to break free of social expectation and stereotyping— Wright as the descendant of slaves and field hands in a discriminatory society; Welty as a woman whose advantages were supposed to lead to marriage and social position instead of the life of a highly dedicated artist; and Williams as a man of deep feeling whose status as a gay American was not a publishable aspect of his life for most of his career.

Richard Wright (1908–1960). As an African American of limited means, Wright had to leave school and work to help his family. In Memphis, a sympathetic white work supervisor allowed him to use a whites-only library card to "fetch" books that were actually for Wright to read. Thus, like Faulkner, whose lawyer friend Stone ordered books for his protégé, Wright read his way into modernism. His experience with Deep South racial codes and the everyday threat of violence also gave him a kind of modernist experience, too—the feelings of fear, alienation, and powerlessness other young men had found on the battlefields of

Richard Wright

Europe in World War I. In Mississippi, and certainly in Memphis—W. C. Handy's hometown—Wright could not have missed the modernist spirit of blues and jazz, as well. The black music then being played throughout the South and made available to a wider audience through "race records" expressed a rationalized primitivism similar to what Pablo Picasso was doing in his paintings. The use of improvisation and quotation in this music resembled Eliot's use of the same devices in *The Waste Land.* The frank and joking banter about sexuality in the lyrics would have intrigued Freud. A poster for one of Louis Armstrong's early concerts, in fact, refers to him in large letters as a "Master of Modernism," though George Gershwin received more credit than Handy, Armstrong, and the "jazz royalty" (King Oliver, Duke Ellington, and Count Basie) for equating those rhythms with modernist music.

Some of Wright's modernism also came from the cultural criticism practiced by the political left that he encountered in Chicago and New York, but this was true of many more white writers of the period than of African American authors. Like the Nashville and New Orleans writers, he wanted to avoid sentimentalism, but for different reasons. A good cry about racial conditions in America was not what Wright wanted from his readers. His powerful 1940 novel *Native Son* tells the story of the tribulations of a young black man who accidentally kills the daughter of his white employer. Wright wrote mainly in a realist and naturalist style, but he foreshadowed the existential philosophy that was developing in Paris, where he ultimately exiled himself after World War II. His autobiography, *Black Boy,* was published in 1945.

Eudora Welty (1909–). Welty's parents were outsiders in Mississippi. Her father and mother were from Ohio and West Virginia, respectively; they came to Jackson when her father accepted a managerial job in a large insurance company there. Her parents' continued interest in the places from which they came—which led to frequent summer trips to visit Welty's grandparents—doubtless helped to give her some distance on the capital-city Mississippi culture into which she was born. Welty's early schooling was nothing extraordinary, but in her circle of high-school friends were a group of young men who went off to prestigious colleges and achieved successful careers in academia, publishing, and even Broadway musical theater.

By contrast, and against her own ambitions, when Welty left high school her parents preferred for her to attend Mississippi State College for Women in Columbus. Notwithstanding its reputation as a protective institution for young Mississippi women, MSCW allowed her to experience what other Southerners found at Vanderbilt, Sewanee, Tulane, Chapel Hill, and Ole Miss. Like Faulkner at the University of Mississippi, Welty drew illustrations for the college yearbook, worked with the drama club, and wrote for the student newspaper. After two years, she escaped to the University of Wisconsin. There she found a great library and teachers who were more current in the tides of modernism. After that, again following the wishes of her practical-minded father, she enrolled in business school at Columbia University to train for a career that might support her. At Columbia, however, one of her male friends from Jackson was working on a master's degree in English, and she attended the courses he was taking. Finding that the business program was undemanding, she had plenty of time to explore the art and theater available in the city.

The unexpected death of her father in 1931 brought Welty back to Jackson. Like many Southern writers of the period, she tried newspaper work, writing about debutante balls in Jackson and weddings in the Delta for the Memphis paper. As the Depression worsened, Welty found a position as a publicity agent with the Mississippi Advertising Commission, the organization that promoted the New Deal and managed the WPA project to create a state automobile guide. In this position she traveled throughout the state, writing

EUDORA WELTY'S MISSISSIPPI

"No countryside has ever seemed stranger to me than that of Mississippi as I traveled through it in humid and heavy heat toward its capital Jackson, home of Eudora Welty. Fetid and luxuriant swamps stretched into shimmering distance; when these gave way to farm or woodland the strangeness did not depart. Mountain valleys do not surprise when they turn out to be arcane in atmosphere but one does not expect this quality in the flat country. Yet after leaving Memphis I felt I had entered a country that had changed very little this century and had even less intention of doing so in the future."

Paul Binding

From *Separate Country: A Literary Journey through the American South* (New York & London: Paddington Press, 1979), p. 131.

about new farm-to-market roads, canning factories, landing fields, and other New Deal projects. An avid photographer, Welty carried a camera and for her own pleasure photographed people and places. Eventually, she tried to market a book of her stories and photographs, tentatively titled "Black Saturday," which seemed to mimic the titles of Peterkin's South Carolina novels: *Green Thursday, Black April,* and *Scarlet Sister Mary.* The book also resembled Peterkin's collaboration with Ulmann, *Roll, Jordan, Roll.* Welty's stories and photographs were not complementary, however, and her project found no publisher.

By the time she began placing short stories regularly in literary magazines, Welty benefited from the success of *Gone with the Wind.* Following the phenomenal success of Mitchell's novel and the movie adaptation, New York editors prospected in the South for more new women writers, and Welty was discovered. Her first short-story collection, *A Curtain of Green*—seventeen stories that were too varied to constitute a unit—appeared in the bookstores in 1941, the same year that the play version of Wright's *Native Son* was first staged. Welty's first full-length novel, *Delta Wedding,* was published in 1946.

Tennessee Williams (1911–1983). Williams was born in Columbus, Mississippi, the town where Welty first went to college. Like Wright, who as a child had to live with grandparents and moved in and out of the Mississippi Delta and Jackson, Williams was displaced. At the age of eight he was taken from the pleasant home of his Sewanee-educated maternal grandfather, an Episcopal rector, and brought into the apartment culture of St. Louis, Missouri. Williams's father was harsh and disapproving, quick to rebuke and punish his oldest child for the same kinds of uncertainty one sees in the lives of Toomer, Welty, and Faulkner, an uncertainty born from a desire to pursue the "impractical" course of the artist. Like Faulkner, as a young man Williams spent some time in the open culture of New Orleans and later embraced it as one of the places where he felt at home. Unlike Toomer and Faulkner, he did manage to finish college after trying several institutions, taking a bachelor's degree from the University of Iowa in 1938, just as the writing careers of Wright and Welty were beginning to take off. Williams's success in drama, the medium he finally found most congenial—though he wrote poetry and fiction, too—began with *The Glass Menagerie,* which opened in Chicago in 1944 and moved with great critical success to New York in 1945.

FLORIDA

James Weldon Johnson (1871–1938). Johnson, an African American, was the beneficiary of parents who had sufficient financial security and personal success to help him establish a career as a teacher and school principal back in his hometown of Jacksonville after he graduated from Atlanta University. In some ways, then, his experience was similar to that of many of the writers of the upper South who attended Vanderbilt and made careers as teachers and writers. Johnson studied law, become a member of the Florida bar, and founded a short-lived newspaper for the African American community in Jacksonville. During this time he also wrote poetry and obviously felt the lack of scope any highly educated and ambitious man of color would feel in the South. When his musician brother invited him to New York, Johnson entered a world more to his liking, writing lyrics for highly popular music-theater acts by turn-of-the-century African American performers.

When this life failed to satisfy Johnson's restless ambition, participation in Theodore Roosevelt's successful 1904 campaign for president gave him another opportunity: consular appointments in Latin America that provided him with leisure to think and write in a more serious vein, much as diplomatic posts in Europe had done for such nineteenth-century American writers as Washington Irving and Nathaniel Hawthorne. Johnson published essays in leading intellectual journals, including Du Bois's NAACP journal, *The Crisis*.

Johnson's anonymously published *Autobiography of an Ex-Coloured Man* (1912) is a novel exploring the conflicts and ambiguities faced by a gifted person of African descent who has opportunities on both sides of a racially divided society. Political activism for the NAACP, for which he served as field secretary, captured much of his attention in the second decade of the twentieth century, but not long after the Southern Renaissance began to heat up in 1920, he wrote influential introductions to volumes of poetry by African Americans. In 1927, the same year that Faulkner saw his second novel into print and Green had a "Negro" play on Broadway that won a Pulitzer Prize, Johnson's *God's Trombones: Seven Negro Sermons in Verse* was published. It is a witty and moving example of dialect writing that continues to attract an audience and inspire performances. Johnson resumed a teaching career, accepting a position as a professor at Fisk in 1930. His untimely death in an automobile accident cut off a career that might have accomplished with new generations of Nashville students—in this case African Americans—the kind of inspiration that Ransom and Davidson had ignited at nearby Vanderbilt.

Zora Neale Hurston (1903–1960). Hurston's literary reputation has taken a double turn since the brief period in the 1930s when she was publishing some of the most interesting, substantial, and important writing about Southern African Americans. Born in a small "all-Negro" town in central Florida, Eatonville, she made her way by virtue of her intelligence all the way to Columbia University in New York, where she studied cultural anthropology with Franz Boas, one of the founders of the field. Pappa Franz, as Hurston called her teacher at a time when academic culture was quite stilted and self-important, gave her the training and the mandate to go back to her little place in Florida—like Faulkner going back to his "postage stamp of native soil" in Mississippi at the suggestion of Anderson[42]—and to conduct research into the culture that she had taken for granted while growing up. The result was a series of nonfiction and fiction works about African American life, folklore, belief, and humanity different from anything written by the many white authors fascinated with the black experience.

When Hurston's career was cut short by changing literary tastes, the diversions of World War II, and her return to a simple life in Florida as a teacher and domestic servant, she apparently kept writing but published only magazine articles after 1948. Her reputation faded, her work became unknown to succeeding generations, and she died in obscurity in 1960, buried in an unmarked grave. The African American writer Alice Walker—author of the best-selling novel *The Color Purple* (1982)—rediscovered Hurston and began to popularize her work, editing an important anthology, *I Love Myself When I Am Laughing . . . and Then Again When I Am Looking Mean and Impressive: A Zora Neale Hurston Reader* (1979). It is clear to readers now that Hurston's folkloric research, her lively presentation of stories from African American life, and her achievement as a short-story writer and novelist place her in the short list of those writers whose works are essential for an assessment of the Southern Renaissance.

The popularity of Hurston's writing about rural and small-town African Americans in the 1930s appears to have affected and influenced several other writers, most notably Faulkner, who once wrote the young Welty an encouraging letter that was apparently intended for Hurston.[43] In the same period Faulkner emulated Hurston in the stories he wrote about the dignified African American Lucas Beauchamp and his family, stories he later reshaped for the 1942 novel *Go Down, Moses*.

Marjorie Kinnan Rawlings (1896–1953). Rawlings's best writing about her own peculiar habitat, the north-central region of

Florida, coincided almost exactly with the work of Hurston. Both authors portrayed regions of the South with which other Southerners could easily identify. Rawlings, unlike Hurston, was not native to the place where she settled and became an observant and imaginative chronicler. Born, raised, and schooled in Washington, D.C., she studied at the University of Wisconsin (where Welty finished her undergraduate degree). After a brief career in the newspaper business, Rawlings moved to Cross Creek, Florida, where she operated an orange grove. From her observations of local life, she wrote stories and novels, including a landmark work, *The Yearling* (1938). Her first book, the novel *South Moon Under* (1933), and the memoir *Cross Creek* (1942) are her most memorable works. In 1946 *The Yearling* was made into a quite successful motion picture by director Clarence Brown, who then used his feeling for Southern settings in the 1949 movie adaptation of Faulkner's 1948 novel *Intruder in the Dust*.

TEXAS

Katherine Anne Porter (1890–1980). Porter was even more adept at creating an imaginary version of her own life than the inventive Faulkner. Some commentators on her work have declared that, unlike Faulkner, she ceased to know the difference between the somewhat archetypal Southern existence she invented and the actual facts of her own rather severe upbringing. At any rate, both Porter's creativity and her will to be something other than what she might have become gave her one of the most interesting careers of any writer in the Southern Renaissance. She appropriated her pen name—she was christened Callista Russell Porter—with a *K* in place of a *C*, from her forceful paternal grandmother, who took a uniformly negative and harsh course in raising her. As another of the "new" women of the modern era, Porter, in the words of one scholar, truly started her apprenticeship as a writer in "her twenty-fifth year, when she divorced her [first] husband and began doing the things vital to her self-discovery and growth." During this period she acted, wrote reviews and publicity for the theater, and kept notes and a journal that recorded her observations of people, places, and events.[44]

Porter did not produce a book until 1930, when *Flowering Judas and Other Stories* established a position for her that she never lost: that of a discerning and meditative writer of short stories with an enviable style. In 1939 she collected three short novels—*Noon Wine, Old Mortality,* and *Pale Horse, Pale Rider* in a volume with the title of the third novella. Her

Katherine Anne Porter in 1933

one attempt at the novel genre, *Ship of Fools* (1962), took her some twenty years to write. It was a commercial success and resulted in a movie sale but did not match her reputation in the short story or the novella.

In 1938 Porter married her third husband, Albert Erskine, who was the business manager and an editor, like Brooks and Warren, for *The Southern Review*. Like Warren, whom she advised about some of the writers being considered for publication in the review, she supported herself with literary journalism, assignments as a teacher at colleges and universities, and grants and prizes, as well as by marketing her short fiction to popular magazines during the heyday of magazine fiction. At the peak of her career as a writer of short stories, she wrote the introduction for Welty's *A Curtain of Green*. Near the end of her career, Porter's *Collected Stories*, published in England in 1964 and in the United States in 1965, won the kinds of prizes that had eluded *Ship of Fools* three years earlier, receiving both the Pulitzer Prize and the National Book Award.

Some of Porter's most Southern work focuses on the youth of her fictional characters, but the South was not, as it was for many writers of the Southern Renaissance, her perennial subject, a fact corroborated by *The Collected Essays and Occasional Writings of Katherine Anne Porter* (1970). When she did write about the South, as in a piece from this collection titled "Portrait: Old South," she wrote of a purely mythic version of her life: "I am the grandchild of a lost War, and I have blood-knowledge of what life can be in a defeated country on the bare bones of privation."[45] This purely invented biography became, nonetheless, according to a one critic, a paradigm of her subject when she wrote about the South,

> the Old Order and the New. The Old Order was a structured antebellum society that cherished aesthetic ideals at the same time it nurtured inequities indigenous to feudalism. . . . Old Order descendants preserve the past by legend and fragile truths . . . often in conflict with the New Order, made up of persons who consciously reject the romantic values and traditions of the past and of poor whites struggling to enter middle-class respectability.[46]

NOTES

1. Joseph Blotner, *Faulkner: A Biography,* revised edition (New York: Random House, 1984), pp. 61, 138.

2. Blair Rouse, ed., *Letters of Ellen Glasgow* (New York: Harcourt, Brace, 1958), pp. 132, 133.

3. Susan Goodman, *Ellen Glasgow: A Biography* (Baltimore & London: Johns Hopkins University Press, 1998), p. 168.

4. Thomas Daniel Young, *Tennessee Writers* (Knoxville: University of Tennessee Press, 1981), p. 26.

5. See Young, *Gentleman in a Dustcoat: A Biography of John Crowe Ransom* (Baton Rouge: Louisiana State University Press, 1976), p. 266; and *Selected Letters of John Crowe Ransom,* edited by Young and George Core (Baton Rouge: Louisiana State University Press, 1985), p. 199.

6. H. L. Mencken, "Criticism of Criticism of Criticism," in his *Prejudices: A Selection,* edited by James T. Farrell (New York: Vintage, 1958), p. 7.

7. Donald Davidson, *Southern Writers in the Modern World,* Eugenia Dorothy Blount Lamar Memorial Lectures, 1957 (Athens: University of Georgia Press, 1958), pp. 33–34.

8. Young, *Tennessee Writers,* p. 28.

9. Robert Bain, Joseph M. Flora, and Louis D. Rubin Jr., eds., *Southern Writers: A Biographical Dictionary* (Baton Rouge: Louisiana State University Press, 1979), p. 444. Ransom's judgment about Tate is almost a direct repetition of what Davidson said about his earliest encounters with Ransom. "I could write nothing of that kind," Davidson recalled of the first poetry Ransom shared with him; "I was not only a long way off from writing poetry. I did not even know how to read poetry." See Davidson, *Southern Writers in the Modern World,* pp. 14–15.

10. Allen Tate, "The New Provincialism" (1945), in his *Essays of Four Decades* (Chicago: Swallow Press, 1968), p. 543.

11. Young, *Tennessee Writers,* p. 29.

12. Robert Penn Warren, "Introduction: Faulkner: Past and Future," in *Faulkner: A Collection of Critical Essays,* edited by Warren (Englewood Cliffs, N.J.: Prentice-Hall, 1966), p. 1.

13. Laurence G. Avery, ed., *A Southern Life: Letters of Paul Green, 1916–1981* (Chapel Hill: University of North Carolina Press, 1994), pp. xx–xxi.

14. Nicholas Natanson, *The Black Image in the New Deal: The Politics of FSA Photography* (Knoxville: University of Tennessee Press, 1992), p. 239. Green and Wright were photographed in the University of North Carolina library where, later, African American novelist and poet Margaret Walker Alexander—who wrote a biography of Wright—was not allowed to work in the main reading room of the Southern Historical Collection while researching her family history for *Jubilee* (1966).

15. Avery, ed., *A Southern Life: Letters of Paul Green, 1916–1981,* p. xx.

16. Richard S. Kennedy, *The Window of Memory: The Literary Career of Thomas Wolfe* (Chapel Hill: University of North Carolina Press, 1962), p. 334.

17. Peterkin's biographer justly observes that though the white writer Peterkin may have been regarded by Americans during her lifetime as the "top Southern writer and 'Negro novelist,'" her work and that of such writers as Green, Heyward, and Bradford

also coincided with a renaissance of writing by African Americans. Their works included Jessie Redmon Fauset's *Plum Bun* (1928), Claude McKay's *Home to Harlem* (1928), Rudolph Fisher's *The Walls of Jericho* (1928), Wallace Thurman's *The Blacker the Berry* (1929), and Nella Larsen's *Quicksand* (1928). See Susan Millar Williams, *A Devil and a Good Woman, Too: The Lives of Julia Peterkin* (Athens & London: University of Georgia Press, 1997), p. 150.

18. Williams, *A Devil and a Good Woman, Too: The Lives of Julia Peterkin,* p. ix.

19. Davidson, quoted in Williams, *A Devil and a Good Woman, Too: The Lives of Julia Peterkin,* p. xi.

20. Natanson, *The Black Image in the New Deal: The Politics of FSA Photography,* p. 24.

21. Ibid. Natanson evaluates the long list of books similar to *Roll, Jordan, Roll* published during and after the Depression, many of them coming in the wake of the popularity of John Steinbeck's novel of the westward flight of poor dust-bowl farmers, *The Grapes of Wrath* (1939). In Natanson's estimation, few if any of them succeed in avoiding stereotypes, condescension, agrarian nostalgia, or the equally dehumanizing politics of victimization in presenting portraits of the rural South or rural Southerners, black or white.

22. Laurence Stallings, quoted in Williams, *A Devil and a Good Woman, Too: The Lives of Julia Peterkin,* p. 206.

23. Federal Writer's Project of the Works Progress Administration, *Georgia: The WPA Guide to its Towns and Countryside,* introduction and appendix by Phinizy Spalding (Columbia: University of South Carolina Press, 1990), p. 492.

24. Goodman, *Ellen Glasgow: A Biography,* p. 186.

25. Richard M. Weaver, "Contemporary Southern Literature," in *The Southern Essays of Richard M. Weaver,* edited by George M. Curtis III and James J. Thompson Jr. (Indianapolis: Liberty Press, 1987).

26. Sylvia Jenkins Cook, *From Tobacco Road to Route 66: The Southern Poor White in Fiction* (Chapel Hill: University of North Carolina Press, 1976), pp. 62–63, 82–83.

27. Frederick J. Hoffman, *The Art of Southern Fiction: A Study of Some Modern Novelists* (Carbondale: Southern Illinois University Press, 1967), p.18.

28. Weaver, "Aspects of the Southern Philosophy," in *Southern Renascence: The Literature of the Modern South,* edited by Rubin and Robert D. Jacobs (Baltimore: Johns Hopkins Press, 1953), p. 29.

29. Doris Betts, "Daughters, Southerners, and Daisy," in *The Female Tradition in Southern Literature,* edited by Carol S. Manning (Urbana: University of Illinois Press, 1993), p. 268.

30. W. E. B. Du Bois, "Georgia: Invisible Empire State," *Nation,* 120 (21 January 1925); reprinted in *These United States: Portraits of America from the 1920s,* edited by Daniel H. Borus (Ithaca & London: Cornell University Press, 1992), p. 94.

31. Ibid., p. 103.

32. Federal Writers' Project of the Works Progress Administration, *Mississippi: A Guide to the Magnolia State* (New York: Viking, 1938), pp. 141–142.

33. Ibid., p. 141.

34. Davidson to Tate, 26 October 1929, in *The Literary Correspondence of Donald Davidson and Allen Tate,* edited by John Tyree Fain and Thomas Daniel Young (Athens: University of Georgia Press, 1974), p. 236.

35. William Faulkner, "Books and Things," *Mississippian,* 10 November 1920; reprinted in *William Faulkner: Early Prose and Poetry,* edited by Carvel Collins (Boston: Little, Brown, 1962), p. 71.

36. Daniel Singal, *The War Within: From Victorian to Modernist Thought in the South, 1919–1945* (Chapel Hill: University of North Carolina Press, 1982), pp. 9–10.

37. Cowley recalled this remark of Faulkner's at a University of Mississippi writers' conference in 1972.

38. William Slavick, *DuBose Heyward* (Boston: Twayne, 1981), p. 112.

39. Davidson, quoted in Fred Hobson, *Tell About the South: The Southern Rage to Explain* (Baton Rouge: Louisiana State University Press, 1983), p. 238.

40. Howard Odum, quoted in Hobson, *Tell About the South,* p. 241.

41. Singal, *The War Within,* p. 156.

42. "Interview with Jean Stein vanden Heuvel," in *Lion in the Garden: Interviews with William Faulkner, 1926–1962,* edited by James B. Meriwether and Michael Millgate (New York: Random House, 1968), p. 255.

43. Joan St. C. Crane, "William Faulkner to Eudora Welty: A Letter," *Mississippi Quarterly,* 42 (Summer 1989): 223–227.

44. Virginia Spencer Carr, introduction to Katherine Anne Porter, *Flowering Judas,* edited by Carr (New Brunswick, N.J.: Rutgers University Press, 1993), p. 4.

45. Porter, *The Collected Essays and Occasional Writings of Katherine Anne Porter* (New York: Delacorte, 1970), p. 160.

46. Darlene Unrue, *Understanding Katherine Anne Porter* (Columbia: University of South Carolina Press, 1988), p. 47.

RELEVANCE OF THE SOUTHERN RENAISSANCE

WHY THE SOUTHERN RENAISSANCE IS STUDIED

When H. L. Mencken's 1917 essay "The Sahara of the Bozart" was republished in 1920 in the author's *Prejudices: Second Series,* it elicited specific responses from the young Southerners who constituted the first generation of writers of the Southern Renaissance. They were, however, predominantly in Mencken's favor rather than against him. Bright young Southerners admired him for his brashness and vivid language, and they wanted most of the things Mencken had said the South lacked. DuBose Heyward of South Carolina was moved by the essay to establish the Poetry Society of South Carolina in 1920, and perhaps there was wit behind forming a "poetry" society instead of just a literary one, for the name responded directly to Mencken's assertion that "Down there a poet is now almost as rare as an oboe-player, a dry-point etcher or a metaphysician."[1] The Society's first yearbook, published in 1921, characterized Mencken as a "sort of literary General Sherman"—a reference to the Union Civil War general who led the destructive "March to the Sea" and ordered the burning of Atlanta. But the same piece in the yearbook admitted that some of the "truths" in Mencken's essay could not be denied.[2]

Having editorialized in their first issue on aspects of Southern culture that they themselves fled, the editors of *The Fugitive* in Nashville sent a copy to Mencken in 1922, and he acknowledged the gift humorously in the Baltimore *Evening Sun,* writing that it represented "at the moment, the entire literature of Tennessee."[3] Since the nine poets represented in the volume had used silly pseudonyms, however, Mencken believed it was all the work of one writer. The Nashville poets were probably pleased and had a laugh, for the record shows that they read and admired Mencken; they lamented their region's pretensions as much as they regretted its lack of interest in the arts, old or new.[4] In New Orleans, the founders of *The Double Dealer* may have felt more confident about the "bozart" to be found in the French Quarter's bohemian culture,[5] but in

Walker Evans photograph of an Alabama tenant-farmer family
singing hymns, 1936

1920 their initial plan for a sophisticated "scandal sheet about local
affairs" turned serious in the wake of Mencken's essay, and they immediately fashioned a lively "bold and responsible" little magazine that published not only such promising Southerners as William Faulkner and
Allen Tate but also Sherwood Anderson and Ernest Hemingway.[6]

In Richmond, Mencken's essay was used to prod a Virginia audience the way the slogan "Banned in Boston" once helped to sell racy novels. In the first issue of *The Reviewer*, the new independent literary
magazine there, an editor quoted "The Sahara of the Bozart" liberally,
teased readers by revealing that the essay had much more to say on the
subject, some "unjust, some merely unsound," and then admitted that
"the main outline of his argument, the outstanding deductions, are so
true that it were petty to cavil at the weaknesses."[7] The lead piece in the
October 1921 issue of *The Reviewer* was by Mencken himself.

Many young people in the South came to admire and imitate Mencken's brash critical style, liked the magazines he edited, and knew that he was as hard on the rest of the boobs in America as he was on the ones he believed to be running the South. Careful readers of the essay would also have noted that "The Sahara of the Bozart" actually documents that Mencken possessed a view of the Old South that was mythic in its own way. He thought that the society of Virginia in Thomas Jefferson's time was the only culture yet erected on the continent but that following the Civil War the whole South had been taken over by rednecks. Southerners who may or may not have agreed with this opinion still found in the Baltimore writer a kindred spirit, one who vividly said things that they themselves had thought and were even trying to say themselves.

The Vanderbilt fugitives who were fleeing the "high class Brahmins" of the New South, the double dealers in New Orleans who were fed up with the syrupy sentiment of "moonlight and magnolias" literature, and Southern independents such as Faulkner who wanted to keep the hoopskirts out of their fiction actually had a champion. Mencken's essay was just one of many he wrote attacking the intellectual and aesthetic slackness of American culture, mocking its false piety and hypocritical Puritanism and attempting to promote a sensible high culture. "The Sahara of the Bozart" propitiously alerted the Southern press—which took exception to his claims—that a renaissance was needed. It did so just as the seeds of a modernist literary and intellectual revolution were being sown in Southern soil, more or less simultaneously all over the region. Thus, Mencken gave the Southern press reason to welcome its new literary heroes, helping their cause. Perhaps his essay and the discussions it generated even had a hand in inspiring the creation of book columns in more and more Southern newspapers during the era.

The Southern writers of the 1920s whose work answered at least a part of Mencken's charge had read enough great literature to understand that "The Sahara of the Bozart" was deliberate hyperbole, the wit of satire. Many of them knew something about the painters and poets of France and the "Secessionists" of Vienna who had rebelled against the stilted, officially sanctioned artistic styles of their day late in the nineteenth century. Mencken, they understood, was not taking comfort in contrasting a richly endowed North with the poor devastated South. He was, in fact, promoting a national rebellion against mediocrity, self-satisfaction, officious moralism, and censorship of the arts. The Southerners had also read the cultural criticism found in such different writers as Anderson, Mark Twain, Edith Wharton, Edward Arlington Robinson,

Edgar Lee Masters, Sinclair Lewis, and Virginia's James Branch Cabell (the only significant writer in the South, Mencken had extravagantly exclaimed, unaccountably omitting the ultimately more important Ellen Glasgow, a friend of Cabell's in Richmond). Mencken's appeal was similar to that of all great naysayers who punctured pretensions and institutionalized hypocrisies. In the "Sahara" essay and others, he attacked the booster-ridden cities and exhausted backwaters of an age noted for neither its sensitivity nor its morality.

Along with other young Americans, many of the writers of the Southern Renaissance had been involved in World War I, and all had watched its fearful progress. After the great cultures of Europe had beaten one another senseless and killed nearly an entire generation of the young, including many promising artists, even Mencken's yardstick for the beaux arts—European achievement in the arts—was suspect. The entire generation of the 1920s seemed to know that from Minneapolis to Memphis grasping boosters, bogus preachers, and industrialist lords of progress mouthed false pieties like those that perplex Jay Gatsby in F. Scott Fitzgerald's 1925 novel *The Great Gatsby* and bother Hemingway's Frederick Henry in *A Farewell to Arms* (1929). Gatsby's understanding of how the great American fortunes were built makes him comfortable dealing in illegal commodities and accepting the friendship of the man who fixed the 1919 World Series. When challenged about this man's behavior by the narrator of the novel, Nick Carraway, who thinks to himself that "It never occurred to me that one man could start to play with the faith of fifty million people," Gatsby's unperturbed reply is, "He just saw the opportunity."[8] When Henry thinks about his experience in the European war, he is

> always embarrassed by the words sacred, glorious, and sacrifice and the expression in vain. We had heard them, sometimes standing in the rain almost out of earshot, so that only the shouted words came through, and had read them, on proclamations that were slapped up by billposters over other proclamations, now for a long time, and I had seen nothing sacred, and the things that were glorious had no glory and the sacrifices were like the stockyards at Chicago if nothing was done with the meat except to bury it. . . . Abstract words such as glory, honor, courage, or hallow were obscene beside the concrete names of villages, the numbers of roads, the names of rivers, the numbers of regiments and the dates.[9]

It was not Mencken alone, thus, as M. Thomas Inge has written, who inspired the flowering of literature in the South; nor was it eighteenth-century Southern culture, which Mencken and many Southerners extravagantly admired. It was not specifically the Civil War, either, for though writers of the Southern Renaissance had great-grandfathers, and perhaps even grandfathers, who had experienced the war, the celebrations

Allen Tate in 1952

of the late Confederacy that they witnessed occasionally or read about, and the anecdotes they heard on stifling porches during long summer evenings, obliterated the harsh realities that had been the lot of the dead and wounded. Survivors and those with memories at second and third hand now told nostalgic tales of adventure and camaraderie. They came to reunions to see old friends and to bask in a glory they had missed when they were losing the war.

The shock of World War I for young Americans, it has been said, resulted from the dual deceptions about warfare created by nostalgia regarding the Civil War and magnification in the press of America's easy triumph in the short-lived Spanish-American War.[10] In *A Farewell to Arms* Henry speaks aptly about soldiering:

> The whole thing seemed to run better while I was away. The offensive was going to start again I heard. The division for which we worked were to attack at a place up the river and the major told me that I would see about the posts for during the attack. The attack would cross the river up above the narrow gorge and spread up the hillside. The posts for the cars would have to be as near the river as they could get and keep covered. They would, of course, be selected by the infantry but we were supposed to work it out. It was one of those things that gave you a false feeling of soldiering.[11]

False feelings were everywhere, some of them imposed by the calculating or the unthinking, some of them harbored by a generation that did not know exactly how it was supposed to feel.

Tate, born the same year as Hemingway but a stranger to war, expressed one version of the Southern mood in "Ode to the Confederate Dead," his homage not to the Lost Cause but to T. S. Eliot and the modernist culture of alienation. In the long poem, an uncertain man peers into a Civil War military cemetery on a windy fall afternoon, trying to figure out the "immoderate past" when men rose up so resolutely to do battle. He sees the leaves "Dazed by the wind . . . plunge and expire" like infantry charging a position and wonders what allowed the dead soldiers to curse the coming dark that would end a day's battle, so eager they were to fight. The coming dark means something else to him (as it does to Hemingway's Nick Adams in the 1925 short story "Big Two-Hearted River" when he looks down the river at the shadows where he chooses not to fish yet). Tate's thinker leaves the "desolation in the plot / Of a thousand acres where these memories grow" and his confrontation with the "immoderate past" without understanding, unsure of what to do next, even in the everydayness of his own life.[12]

Feelings such as those expressed in Tate's poem were fed by seeing, and in some cases surviving, the senseless brutality of a war that did not end all wars, watching life resume after the war as the empty busyness of routine existence in factory or office, hearing the uncovered falseness of slogans, and facing the new freedom to work out life for one's self outside the former nearly absolute restrictions or expectations of family, clan, community, and church. The forces that found young people everywhere and made them modernists had as much to do with the new literature of the South as they did with the new literature (and painting and music) of Europe and the American Midwest. One with Pablo Picasso, Igor Stravinsky, Ezra Pound, Eliot, and even with Charles Darwin and Sigmund Freud—whether they knew it yet or not—the writers of the Southern Renaissance who continue to matter most started by getting the feeling of the modern era. Much of it they got from reading widely and sharing ideas with others who also read. Some of it they got by traveling far enough from home to feel skeptical about themselves and their once-secure positions in the world. They rapidly turned their skepticism toward everything else, but through art rather than cynicism.

This surplus of critical intelligence did not mean that the writers of the Southern Renaissance retained no values or failed to find positive cultural memories in the recent or even the remote past. These young women and men had questions and did not accept easy answers, and as they read widely and compared their own writing with one another and with the great writing of the past, they discovered that feelings of flight from one's contemporary culture were common among the greatest artists of the past. Flight of one kind or another had been the lot of the classical writers whom they had studied piously in small-town Latin schools, the venerated giants of the Renaissance in Europe (from Dante and Cervantes to William Shakespeare and Christopher Marlowe), the great poets and novelists of the nineteenth century, the European dramatists of the turn of the century, and the modernists. Like the Buddhist fleeing Buddha—who may do so only in Buddha's hand, goes the story—the Southerners who started, literally or figuratively, walking toward the door were always carrying the South with them. For all of them, depending on where they had grown up and where they had formed their new ideas, what they carried was different. Yet, all of it related to their Southern heritage. They existed within a kind of cousinship of shared relationships that the Fugitives liked to evoke, addressing one another and new friends as "Dear Cousin."

If "The Sahara of the Bozart" aroused the pride or confirmed the critical judgments of the new generation in the South, another Mencken essay may have promoted both the craftsmanship and the congenial but stringent self-criticism for which some of the Fugitives later became world-famous. In "Criticism of Criticism of Criticism," from *Prejudices: First Series* (1919), Mencken promoted a literary criticism based upon craft judgments, not biographical or narrowly moralistic ones. The essay promotes, even as it enlarges upon, the views of Professor Joel Spingarn, who had left Columbia University to serve in World War I as a major, a fact that appealed to Mencken, apparently, as an indicator that Spingarn, unlike other professors of the day who made critical judgments, knew something of the world. Spingarn had written a book titled *The New Criticism* (1911)—a title John Crowe Ransom used in 1941—advocating an analytic and creative criticism based on the doctrine that (in Mencken's paraphrase) the "poem was the thing," and the "character and background of the poet" were *not* the thing. This theory, Mencken writes,

> imposes a heavy burden upon the critic. It presupposes that he is a civil and tolerant man, hospitable to all intelligible ideas and capable of reading them as he runs. This is a demand that at once rules out nine-tenths of the grown-up sophomores who carry on the business of criticism in America. Their trouble is simply that they lack the intellectual resilience necessary for taking in ideas, and particularly new ideas. The only way they can ingest one is by transforming it into the nearest related formula—usually a harsh and devastating operation. This fact accounts for their chronic inability to understand all that is most personal and original and hence most forceful and significant in the emerging literature of the country. They can get down what has been digested and redigested, and so brought into forms that they know, and carefully labeled by predecessors of their own sort—but they exhibit alarm immediately they come into the presence of the extraordinary . . . and here we have an explanation of [critic William Lyon] Phelps's inability to comprehend the colossal phenomenon of Dreiser . . . and of all the fatuous pigeonholing that passes for criticism in the more solemn literary periodicals.[13]

Mencken's essay, which comes to its own conclusions regarding a new criticism that would judge a work by its clarity, sincerity, the force and charm of its ideas, the technical virtuosity of the artist, and the artist's originality and courage, sounds like a plan for the program of self-criticism that the Fugitives practiced on one another during their early meetings in Nashville. It prefigures the criticism they practiced as teachers and later wrote as critics and popularizers of their own "New Criticism."

To speak, then, of the relevance of the Southern Renaissance is to consider several matters. The literary renaissance in the South of the 1920s has perhaps failed to receive quite as much credit as it deserves for being another theater of American modernism. It ranks with the imagist group, the Midwestern expressionists, and the expatriates. One aspect of its relevance is the way its members discovered and fostered new attitudes about both literature and society, inspiring a generation of young people who tried not to become mired in sentimentality and false morality or fooled by official dogma. Another matter is how the Southern division of the modernist movement set many of its writers in search of a new aesthetic, one that demanded craft but did not reject the subject of history. Still another matter is its ethical stance, which at its best evolved not as a new dogma that could easily become false over time but as a critical and increasingly humanistic perspective that continued to question the Southern status quo regarding economics, religious practice, education, and race.

Like writers from other regions, the Southerners had some ideas about how to restore the power of human expression, but instead of stripping language to the basic words that describe acts directly or what one can see—the project of writers such as Hemingway or the poet William Carlos Williams—they dipped into their traditions of stump and courtroom rhetoric, tale-telling, exaggeration, extravagance, languor, and intransigence. The Southerners' ear for the circumlocutions of memory gave them congeniality with the descent into the stream of consciousness as well as the eccentric ideolect of the individual narrative voice. For all that the Fugitives, particularly, are seen as deep-seated cultural conservatives, Ransom reviewed Freud appreciatively

ECONOMIC AND LITERARY EXPLOITATION

"The impact of national forces—economic, political, and social—has made for quick and uncharacteristic change, partly encouraged and in part resisted. An element of outside exploitation has caused the South to revert somewhat to a colonial, rather than a regional status. In the field of literature, commercial and editorial pressures have encouraged a similar exploitation, in books that frequently have the tone of exposé and reform worked through the fabric of explanation.... Confusion at home and abroad have led to lumping together as essentially kin the novels of Caldwell and of Faulkner, with no recognition of the purposes or limits of fiction, no recognition of Faulkner's success as contrasted with [T. S.] Stribling's failure in the creation of literature. The same confusions have led critics to deny there could be artistic reality in the dissimilar but valid Mississippi novels of Faulkner and of Stark Young—that there could be varying strata of people worth writing about, as there are varying geological strata worth studying."

Edd Winfield Parks

From *Segments of Southern Thought: Essays in the Re-evaluation of Southern Life and Literature, Old and New* (Athens: University of Georgia Press, 1938), p. 127.

in a national magazine one year before the Scopes "Monkey Trial" in Dayton, Tennessee, and two years before his friend Tate wrote his ironic "Ode to the Confederate Dead" imitating the form and thought of Eliot's psychological style.[14] More than simply disbelieving the falsified past, the writers of the Southern Renaissance began to attempt a correction of the record, some in biographies, some in magisterial essays, and some, like Faulkner, in works of the imagination. In turn, all these efforts helped to inspire not only another generation of creative writers but also one or two generations of professional historians of the South, who began to look at the record more closely and write what they found, often quoting from fiction and poetry to dramatize their data.

If the modernist movement is relevant as a subject today—and though it is debated, it certainly remains important—so is the Southern Renaissance. The writers of the period enrolled in the ranks of the modernists, even though they did not all always create the kinds of works that immediately proclaimed themselves as disorienting and destabilizing challenges to establishment art. Historian Daniel J. Singal, in *The War Within: From Victorian to Modernist Thought in the South, 1919–1945* (1982), argues that the "crowning blow" to Victorian thought "came from cultural anthropology. Its field studies proved consistently that 'savage' life was not as different from civilized life as the Victorians had supposed," and civilization "could no longer be construed as some vague spiritual quality [only] cultured people possessed"; "it was a set of traits and practices people invented to adapt to the particular environment they found themselves in," and thus, all organized human life was civilized.[15]

There was, of course, no specific day when this information hit even the rising generation of Southern writers, much less the general populace, but no culture ever needed such information more than the South, where myths of race and class had solidified into customs and laws that kept a large part of the population, black and white, in a subject position and culturally invisible to much of the middle class. The importance of African American life to the Southern Renaissance as a subject, a dramatic force, and a source of ideas and feelings mediated through modernist music—blues and jazz—is incalculable. Zora Neale Hurston was not the only anthropologist researching and writing in the South.

In different ways, the best writers of the Southern Renaissance applied the modernist slant to something that was more important to the Southern experience than anyone before them was able to express. Their subject increasingly became an enlarged sense of exactly what the Southern experience was. What is especially relevant about the best writing of the Southern Renaissance, then, is the way it combines knowledge and imagination, the past with the modern reaction to the past, traditional ways of telling stories with ways made relevant by modern psychology, anthropology, philosophy, theology, and history. To read the work of Glasgow or the contemporary Mississippi writer Ellen Gilchrist is not only to encounter stories that sound true-to-life but also to discover the tracks of deeply read philosophical thinkers. From Katherine Anne Porter to Walker Percy it is the same. The great writers of the first two decades of the Southern Renaissance did not stumble out of the woods mumbling folktales, nor did they drop the plow and rush inside to write poems, and no amount of listening to uncles and aunts talking on the summer porch could, alone, provoke into being novels such as *The Sound and the Fury; Look Homeward, Angel; All the King's Men; Native Son;* or even that marvelous and touching novel that begins and ends with talking on a porch, Hurston's *Their Eyes Were Watching God.* Like Prometheus, they brought fire to humankind, which is a way of saying they brought imagination to everyday human affairs. Their field of play was the slowly vanishing transitional South. Like Prometheus, many of these writers were punished for their assertiveness, cursed by another Southern tradition—alcoholism—that shortened their productive lives, or simply reviled by their townspeople.

WORLD WAR I

"With the war of 1914-1918, the South reentered the world—but gave a backward glance as it stepped over the border: that backward glance gave us the Southern renascence, a literature conscious of the past in the present."

Allen Tate

From "The New Provincialism," in his *Essays of Four Decades* (Chicago: Swallow Press, 1968), p. 545.

The writers of the first generation of the Southern Renaissance did more, however, than make the small, brief mark against time that Tate believed was their fate. They initiated a tradition that hundreds of later writers also embraced. The movement will be over only when the South is no different from any other place in America, an end that some writers have already envisioned but that seems in certain respects doubtful, if only because the writing that already exists helps to keep a distinctive South present.

In 1929, the year that Faulkner's *The Sound and the Fury* and Thomas Wolfe's *Look Homeward, Angel* were published, an essay titled "The Mind of the South" appeared in Mencken's *American Mercury,* but Mencken did not write it. The author was a Southern journalist who had grown up in ordinary circumstances in North Carolina. The title was later attached to his seminal book-length meditation on what he knew about the South—especially the white communities of the Piedmont South. *The Mind of the South* was published in 1941, the year of Richard Wright's *12 Million Black Voices,* Eudora Welty's *A Curtain of Green,* and of course America's entrance into World War II.

Wilbur J. Cash's *The Mind of the South* remains a much-discussed contribution to the debate about Southern culture and its myths, a debate he did not live to join since he committed suicide in Mexico City the year his book appeared, a victim of depression and, possibly, the alcoholism from which writers from Faulkner to William Styron have suffered.[16] In his 1929 essay in Mencken's *American Mercury,* Cash sounded like Mencken himself: "the mind of that heroic region, I opine, is still basically and essentially the mind of the Old South. It is a mind, that is to say, of the soil rather than of the mills—a mind, indeed, which, as yet, is almost wholly unadjusted to the new industry." Cash argues that the South's

> salient characteristic is a magnificent incapacity for the real, a Brobdingnagian talent for the fantastic. The very legend of the Old South, for example, is warp and woof of the Southern mind. The "plantation" which prevailed outside the tidewater and delta regions was actually no more than a farm; its owner was, properly, neither a planter nor an aristocrat, but a backwoods farmer; yet the pretension to aristocracy was universal. Every farmhouse became a Big House, every farm a baronial estate, every master of scant red acres . . . a feudal lord. . . . It is not without a certain aptness, then, that the Southerner's chosen drink is called moonshine. Everywhere he turns away from reality to a gaudy world of his own making."[17]

After mentioning the contrast to this "moonshine" just then being expressed in honest terms by a few South Carolina writers and the sociologists and playwrights at Chapel Hill, Cash closes by observing, "Eventually, of course, must come change. Perhaps, indeed, the beginning of it is already at hand. For, undeniably, there is a stir, a rustling upon the land, a vague, formless, intangible thing which may or may not be the adumbration of coming upheaval. Tomorrow—the day after—eventually—the cotton-mill peon will acquire the labor outlook and the explosion will follow." But, he laments, "I suspect that the South will merely repeat the dismal history of Yankeedom, that we shall have the hog . . . and nothing else . . . merely exchange the Confederate for that dread fellow, the go-getter . . . the Hon. John LaFarge Beauregard for [Sinclair Lewis's] George F. Babbitt. I suspect, in other words, that the last case will be infinitely worse than the first."[18]

Cash remains an important voice of the Southern Renaissance, but many voices ran counter to his pessimistic view, including the African American social scientist, teacher, and editor W. E. B. Du Bois, who himself wrote an interesting piece about the South several years before Cash's essay appeared. In 1925 *The Nation* ran a series of forty-eight essays on each of the United States, almost all of them written by well-known writers. Du Bois, the author of *The Souls of Black Folk* (1903), in which he had sought to promote the value of both classical and folk knowledge and the contributions of African Americans to national life, had taught at Atlanta University and knew the South. He wrote as eloquently about Georgia as any native child could have wished, in a voice that anticipated Wolfe and Faulkner. Yet, as Du Bois observed as an African American in the South, "few speak of the beauty of Georgia.

. . . [which] connotes to most men national supremacy in cotton and lynching, Southern supremacy in finance and industry, and the Ku Klux Klan."[19] Du Bois, unlike Cash, who condescended to the "mill peon" and ignored African Americans, had a vision that included the poor of both races, observing that their positions were maintained by the lords of industry and agriculture, who had a vested interest in keeping the price of labor low and did so by keeping poor classes of both races apart so they could not organize, earn more, own land, and vote.

What Du Bois saw in Georgia, eventually other writers saw there, too—Erskine Caldwell in his 1932 novel *Tobacco Road,* Lillian Smith in *Killers of the Dream* (1949)—the contradictions inherent in the highly promoted antipathy between rural and urban poor of both races. Near the end of the first wave of the Southern Renaissance, Faulkner found new ways to handle the issue as well, in *The Hamlet* and *Go Down, Moses,* and resumed his career following a hiatus during World War II with *Intruder in the Dust,* in which blacks and whites unite to seek justice. The South's issues and problems, thus, were as much the subjects of Southern Renaissance writers as were its history and larger fate. As is often the case, imaginative literature opened questions that society, politics, and even religion had closed, making the Renaissance, especially in its prime, relevant on all counts.

Dust jacket for Faulkner's 1940 novel, the first volume in his trilogy concerning the Snopes family

It is conventionally remarked that what made the Southern Renaissance remarkable during this period was the exceptionally large number of excellent writers who appeared on the scene and wrote books, poems, or plays of lasting merit. Depending on who is counting, the number runs from four hundred to more than five hundred authors doing serious writing for the period 1919–1941, and Lewis Lawson counts more than four hundred novelists alone who published a first book after 1940 and before 1983. But in reality, there were not many who succeeded extraordinarily in the first generation of the Southern Renais-

COLONELS INTO CAPITALISTS

"[T]here had been some vocal discontent with the domination of the southern myth ever since the 1880s. And this discontent became increasingly aggressive as southern cultural patterns became more rigid in the last years of the century because of the failure of the Populistic impulse and of the introduction of segregation and Negro disfranchisement. In a sense certain Confederates were responsible for the growing disenchantment with the myth. Defeated by the Yankees, they seemed determined to champion the myth but to practice the opposite; many Confederate Brigadiers became Southern Bourbons, those Southerners of upper class who aligned themselves with Northern capitalists intent upon exploiting the South. Many became involved in questionable activities, in railroad manipulation, land grants, and speculation, and others lent their names to notorious schemes."

Lewis Lawson

From *Another Generation: Southern Fiction Since World War II* (Jackson: University Press of Mississippi, 1983), p. 5.

sance. Only about thirty writers have achieved the first rank (as yet) of public or scholarly interest, and this includes several remarkable African American writers who were for a long time even more neglected by literary history than, say, Faulkner was until he received the Nobel Prize in 1950.[20]

What the most-talented and now best-known writers of this first generation achieved is indeed remarkable, and one suspects that their achievement had to do not only with how smart they were, how much they read, and how lives lived in simpler times allowed them to absorb experience without the distractions of the current age, but also with their consciousness of a cohesive, enveloping culture from which they fell—on purpose—with all the shock of the new the world could muster. Like the orchard thieves of Eden, as Twain called Adam and Eve, the members of the Southern Renaissance endured expulsion because they lost their innocence and gained forbidden knowledge of the standards of another realm. What they learned they applied inventively to what they innately knew but had lost, even when they settled back within it. The best of them found ways to regard what was lost through the lens of influences that resonated with the power of classical, medieval, renaissance, and eighteenth- and nineteenth-century literature, as well as modernist artistic expression. This absorbing of influences was not cut-and-paste work. The process of great writing goes deeper than that, and the sophistication of their depth of vision into their own culture, into the culture of speaking and writing in general, and into aspects of world culture gave compelling power to the best work of these writers.

What makes the writing of the Southern Renaissance relevant is its intelligence—about writing, Southern culture, language, and human feelings. That is the general relevance. What made it relevant to its times was the way in which the writers created variations on the spirit of the times: the modernist moment, first, and then the complicated descent through the Depression, another and even more economically costly world war, and what is now being called the American Century.

Works by writers of the Southern Renaissance have traveled well to other cultures and to subsequent generations. People have laughed and cried in other languages over these books, and they have seen their own lives and cultures X-rayed—revealed by virtue of the shadowy obverse that is art. As is known from the record of international responses by writers, philosophers, teachers, and readers, the work of the Southern Renaissance has demonstrated relevance to world culture for quite a long time, spawning literary movements even in some of the far-flung regions Mencken named as culturally arid when he sought images of the South's benightedness.[21]

HISTORICAL FOUNDATIONS OF THE SOUTHERN RENAISSANCE

Slavery had made much of the South a society with a large African American population, and race consciousness bred by slavery and politics helped make the South—and even, for a time, most of the American nation—a place where, regardless of history, racial definitions and separation were enforced by custom and legal codes even after the practice of slavery was forcibly ended. That these codes persisted, became more complex, and fostered violence in the South affected the Southern experience even more gravely than fighting and losing the Civil War affected the states that made up the Confederacy.

How is it, then, that such experience created a literary renaissance that is remarkable not only for its creativity but also for its increasingly critical perspective on Southern culture? What makes the South distinctive within the United States is a matter for considerable debate. After considering several factors, many commentators have centered first upon the South's climate and topography: the heat and humidity, the violent weather—tornadoes and hurricanes—the floods and droughts, the valleys and floodplains of incredibly rich soil, the long growing season, the mosquitoes, the lush vegetation, and the sparsity of settlement (even today an automobile trip through the South is characterized by views of enormous open spaces, great forests, and the threatening look of strange, looming roadside forms made by draped kudzu).

Topography and weather, it is then said, imposed a history on the South: pushed it into large-scale commercial agriculture of big cash crops marketable on a world stage—sugarcane, indigo, rice, cotton, and tobacco—and doomed it first to accept, then promote and profit from,

GENDER IN THE SOUTH

"During the Southern Renaissance . . . writers from the most canonized to the most obscure carried on the cultural work of revising gender. As women found new ground and focus for their identities, locating them within rather than outside the woman's body, men simultaneously explored new possibilities for manhood yet reacted with anxiety to the new freedom of women. Perhaps it was too much, too soon, certainly there was an air both of giddiness and of terror for all concerned. Yet, their experiments with gender were as serious as their experiments with racial boundaries and with modernist fictional form. After all, any rewriting of gender in the form of narrative must take as an assumption that culture, rather than nature, constructs gender itself. Otherwise writing could make no difference at all. The work of these women and men with gender thus deserves to become visible as a major component of and contributor to the Southern Renaissance."

Anne Goodwyn Jones

From "The Work of Gender in the Southern Renaissance," in *Southern Writers and Their Worlds*, edited by Christopher Morris and Steven G. Reinhardt (College Station: University of Texas at Arlington/Texas A&M University Press, 1996), pp. 55–56.

and, finally, fiercely defend the practice of slavery, out of which developed a virulent racism that divided Southern society, doomed its educational system for decades, and put a curse on the nation. As historian David L. Smiley has observed, the "climate-determined South was largely mythic, however, and it appeared as so self-serving—an excuse for such glaring inequities in the status quo—that it has been under constant attack. The idea [of a single-climate South] was also difficult to defend in a region that extended through 15 degrees of latitude, and from sea level to the forested heights of Appalachia, from humid woodlands to semi-arid plains."[22]

Smiley goes on to cite several "central" themes that historians and journalistic commentators have raised, from the influence of frontier violence, sexual domination (white men over black women and white women over malleable men), isolation and indifference to community values such as road and bridge building, and "such phenomena as fireworks at Christmas and a quiet Fourth of July, mockingbirds, xenophobia, a chivalric respect for the ladies, a slovenly and dialectic speech pattern, and shoeless, clay-eating poverty. Pellagra, malaria, and hookworm have also provided thematic interpretations," as have religious fervor, one-party politics, and states' rights.[23] None of these explanations mentions the Civil War—which the South preferred, in a states' rights mood, to call "The War Between the States"—and most of them ignore the presence, long history, influence, and continued push for equality of African Americans and all that goes with their struggle, including special legal codes in the past and the Civil Rights movement in the modern era.

In a wise summary, Smiley—whose observations represent a distillation of scores of books about the South—notes that these themes can all be subsumed under the theory of the great Southern historian C. Vann Woodward that "the central theme of southern history" is "southern history itself."[24] Woodward believed that this history not only set the South apart from the rest of the American nation, both its national culture and its other regional cultures, but also ironically gave the South a history more in keeping with, and common to, the histories of other cultures throughout the world. He expresses this situation eloquently in *The Burden of Southern History* (1960), specifically in a chapter appropriately called "The Irony of Southern History." His argument is set up so well that it is worth quoting at length:

> In a time when nationalism sweeps everything else before it . . . the regional historian is likely to be oppressed by a sense of his unimportance. America is the all-important subject, and national ideas, national institutions, and national policies are the themes that compel attention. Foreign peoples, eager to know what this New-World colossus means to them and their immediate future, are impatient with details of regional variations, and Americans, intent on the need for national unity, tend to minimize their importance. New England, the West, and other regions are occasionally permitted to speak for the nation. But the South is thought to be hedged about with peculiarities that set it apart as unique. As a standpoint from which to write American history it is regarded as eccentric and, as a background for an historian, something of a handicap to be overcome.

> Of the eccentric position of the South in the nation there are admittedly many remaining indications. I do not think, however, that this eccentricity need be regarded as entirely a handicap. In fact, I think that it could possibly be turned to advantage by the Southern historian, both in understanding American history and in interpreting it to non-Americans. For from a broader point of view it is not the South but America that is unique among the peoples of the world. This peculiarity arises out of the American legend of success and victory, a legend that is not shared by any other people of the civilized world. The collective will of this country has simply never known what it means to be confronted by complete frustration. Whether by luck, by abundant resources, by ingenuity, by technology, by organizing cleverness, or by sheer force of arms America has been able to overcome every major historic crisis—economic, political, or foreign—with which it has had to cope. This remarkable record has naturally left a deep imprint upon the American mind. It explains in large part the national faith in unlimited progress, in the efficacy of material means, in the importance of mass and speed, the worship of success, and the belief in the invincibility of American arms. . . .

> The South has had its full share of illusions, fantasies, and pretensions, and it has continued to cling to some of them with an astonishing tenacity that defies explanation. But the illusion that "history is something unpleasant that happens to other people" is certainly not one of them. . . . For the inescapable facts of [Southern] history were that the South had repeatedly met with frustration and failure. It had learned what it was to be faced with economic, social, and political problems that refused to yield to all the ingenuity, patience, and intelligence that a people could bring to bear upon them. It had learned to accommodate itself to conditions that it swore it would never accept, and it had learned the taste left in the mouth by the swallowing of one's own words. It had learned to live for long decades in quite un-American poverty, and had learned the equally un-American lesson of submission. For the South had undergone an experience that it could share with no other part of America—though it is

shared by nearly all the peoples of Europe and Asia—the experience of military defeat, occupation, and reconstruction. Nothing about this history was conducive to the theory that the South was the darling of divine providence.[25]

In *Inventing Southern Literature* (1998), the literary scholar Michael Kreyling makes the postmodern statement that whereas "contemporary literary critics and historians are weaned on the idea of the constructedness of meanings . . . critics of southern literature . . . have been more rigorously schooled than others in the orthodox faith that our subject is not invented by our discussions of it but rather is revealed by a constant southern identity."[26] This is a useful point, with application to the subject at hand, for the Southern Renaissance certainly was created by discussion, and perhaps so was the region's distinctiveness, a point argued thoroughly in historian Michael O'Brien's landmark *The Idea of the American South, 1920–1941* (1979). Finally, in an introduction to a symposium that encouraged comparative studies of the South against other national and regional cultures, *What Made the South Different?* (1990), Kees Gispen notes that what emerges "time and again" from such analyses "is the overwhelming importance of incongruity," the contradictions in Southern culture: "The South was not a case of capitalism *or* slave system, tradition *or* modernity, bourgeois liberalism *or* patriarchal conservatism, but rather their simultaneity, confrontation and amalgamation: capitalism *and* slavery, tradition *and* modernity, liberalism *and* conservatism, shading into one another as though aligned in a continuous spectrum and combining in the unexpected ways of a hybrid."[27]

Gispen might also have noted that contradictions are a hallmark of human behavior in general, whether they take the name of ambiguity, failure to stick to the point, contrariness, or creativity. Hybridity and contingency are other terms to use in speaking of the South and its art, for they apply to the literature as well as to the important musical traditions, which originated as folk expression, rose into prominence, and received formal structure—as did the Southern penchant for storytelling—in the period essentially cognate with the literary renaissance. These musical traditions include blues, jazz, gospel, and what has been called "country" music. Contingency is the great subject of blues: the uncertainty of the weather, love, happiness, and life itself, evoked in stories told with verve and humor. Hybridity was the great triumph of Southern music: Mississippi's Jimmie Rodgers, a white railroad man, blended a cowboy yodel with the twang of the blues, Bessie Smith and Ray Charles carried the passion of gospel into the realm of more earthly passion, and Elvis Presley drew the strands together any way he wanted.

The South, bastion of states' rights, talked about itself as a unity, though confederation never worked. The South built monuments to its failures, sometimes with irony: a town in Alabama raised a monument to the boll weevil because the insect's depredations—which temporarily contributed to an economic crisis throughout the cotton-growing South— freed the town from one-crop agriculture. In Oxford, Mississippi, disputes about the placement of the traditional monument to the Confederate soldier (Faulkner's grandmother was involved) resulted in rival monuments, neither of which faces the traditional North, opposing the enemy. One even faces the South, looking hopelessly for reinforcements, as one wit has said. The memorial carved on the side of Stone Mountain, near Atlanta, showing Robert E. Lee, Jefferson Davis, and Stonewall Jackson riding home with their hats off, is a monument to defeat.

THE SOUTHERN RENAISSANCE AND THE MODERNIST MOVEMENT

Tate's identification of the Southern Renaissance as having happened "between the two world wars" draws attention to the strong relationship between the specific Southern phenomenon and modernism, or the modernist movement. Although modernism is traced back to at least 1890 in a landmark study of the movement's origins in Europe,[28] it certainly reached a high point for literature in the English-speaking world between the two world wars. Stressing the "Southernness" of this regional expression of modernism, identifying it solely with Southern cultural conservatism, and even trumpeting its existence pridefully as a purely Southern phenomenon represents a form of regional chauvinism and has caused some inattention to the point that the Southern Renaissance was, in reality, a "southern branch office of the midwestern division of the North American franchise of that international movement in the arts" that flourished first in Europe.[29]

The reaction against modernity that became the modernist movement, as is now well recognized, revolutionized the arts long before the cultural disaster of World War I. Before 1914, the year the war began, there was new painting, music, fiction, drama, and poetry, as well as new anthropology and psychology and new or newly influential philosophies of time, memory, and being. Those pre–World War I creative tides found their way to America quite rapidly. Freud was invited to lecture on psychoanalysis at Clark University in Worcester, Massachusetts, some thirty miles from Harvard University, in the fall of 1909. Examples of the strange new paintings by "Les Fauves"—the "wild beasts" who experimented with violent color—and by such Cubists as Picasso were displayed in New York in 1913 in the famous Armory Show and traveled on to Chicago; newspaper and magazine coverage of the exhibition, and parodies of its art, reached a wide audience. Such adventurous, noncommercial "little" magazines as *Poetry: A Magazine of Verse* and *The Little Review* were founded in Chicago in 1912 and 1914, respectively, and began to popularize new writing from America and abroad. Two of the most visible writers were Eliot and James Joyce, who were so influential that the critic Stanley Sultan has defined "modernism"—rashly, one might add—as that period in twentieth-century letters that felt the impact of their work.[30]

The nationalistic tides that led to World War I and the squandering of energy, wealth, culture, and human life that occurred during the war miraculously did not stop the new century's creative currents; rather, the war seemed to intensify them. For young Americans who made it to the European war, or wished they had, the exposure to new ideas took on special power, for the war had in many respects confirmed the new theories of psychology and anthropology, revealed the darkness beneath genteel bourgeois society and the hypocrisy of its political and religious platitudes, and validated discordant, violent, and otherwise nonconforming expression in the new art, literature, and music.

What occurred makes simple sense. Among those affected by the rising tide of modernity, the disillusionment inspired by modern warfare, and the doubts about social and political pieties were many young Southerners of intelligence and imagination. If they did not leave home, they happened upon revolutionary ideas and images in the "little" magazines, especially *The Little Review*, and in such commercial magazines of the arts and ideas as *The Dial, The Smart Set, Vanity Fair,* and *The New Republic*. If they did leave home, it was to attend modest but intellectually stimulating universities, serve in the Great War, or find employment in cities where, as newspaper writers or simply postwar travelers, they encountered realities different from those they had been raised with in provincial Southern towns. Those young people who lacked such experiences themselves often encountered better-informed companions, usually a little older, who had studied at a good university, traveled abroad, or served in the war.

Young Southerners could not personally remember their own Great War—the Civil War. But most of them were not allowed to forget it, especially since this generation, born in the 1890s for the most part, had grown up in the era when the South was most active in commemorating the "Lost Cause" of Southern independence. They lost no time in responding to the war in Europe in their own ways, and the sentimentality of Southern celebrations of defeat inspired many of them to write in any other manner than the sentimental. Southern culture was conservative, but not really more so than the culture of the rest of rural and small-town America, and much of that conservatism, both in the South and elsewhere, was hypocritical or simply ill informed. Modernism was also conservative, but it was conservative about what its practitioners thought was a higher order of human concerns. The modernist opposition to "modernity" resisted the transformation taking place in capitalistic industrial society that promoted standardized work and products and inhuman efficiency at the expense of individuality and self-satisfaction. Personal craft, time, and feelings were, in the view of many, being streamlined out of existence. The vagaries of the human imagination were ruled out, as was the individual signature on human labor made by a person who advanced or altered a tradition by reflection or even by happy accident. Science would explain everything, including society, and technology would make it work rationally and regularly. The machine age, as this period of an ethos (and aesthetic) of streamlining is sometimes called, had its attractions: museums have collected its vacuum cleaners, teapots, lampstands, and locomotives, and everyone still seems to want its automobiles, as they began to do with a vengeance in this era. Unfortunately, its highest achievement, looked at one way, was the great machine-driven war of 1914–1918, in which all the new tools and products of heavy industry were brought to bear upon the process of multinational murder and destruction, and that was not even its ultimate outcome. Such "modernists" as Adolf Hitler in Germany, Benito Mussolini in Italy, and Joseph Stalin in Russia attempted less than a generation later to fashion new societies perfected under the rules of inhuman control, social uniformity, and efficient organization learned, one might say, by watching the automobile-factory assembly line.[31]

Before and between the two world wars, modernism, as a movement of thought and imagination, was a warning, a protest, and a demonstration of alternatives. Its artists found radical-looking ways to express their conservative concerns, though often their sources and images derived from the most ancient and deeply ingrained qualities of human thought: myth, "primitive" culture and art, evolutionary biology, historical linguistics, and depth psychology. Verse was set free, as were the language and subject matter of fiction, the making of paintings and sculptures, the critical perception of places and cultures, and even memory and desire. The critic Harry Levin has argued that modernists felt "belated and up-to-date simultaneously," working "experimental transformations into traditional continuities."[32] Richard J. Calhoun asserts that the Southerners whose literary coming of age coincided with modernism derived their power from a "tension" that existed because of their desire to be unsentimental Southerners and, at the same instant, to be technically modern.[33] Their conservatism derived from a real love of the places where they had grown up; their modernism, from all the reasons they had discovered to mistrust what they were told about those places.

Anyone who has read Fitzgerald's *The Great Gatsby* is aware of the modernist's critique of the machine—Gatsby's past in a machine-gun battalion, the negative role of automobiles—and the effects of World War I. The war irrevocably interrupts Gatsby's courtship of Daisy Fay, which he cannot resume with the same innocence the world had before the war began. Symbolically, Gatsby's dubious postwar economic success and his life are ended at the hands of a madman, George Wilson, whose name suggests the leaders of the Allied powers in the war (King George V of England and Woodrow Wilson of America) and who is an automobile mechanic. Hemingway's short-story collection *In Our Time* (1925) dramatizes similar modernist perceptions, from the violence that pervades the tiny between-chapter vignettes to the estrangement toward even the natural world that the war has fostered in the young veteran Nick Adams. Fitzgerald's Gatsby gives garden parties that do not really succeed; Hemingway's young Nick recalls the conjunction of locker-room bragging and suicide in "Indian Camp" and experiences the fear of fishing in a burnt-out land in "Big Two-Hearted River." Whether the text is Eliot's poem *The Waste Land* (1922) or Elmer Rice's now little-known expressionistic play *The Adding Machine* (1923), the voice of American modernists is not just a whine of despair in a bad time but a critique of what has occurred in the industrialized world, a dramatization of the way people caught in the cogs of modernity feel. Charlie Chaplin's witty movie *Modern Times* (1936) is a graphic protest of the same things. Ironically, the motion-picture medium requires the same technology as that in which the little tramp is caught as he works on an assembly line: he falls into a machine and is rolled in and out on a cogwheel.

The South of the period between the two world wars might not have seemed to be in the thrall of the factory system and the inhumane regimentation it represented, especially when critics in the North chided it for not having reaped the benefits that nineteenth-century robber barons had bestowed upon the country's urban centers—great libraries, museums, endowments for symphonies, and patronage for opera and theater, all funded from the enormous profits achieved by monopolists. The South was, however, feeling the results of its own dabbling in regimentation and industry, even though the industry was primarily what is today called agribusiness. There were, and are, many Souths, and the era of the Southern Renaissance was the period historian Numan Bartley identifies as coincident with a national impression that the former Confederacy had become the "benighted South"—a region of ignorance and sentimentality, of poverty and injustice, of bad roads and bad morals, and of "redneck" ideas not only in politics but also in culture. Even if one accepts this view of the South, however, there is room to recognize that in the 1920s farming was moving toward increased mechanization and rationalization. Industry was on the rise along the Piedmont corridor, with textile mills being established from North Carolina to Mississippi and tobacco-processing and soft-drink companies starting their climb to the kind of wealth that endowed universities. Southern cities were now regional headquarters for food processing and hardware distribution that sent traveling salesmen into the countryside and standard brands into the stores of county-seat towns. As in the slave-plantation era, Southern agriculture was once again practiced on a large scale, with hordes of laborers who, like millworkers,

The Richmond writer James Branch Cabell, whose controversial 1919 novel *Jurgen* won praise even from H. L. Mencken, who considered the South to be a cultural wasteland

worked at backbreaking jobs for long hours regardless of age, gender, or condition and lived in cheap housing they could never own. Like millworkers, these agricultural laborers were dependent on credit at the company store and subject to dismissal on any grounds whatsoever. The South had apparent leisure because most of its enterprises followed the seasonal rhythms of agriculture, but for the many who owned no land and could not even plant a kitchen garden, this meant being periodically out of work, on reduced incomes, or dependent on a ruthless system of finance capitalism that kept them poor and servile.

In every way, then, the mixed blessings of modernity had an impact upon the South, and even the slow passage of Southern time brought radical changes in thinking and action that produced reflection on the part of the region's writers. The high point of this phenomenon in the beaux arts was from 1919 to 1941, from Cabell's *Jurgen* to Faulkner's *Go Down, Moses*, Wright's *Native Son*, and Welty's *A Curtain of Green*. The shadow of the wasteland somehow made the "Sahara of the Bozart" bloom.

NOTES

1. H. L. Mencken, "The Sahara of the Bozart" (1920), in *Defining Southern Literature: Perspectives and Assessments, 1831–1952,* edited by John E. Bassett (Madison & Teaneck, N.J.: Fairleigh Dickinson University Press / London: Associated University Presses, 1997), p. 284.

2. "The Worm Turns, Being in Some Sort a Reply to Mr. H. L. Mencken," *Year Book of the Poetry Society of South Carolina,* 1 (1921); quoted in Fred Hobson, *Serpent in Eden: H. L. Mencken and the South* (Chapel Hill: University of North Carolina Press, 1974), p. 31.

3. Mencken, quoted in Hobson, *Serpent in Eden: H. L. Mencken and the South,* p. 73.

4. Hobson, *Serpent in Eden: H. L. Mencken and the South,* p. 72.

5. Robert M. Crunden, *American Salons: Encounters with European Modernism, 1885–1917* (New York & Oxford: Oxford University Press, 1993), pp. 125–144.

6. Ibid., p. 31.

7. Ibid.

8. F. Scott Fitzgerald, *The Great Gatsby* (New York: Collier, 1986), p. 74.

9. Ernest Hemingway, *A Farewell to Arms* (New York: Scribners, 1957), pp. 184–185.

10. Michael Reynolds, *The Young Hemingway* (Oxford: Blackwell, 1986), pp. 34–35, 42.

11. Hemingway, *A Farewell to Arms,* p. 17.

12. Allen Tate, "Ode to the Confederate Dead," in *The Swimmers and Other Selected Poems* (New York: Scribners, 1970), pp. 17, 18.

13. Mencken, "Criticism of Criticism of Criticism," in *Prejudices: A Selection,* edited by James T. Farrell (Baltimore: Johns Hopkins University Press, 1996), pp. 6–7.

14. John Crowe Ransom, "Freud and Literature," review of *Group Psychology and the Analysis of the Ego* (1921) and *Beyond the Pleasure Principle* (1920), *Saturday Review of Literature,* 4 October 1924, pp. 161–162.

15. Daniel Joseph Singal, *The War Within: From Victorian to Modernist Thought in the South, 1919–1945* (Chapel Hill: University of North Carolina Press, 1982), p. 6.

16. Paul D. Escott, ed., *W. J. Cash and the Minds of the South* (Baton Rouge: Louisiana State University Press, 1992), pp. 40–41.

17. W. J. Cash, "The Mind of the South," *American Mercury,* 17 (October 1929): 185.

18. Ibid., p. 192.

19. W. E. B. Du Bois, "Georgia: Invisible Empire State," *Nation* (21 January 1925); reprinted in *These United States: Portraits of America from the 1920s,* edited by Daniel H. Borus (Ithaca & London: Cornell University Press, 1992), p. 94.

20. Using the chapters about literature in the WPA guides to the Southern states, one can count nearly five hundred writers of fiction, poetry, drama, and popular history at work during the period 1919 to 1941 in the South. Most of the names are now unfamiliar, including several authors who won the Pulitzer Prize, though summaries of specific works offer interesting projects for modern students who would like to recover an overlooked talent. In *Renaissance in the South: A Critical History of the Literature, 1920–1960* (Chapel Hill: University of North Carolina Press, 1963), John M. Bradbury includes an appendix that lists nearly five hundred active authors from the South within his somewhat longer period—poets, dramatists, and fiction writers. Not

all the authors on Bradbury's lists were part of the Southern Renaissance, despite their having lived and written in Southern states and about Southern places, people, and events. See also Lewis Lawson, *Another Generation: Southern Fiction Since World War II* (Jackson: University Press of Mississippi, 1984), pp. 145–151.

21. Thomas L. McHaney, "Watching for the Dixie Limited: Faulkner's Impact upon the Creative Writer," *Fifty Years of Yoknapatawpha: Faulkner and Yoknapatawpha, 1979*, edited by Doreen Fowler and Ann J. Abadie (Jackson: University Press of Mississippi, 1980), pp. 226–247.

22. David L. Smiley, "History, Central Themes," in *Encyclopedia of Southern Culture*, edited by Charles Reagan Wilson and others (Chapel Hill: University of North Carolina Press, 1989), p. 1110.

23. Ibid.

24. Ibid.

25. C. Vann Woodward, *The Burden of Southern History*, revised edition (Baton Rouge: Louisiana State University Press, 1968), pp. 187–188, 190–191.

26. Michael Kreyling, *Inventing Southern Literature* (Jackson: University Press of Mississippi, 1998), p. ix.

27. Kees Gispen, introduction to *What Made the South Different?*, edited by Gispen (Jackson: University Press of Mississippi, 1990), p. xvii.

28. Malcolm Bradbury and James McFarlane, eds., *Modernism: 1890–1930* (Harmondsworth, U.K. & New York: Penguin, 1976).

29. McHaney, "Literary Modernism: The South Goes Modern and Keeps on Going," in *Southern Literature in Transition: Heritage and Promise*, edited by Philip Castile and William Osborne (Memphis: Memphis State University Press, 1982), p. 43.

30. Stanley Sultan, *Ulysses, The Waste Land, and Modernism: A Jubilee Study* (Port Washington, N.Y.: Kennikat Press, 1977), p. 81.

31. British novelist Aldous Huxley, of course, made this point in *Brave New World* (1932), a novel in which modern time is reckoned "B.F." and "A.F."—that is, Before Ford and After Ford. American playwright Elmer Rice made it even earlier in a drama titled *The Adding Machine* (1923), in which a workingman, Mr. Zero, is put out of a job by the new mechanical wonder.

32. Harry Levin, "What Was Modernism?" in his *Refractions: Essays in Comparative Literature* (New York: Oxford University Press, 1966), p. 287.

33. Richard J. Calhoun, "Southern Writing: The Unifying Strand," *Mississippi Quarterly*, 27 (Winter 1973–1974): 108.

HALLMARK WORKS OF THE SOUTHERN RENAISSANCE, 1919–1941

James Branch Cabell. *Jurgen*. New York: R. M. McBride, 1919.

Cabell's daring novel *Jurgen* is perhaps as important for the Southern Renaissance as the firing on Fort Sumter was for the Civil War. In the period right after World War I, when the South was regarded as a benighted region without any modern cultural expression to counter an overwhelmingly sentimental literature, Cabell published a novel that one critic has called "a naughty boy's version of *The Waste Land*"[1]—three years before T. S. Eliot's poem was published. In a literal sense, *Jurgen* is not about the South. The surface narrative is a medieval legend about a middle-aged poet who is given back his youthful body but keeps his wry and lecherous adult mind. He has a series of fantastic adventures, most with sexual overtones, on his way to realizing that love—and much else—is illusion. But the frankness of the novel delighted the postwar generation in the South, whose own delayed and disillusioned embrace of youth in the Jazz Age was foreshadowed by Cabell's allegory. When it was attacked for obscenity, the reputation of *Jurgen* became even more delicious, and the novel prompted H. L. Mencken to proclaim the Richmond writer as the sole exception to Southern cultural aridity. Young Southerners, whether they knew it or not, may have found in Cabell's allegory a version of postwar changes in a medieval—that is, feudal—South, a suffocating gentility increasingly supplanted by new freedoms for women as well as for men, and the parlor singing of church tunes challenged by the rhythms and lyrics of the blues and jazz to which young people danced suggestively.

Jean Toomer. *Cane*. New York: Boni & Liveright, 1923.

Cane may be the first modernist work to come out of the Southern experience, a sensual and lyrical evocation of African American life employing alternating stories, poems, and a play. *Cane* presents a juxtaposition of seemingly unrelated pieces that nonetheless add up to a

110

Jean Toomer

coherent context for the final drama, the failure of Cane's autobiographi-
cal light-skinned protagonist to find a meaningful life in the South from
which his forebears fled. Though Toomer was raised in Washington,
D.C., his grandfather had served as a governor of Louisiana during
Reconstruction, and the writer's move to the South—to a small town in
Georgia, where he taught school—qualified him as a member of the
Southern Renaissance. Although he is more usually identified with the
Harlem Renaissance, Toomer was one of many writers of this group who,
though born in the North or East, sought to reestablish lost roots in the
South and to express the Southern experience of African Americans. He
was also one of many black writers who wrote works with a "radical
admixture of forms," as Robert Stepto has observed, in a way that was not
necessarily an imitation of the fragmentary constructions of high modernism. The free mixture of genres is perhaps something uniquely African American, Stepto argues.[2] If he is right, perhaps Toomer's experiment
is analogous to the improvisation and quotation present in the music and
lyrics of jazz.

Ellen Glasgow. *Barren Ground*. Garden City, N.Y.: Doubleday, Page, 1925.

Like her Richmond neighbor Cabell, Glasgow published important work twenty years or more before the Southern Renaissance was
acknowledged, including the realistic 1900 novel about her native
place, *The Voice of the People*. But *Barren Ground*—published the same
year as F. Scott Fitzgerald's *The Great Gatsby* and Ernest Hemingway's *In
Our Time*—attracted national attention to a new quality in Southern
writing. The novel is a lean account of how, in Cecilia Tichi's apt summary, Dorinda Oakley, "without money, a sheltering family, or marriage,
single-mindedly bends land and society to her will in a triumph of fortitude—and renunciation" in order to achieve success.[3] Both style and
subject emphasize the blood and irony that Glasgow recommended as
an antidote to the myth-minded sentimentality in much Southern writing that preceded her. In quite a different way from *Jurgen, Barren
Ground* is deeply allegorical, a forecast of what the still-destitute South
might accomplish if it worked hard, managed well, united agriculture
and commerce, and avoided sentimentality and false piety at all costs. It
is also a narrative about what a Southern woman was required to put
aside in order to achieve personal independence—for example, as a
successful but conflicted woman writer such as Glasgow herself. Such
subsequent novels by Glasgow as *The Sheltered Life*, published in 1932,
and *Vein of Iron*, published in 1935, are also hallmarks of the Southern

Renaissance, but by virtue of its early date *Barren Ground* deserves special notice.

Paul Green. *In Abraham's Bosom*. In his *The Field God and In Abraham's Bosom*. New York: R. M. McBride, 1927.

Promoting a Southern tradition in the new, frank, and socially committed drama of the 1920s was a highly unlikely possibility, given that theaters were even rarer than bookstores in the South.[4] Yet, at the University of North Carolina in the period leading up to the 1920s and after, that is exactly what Frederick Koch, a professor of dramatic arts from the Midwest, did. He founded The Carolina Playmakers, a student theater group, and encouraged students to write plays about regional life for the developing American theater. Though Thomas Wolfe remains Koch's best-known student, North Carolinian Paul Green was his greatest success. A one-act version of *In Abraham's Bosom* was published in 1926 in a collection of Green's plays, *Lonesome Road: Six Plays for the Negro Theatre*. An expanded version of the play succeeded both financially and critically on Broadway and won a Pulitzer Prize in 1927. More impor-

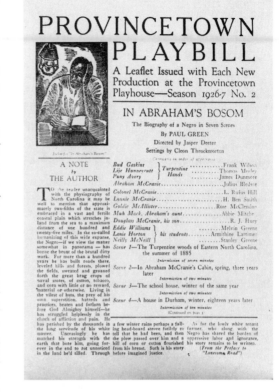

Playbill for Paul Green's Pulitzer Prize-winning 1926 play

tantly, it was the most morally serious treatment of African American life written by a white Southerner of the time, though other white Southerners were experimenting with black characters and voices (for example, DuBose Heyward, Roark Bradford, and Julia Peterkin).

The protagonist of *In Abraham's Bosom* is a racially mixed young man who is acknowledged to be the son of a white planter. The young man's ambitions prompt him to start a school for black people in the plantation community where he grew up. His efforts are resisted by both sides, white and black, of the community, and his dreams of greater opportunity for himself and his race are thwarted at every turn. Finally, he is pushed into murdering his white half brother, who has always resented and opposed him, and he dies at the hands of a mob as he defiantly proclaims the future success of African Americans.

BIRTH OR REBIRTH?

"[T]he period now somewhat misleadingly called the Southern Renaissance . . . was more precisely a birth, not a rebirth. . . . I take it to be a commonplace of literary history that no writer of Mr. Faulkner's power could emerge from a literary and social vacuum. It is part of Mr. Faulkner's legend about himself that he did appear, like the sons of Cadmus, full grown, out of the unlettered soil of his native state, Mississippi. But we are under no obligation to take his word for it."

Allen Tate

From "A Southern Mode of the Imagination," in his *Essays of Four Decades* (Chicago: Swallow Press, 1968), p. 577.

William Faulkner. *Soldiers' Pay*. New York: Boni & Liveright, 1926.

Faulkner's first novel, written with great rapidity in the exotic environment of New Orleans, is a Southern version of such post–World War I novels of disillusion and despair as John Dos Passos's *Three Soldiers* (1921), Fitzgerald's *The Great Gatsby,* and Hemingway's *The Sun Also Rises* (1926). The first chapter of *Soldiers' Pay* begins as an ironic romp with three returning American servicemen drunk on a train headed South, one of them a pitiful air cadet who never flew before the war ended. Attention soon shifts to a fourth serviceman, a severely wounded airman from Georgia who was shot down abroad. A war widow appears and helps a hardened foot soldier named Gilligan take the wounded airman back to his hometown of Charlestown, Georgia, several miles south of Atlanta. The second chapter introduces an entirely new cast of characters, including one who talks like Cabell's Jurgen. Faulkner shows off his knowledge of Sigmund Freud's ideas about the psychopathology of everyday life. *Soldiers' Pay,* more than Faulkner's first book, the 1924 poetry collection *The Marble Faun,* announced the debut of one of the greatest talents of the Southern Renaissance in the genre he went on to master. Margaret Mitchell, who ten years later published a truly monumental first novel, *Gone with the Wind,* found *Soldiers' Pay* noteworthy among "thousands of stories . . . of the return of the soldier, and the bitterness and disillusion that changed conditions produced in him" because it was "a homecoming that will be especially interesting to Southerners" and evoked truly the "atmosphere of the small Southern town where the duck-legged Confederate monument ornamented the courthouse square."[5]

Allen Tate. "Ode to the Confederate Dead." In his *Mr. Pope and Other Poems*. New York: Minton, Balch, 1928.

"Ode to the Confederate Dead" was conceived in imitation of Eliot's *The Waste Land* and perhaps in parody of nineteenth-century Southern poet Henry Timrod's "Ode Sung at the Occasion of Decorating the Graves of the Confederate Dead" (1867). Tate's modernist poem, as he explains in the essay "Narcissus as Narcissus" (1938), is about "solipsism, a philosophical doctrine which says that we create the world in the act of perceiving it; or about Narcissism, or any other *ism* that denotes the failure of the human personality to function objectively in nature and society." In the modern era, he observes, both nature and society "offer limited fields for the exercise of the whole man, who wastes his energy piecemeal over separate functions that ought to come under a unity of being." More simply put, the poem is, in Tate's good summary, "about a man stopping at the gate of a Confederate graveyard on a late autumn afternoon," where the falling leaves and the desolation allow him to think both of the unself-conscious bravery of charging soldiers and his own uncertainty.[6] Thus, like Eliot's "The Love Song of J. Alfred Prufrock" or *The Waste Land* and other modernist works, it is about the modern consciousness, now sited specifically in a deeply Southern mind.

Fugitives: An Anthology of Verse. New York: Harcourt, Brace, 1928.

Following the success and national attention accorded their modest little magazine, *The Fugitive*, the poets and critics known as the Fugitives, who taught and studied at Vanderbilt University, were able to publish an anthology of their work for a national audience. *Fugitives: An Anthology of Verse* marked the end of a close association between the members of the group, at a time when almost all of them had already published, or were about to publish, poetry collections of their own, as well as other kinds of work. The anthology, however, serves as a fitting summary and constitutes a list of hallmarks for each of the main figures in the movement. Four collections of John Crowe Ransom's poems had already been published: *Poems About God* (1919), *Chills and Fever* (1924), *Grace After Meat* (1924), and *Two Gentlemen in Bonds* (1927). Tate's *Mr. Pope and Other Poems* and a biography, *Stonewall Jackson, the Good Soldier,* both appeared in 1928; a biography by Robert Penn Warren, *John Brown: The Making of a Martyr,* came out the following year. Donald Davidson's poetry collection *The Tall Men* was published in 1927, and Andrew Lytle's biography *Bedford Forrest and his Critter Company* came out in 1931. At their best, the chief members of the group wrote poems on the Southern experience that evoke deep and ironic feelings of family, history, Southern solidarity, folklore and legend, and the religious scrutiny of the guilty self. Like much other literature of the Southern Renaissance, their early poems represent a fresh, sharp, and unsentimental literature of memory that can touch chords of feeling in anyone who remains conscious of lost origins or the contrast between childhood experience and mature responsibility.

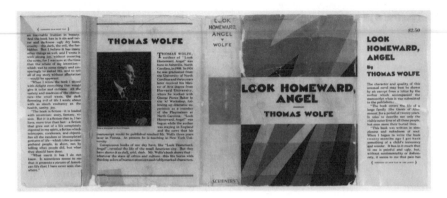

Dust jacket for Thomas Wolfe's first novel

Thomas Wolfe. *Look Homeward, Angel*. New York: Scribners, 1929.

In a frank and lyrical manner, Wolfe evokes the life of an eccentric Southern family who produced someone much like himself. Eugene Gant is a prodigy with the conflicting desire to belong to and escape from both his family and the South. The story told in Wolfe's first novel literally sweeps a sympathetic reader away with a flood of vivid language as it recounts the strange juxtapositions that account for Eugene's origins and depicts his development into a sensitive youth who wants to be a writer. Wolfe drew freely on the life of his hometown, Asheville, North Carolina—Altamont in the novel—and his college experiences at the University of North Carolina in Chapel Hill, where he studied literature, philosophy, and playwriting. Faulkner, whose novels *Sartoris* and *The Sound and the Fury* were published in the same year as *Look Homeward, Angel,* later placed Wolfe at the top of a list of American writers he was asked to rate, because, he said, "Wolfe tried to do the greatest of the impossible . . . he tried to reduce all human experience to literature."[7] The uncut version of *Look Homeward, Angel,* with Wolfe's original title— *O Lost*—has now been published.[8]

Faulkner. *Sartoris*. New York: Harcourt, Brace, 1929.

Sartoris, initially conceived as "Flags in the Dust," suffered a fate somewhat similar to Wolfe's *Look Homeward, Angel*. After Faulkner's first publisher rejected "Flags in the Dust," he had to shop his manuscript to several other firms. Harcourt, Brace accepted it, on the condition that he cut and retitle the novel; *Sartoris* was the result. Like *Look Homeward, Angel,* Faulkner's book is a family chronicle, a long-established form in Europe, and like Wolfe's novel, it carries the form into new territory. *Sartoris* bears some resemblance to the German writer Thomas Mann's influential family-chronicle novel *Buddenbrooks* (1900), but it is also a clever adaptation of the novel of life after the war, as is *Soldiers' Pay*. *Sartoris* depicts the generation returning from World War I to a sleepy and just-changing South, but Faulkner also portrays characters who represent the still-living memories of the Civil War, setting the two periods into dramatic conflict. Though not as successful as *Look Homeward, Angel* (or Hemingway's *A Farewell to Arms,* a postwar novel published in the same year), *Sartoris* is a hallmark for the Southern Renaissance because in writing the book, as Faulkner once said, he discovered that the region of Mississippi he grew up in "was worth writing about and that I would never live long enough to exhaust it. . . . It opened up a gold mine of other peoples, so I created a cosmos of my own."[9] His cosmos, to which he gave the fictional name Yoknapatawpha County, with its county seat of Jefferson, is the setting for more than a dozen of his subsequent novels and scores of short stories. From the experience of writing "Flags in the Dust" Faulkner constructed a body of work that is both local to north Mississippi and expressive of a great deal of the entire South.

Just as Wolfe based the Gants on his own family, the Sartorises are modeled on Faulkner's family, with the generation of his parents (unlike in Wolfe's case) left out. Young Bayard Sartoris's twin brother, John, was killed in World War I, in which they were both dashing pilots for the Royal Air Force. Bayard returns to the house of his grandfather, also named Bayard, whom the novel has already established as lost not only in deafness but also in the powerful grip of a dead past. John, whose death in combat young Bayard envies, has an historical counterpart in the twins' great-grandfather, John Sartoris, the founder of the family fortune and the older Bayard's father. This great-grandfather survived an illustrious career in the Civil War to build a railroad, but he was murdered by a former business partner before the twins were born.

Pride and disdain for the Sartoris tradition of foolhardiness and daring survive in Jenny DuPre, the great-grandfather's sister, widowed by the Civil War and now in command of the family home. Foolhardiness masked as courage results in the untimely deaths of both the older Bayard and his restless grandson of the same name. A male child born to the younger Bayard's widow, Narcissa, nonetheless ensures that the fatal flaws of the Sartorises will continue into succeeding generations, despite her attempt to change matters by refusing to name the child with one of the traditional family names.

Faulkner. *The Sound and the Fury*. New York: Cape & Smith, 1929.

   The Sound and the Fury is in the tradition of the family-chronicle novel, too, but the presentation is far different from the chronological narrative still familiar to, and preferred by, readers of Faulkner's day. The family in this case is named Compson. Like the members of the Sartoris family, the Compsons reappear in other works throughout Faulkner's career, along with the Snopes family of former sharecroppers; the McCaslins and the Sutpens, both plantation families with troubling heritages; and the Priests, who are used to tell a more positive story in the author's last novel, *The Reivers* (1962). Though *The Sound and the Fury* was radically new in structure at the time it was published, none of Faulkner's first three novels featured a purely conventional chronological narrative, nor were any of them constructed in the same way. With *The Sound and the Fury*, however, the author outdid himself with a completely modernist frame.

   The story is told in four independent segments, each identified with a different specific day. The first two are stream-of-consciousness narratives recording the impressions of the brothers Benjy and Quentin Compson, respectively. The third section uses the similar technique of interior monologue, expressed by the third brother, Jason, and the fourth is presented from an omniscient perspective, with a shifting, limited point of view that begins with the Compson children's old black nurse, the housekeeper Dilsey Gibson. The present time of the novel is Easter 1928, but the days are presented out of order, as topsy-turvy as are the individual thoughts and memories of each Compson brother. The days are Saturday, Thursday, Friday, and Sunday, but the Thursday (on which Quentin ends his freshman year at Harvard by committing suicide) is in June 1910, not in April 1928 as in the other three parts. These chronological shifts are not willful dislocations on Faulkner's part. The psychological nature of time and the free association of memory accord well with a story that does not unfold chronologically but is revealed in fragments that may cohere in the mind of the reader only as the novel is read for a second time.

   The Compson parents are outmoded in their attitudes, and their attempts to cling to false and hypocritical values show the failure of the old order. Supposedly based on honor, gentility, and Christian values, the Southern past as embodied in Jason and Caroline Compson is really sustained by greed, lust, rationalization, false pride, and wealth acquired through the work of a captive people once enslaved and now in economic, social, and intellectual bondage. The old values prove most empty when they are used for cruel purposes. The young Compsons are classic examples of abused children, punished and turned to self-criticism by the hypocritical or narrow-minded demands of their unhappy parents. Benjy, who is called an idiot or a loony, is more likely a child deprived of speech by a childhood illness, someone who—like the Southerner Helen Keller—might be helped if his mother and others did not regard him as a curse, an embarrassment, and a burden. Absent from the Compson household, except in the obsessive memories of all three brothers, is their sister, Caddy. She was denied love in the household, though she gave it selflessly, and so she was pushed to find it elsewhere, with unfortunate results. When she conceived a child out of wedlock, her mother forced her to seduce a prospective husband anyway, and when that relationship failed and Caddy was sent home, her mother stole the child and demanded Caddy's exile, even forbidding her name to be spoken in the household.

Because of these dynamics, the lives of the Compsons naturally work out badly, even in the limited context of four days' time. But the poetry of the voices Faulkner creates, the intricate interrelationships among the fragmented recollections and the feelings they evoke, and the subtle unrolling of the past in terms of present stimuli—these masterful elements create a work that has the texture and effect of symphonic music. *The Sound and the Fury* has become, in consequence, not only a highly influential work that has inspired imitation by many subsequent writers but also one of Faulkner's most frequently taught texts, an imaginative and compelling tragedy in which, as the critic Michael Millgate has observed, "such meaning as at first sight the incidents appear to possess proves on closer inspection to dissolve into uncertainty and paradox."[10]

Donald Davidson and others. *I'll Take My Stand: The South and the Agrarian Tradition*. New York & London: Harper, 1930.

Whether the number twelve—the number of contributors to the volume—was an accident or a deliberate allusion to the apostles, *I'll Take My Stand* was conceived, if not carried out, as a new gospel for a new South. Called the "Agrarian Manifesto," it was written in opposition to Karl Marx and Friedrich Engels's *Communist Manifesto* of 1848, but it equally opposed the creed of urban capitalist industrialism. This collection of essays on various aspects of Southern values was organized and edited by Ransom, who had been the leader of the Fugitive group in Nashville in the 1920s, and his friend Tate. The contributors are described in the unsigned introduction to the volume as

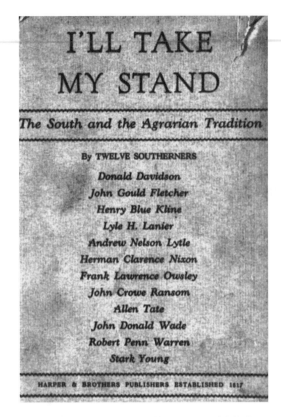

Cover of the 1930 essay collection in which the Nashville Fugitives and other Southern writers championed the traditional agricultural society of the South

Southerners, well acquainted with one another and of similar tastes . . . and perhaps only at this moment aware of themselves as a single group of men. . . . All the articles bear in the same sense upon the book's title-subject: all tend to support a Southern way of life against what may be called the American or prevailing way; and all as much as agree that the best terms in which to represent the distinction are contained in the phrase, Agrarian *versus* Industrial.[11]

Convinced that the world was "groaning under industrialism," which was "an evil dispensation,"[12] the organizers of the symposium offered no plan for national reorganization but, as seen now in light of other acts of the modernists, did offer a concerted cry in the wilderness against the headlong work requirements, regimentation, and purely profit-oriented inhumanity of modern times. The effort was something most of these university men essentially abandoned afterward, not so much in disillusionment as in a spirit of realism. Besides, they realized that they had no answers for the agrarian's hardworking wife, nor, looking back at the old South and even at the new, for the blacks and whites locked in unfair economic and social systems that promised to create recurrent generations of poor and uneducated people.

Erskine Caldwell. *Tobacco Road.* New York: Scribners, 1932.

A great deal of sympathetic literature about poor white farm people came out of the South in the early twentieth century as writers in many different subregions were moved to record their trials in a harsh kind of local color. The coming of the Great Depression in 1929 only intensified the difficulties of the Southern poor, white or black. Increasing attention to the problem, however, helped to create a market for fiction portraying both the misery and the foibles of the Southern lower classes. Faulkner attempted to start his career with a novel about a sharecropping family named Snopes, one of whom, Flem, is clever enough to learn the tricks of materialism and move up in the world through ruthless dealings. Faulkner's conception of the Snopes family was initially comic, though he came to have deep sympathy in his fiction for those of both races caught in the iron grip of sharecropping. In the 1930s his Flem Snopes stories were so popular that magazine editors were begging him for more of them. In 1931 Faulkner's *As I Lay Dying* was published. A more sober tragicomedy about the rural poor, it is a tour de force in which a family named Bundren transports the rotting corpse of the family matriarch through flood, fire, and public disapproval for a quick burial at the county seat, where each of them hopes to find something.

At roughly the same time, Erskine Caldwell, who had written several books out of his experience as a minister's son in rural Georgia, published *Tobacco Road*. The central figure is Jeeter Lester, an impoverished agrarian who cannot farm because he has no credit and resists leaving the land to work in town, as have some of his many children. Left in a depressed and even perverse rural community, Lester, his sick wife, and his pitiful, home-bound children come to a tragic end, without the dignity of intelligent resistance or even passionate error. Sensational because of its representation of the sexual mores of the poor and oppressed, *Tobacco Road* portrays a world in which, as the narrative voice says, "no one ever laughed." Yet, it does so with a kind of black humor that, as Wayne Mixon argues, "makes the novel emotionally bearable and saves the characters from being merely objects of pity"; the book actually leaves many readers feeling that it is highly compassionate.[13]

Although *Tobacco Road* was well reviewed throughout the South, it did not sell well at first, but it was adapted as a remarkably popular play on the New York stage (beginning in 1933, it ran for more than three thousand performances in seven-and-a-half years). The success of the play version boosted the sales of the novel and Caldwell's subsequent career. He was no Agrarian, and he was quick to express his concern that too many of

THE 1962 REPUBLICATION OF *I'LL TAKE MY STAND*

"A reissue of *I'll Take My Stand* has been long overdue.... The book has been much discussed since its original publication in 1930: it has been praised, blamed, revered, distorted, maligned, patronized; but it has not been printed.

"*I'll Take My Stand* is important for several reasons. Perhaps foremost among them (and what has done more than anything else to keep the book alive) is the fact that several of its contributors have become leading artists and men of letters of their generation. For this reason alone the symposium is significant, but the value of the book goes beyond this. I doubt that anyone will deny that there is foolishness in the volume, and a great deal of sentiment and some sentimentality.... But with this foolishness and often excessive sentiment there is also a great deal of highly perceptive literary and social writing which deserves anyone's careful consideration.

Edward M. Moore

From a review of *I'll Take My Stand*, *Sewanee Review*, 71 (Winter 1963): 133.

Erskine Caldwell

his generation of Southern writers were more interested in the past than the present; he particularly had no patience with the Nashville school.[14] The sexual innuendo in Caldwell's many novels and their lurid paperback covers likely fueled their steady sales from bus-station and drugstore racks, making him one of the most widely published Southern writers of his era.

Margaret Mitchell. *Gone with the Wind*. New York: Macmillan, 1936.

No single Southern book has yet had the success and international popularity achieved by Mitchell's bittersweet romance about the period before, during, and after the Civil War. The novel repeats a pattern, perhaps a legend, of the type that is explored in Wilbur J. Cash's 1941 study, *The Mind of the South*: an Irish immigrant settles in the South, becomes wealthy, and builds a pretentious mansion, Tara, that becomes a symbolic focus of the novel. Gerald O'Hara's impetuous and strong-willed daughter Scarlett endures more adventures than many families could claim over the course of several generations: romantic disappointments, the coming of the Civil War, the deaths of many close to her, the burning of Atlanta, and the difficulties of single-handedly restoring the symbolic plantation in the harsh period after the war. In the finale, Scarlett commits the error of not making the match that was most suited to her ambitions and her desires—with Rhett Butler—but at the end of the novel she has not lost her determination:

> With the spirit of her people who would not know defeat, even when it stared them in the face, she raised her chin. She could get Rhett back. She knew she could. There had never been a man she couldn't get, once she set her mind upon him.
>
> "I'll think of it all tomorrow, at Tara. I can stand it then. Tomorrow, I'll think of some way to get him back. After all, tomorrow is another day."[15]

As with the play version of *Tobacco Road*, the 1939 movie version of Mitchell's novel had qualities, including the star power of Clark Gable and Vivien Leigh, that have sustained it as a perennial favorite and helped to keep the novel popular as well.

Faulkner. *Absalom, Absalom!* New York: Random House, 1936.

A novel Faulkner found difficult to write—in part because of financial difficulties and the need to spend increasing amounts of time working as a screenwriter in Hollywood—*Absalom, Absalom!* became in his eyes a likely candidate for a highly profitable Hollywood movie, but *Gone with the Wind* was published earlier in the same year. The cinematic potential of Faulkner's novel has never been tested, but it stands in the opinion of most of his critics as his greatest achievement, not only as an example of narrative art but also as a highly thoughtful and moral exploration of the roots and results of Southern thinking about race and of the recovery of Southern history. Like *Sartoris* and *The Sound and the Fury,* it is a family chronicle. *Absalom, Absalom!* presents the strange and contested story of Thomas Sutpen and his children, as told and reimagined in several intense minds: Sutpen's sister-in-law, a brooding spinster; a jaded small-town lawyer (the older Jason Compson of *The Sound and the Fury*); the lawyer's son Quentin, whose departure for Harvard and debates with his roommate there give the story a modern timeline; and Shreve McCannon, Quentin's roommate. Shreve, a Canadian, is also from a backwoods frontier (like the Mississippi of the Compsons), but because of the absence of racial issues in his own culture, he cannot really comprehend what it is like to live in the South. For all their foibles and lack of complete information, the narrators become so involved in the Sutpen story that Sutpen "abrupts" into their midst; later, the two Harvard boys become, in their imaginations, his sons. The reader and the narrators come to understand that Sutpen's actual sons, whose story is the provocative root of the novel, are separated on either side of the racial divide, much like the mixed-race protagonist and his white half brother in Green's *In Abraham's Bosom.* One of the Sutpen sons was the child of a woman whom the father abandoned because he believed she descended, distantly, from an African forebear.

Zora Neale Hurston. *Their Eyes Were Watching God.* Philadelphia: Lippincott, 1937.

What first pulled young Southerners into writing and then revolutionizing Southern literary art was education.[16] Though an African American from a small town, Hurston was no exception. Her intellectual fortune was that she grew up in an all-black town, Eatonville, Florida, where there were good schools and proud, caring townspeople to recognize and nurture a bright child. Hurston made her way through Atlanta, which had (and still has) an African American educational establishment of the first order, and on to Columbia University. At Columbia

Zora Neale Hurston

she studied anthropology with one of the pioneers of the field, Franz Boaz, a practical investigator of physical and cultural anthropology. Under his instruction, and with his straightforward and untheoretical field methodology as her guide, Hurston returned to the town she had come from and began collecting stories, history, and cultural practices. She turned these—as well as materials she collected in New Orleans and the Caribbean—into such books as the novel *Jonah's Gourd Vine* (1934) and the folklore collection *Mules and Men*, published the following year. In 1937 Hurston's *Their Eyes Were Watching God* was published, a novel as stirring and significant as Kate Chopin's *The Awakening* (1898).

Their Eyes Were Watching God is about a woman's life in a world seemingly run by men to suit men. The summary in the fifth edition of *The Oxford Companion to American Literature* (1983) suggests how Hurston's book has been neglected: it is described simply as a novel "about a black woman finding happiness in simple farm life."[17] The extent to which critical opinion of the book has changed is suggested in a more recent study, *The Oxford Book of the American South* (1997). *Their Eyes Were Watching God* "combined her [Hurston's] past, her learning, and her fiction into a powerful story of a black woman's refusal to accept the limitations and expectations of her time."[18] An even fuller account grants Hurston credit for writing "a modernist novel that incorporates surreal elements into its realism, and that alternates between the sophisticated verbal range of an omniscient narrator and a more intimate folk idiom that represents the consciousness of the heroine." Rooted also in African American tradition by its use of "dialect, folklore, and a mulatto heroine," "the novel is primarily the story of a woman's evolution from loneliness to independence."[19] In this regard, Hurston's writing may be compared with that of Glasgow, Faulkner, and Toomer.

As the novel opens, the central character, Janie, makes her way home after a long absence. She walks a street where people sit on their porches and comment, verbally and in their thoughts, on Janie, what she has done, and how attractive she still is, despite, in their view, having been deceived and abandoned by a much younger man. Janie's friend Pheoby, however, hears a different story when she brings food and the friends sit on the porch as Janie tells her tale. The story goes back to the madness of her mother, who had been raped by a white planter; the well-meaning cruelty of her grandmother, who wanted Janie to marry a well-to-do old man so that she would be protected sexually and financially in the dangerous South; and the attempts of her two husbands to tame her. After the death of her second husband (who died of an illness in the wake of her justifiably putting him down), Janie left town in the company of Tea Cake, who appeared to be a happy and sexually liberating vagabond. He allowed her to be herself, removing her from the class- and color-conscious all-black town and taking her to a tribal life among migrant workers in the Florida swamps. A powerful hurricane not only disrupted their lives but also set in motion events that led to Tea Cake's death at Janie's hands in self-defense, providing closure to what was clearly just a phase in her life, the point from which, still a well-off woman from her second husband's estate, she returns home to tell her story of self-actualization.

Faulkner. *The Hamlet*. New York: Random House, 1940.

Portions of *The Hamlet*, like Faulkner's *Go Down, Moses*, were first published as magazine stories in the late 1930s. *The Hamlet* brought together the first stories about the arrival in Yoknapatawpha County of Flem Snopes and his increasingly rapacious kinsmen, such as the Dickensian figure I. O. Snopes, the virulent Mink, the peaceful Eck, and Eck's bright-eyed son Wallstreet Panic. *The Hamlet* is brilliantly comic, set in a mythic mode, but it says more about economics and social forces than the laughing reader may perceive. Money comes into a barter economy; collection replaces credit; and poor farmers are made to want things that they can neither afford nor, in the long run, use. Even Flem's epic adversary, the sewing-machine salesman V. K. Ratliff, is not immune to some of the temptations the remorseless Flem lays down in his drive to move from the hamlet of Frenchman's Bend to the county seat, Jefferson; and Ratliff, the reader realizes, has brought installment-plan purchases into the county himself.

Snopes, however, will play any pawn, even the helplessness of his idiot cousin Ike or his father's reputation as a barn burner, to forge ahead. The novel ends with Flem's moving from the hamlet to the town. *The Town* is accordingly the title of the second novel in the Snopes trilogy, which was not published until 1957. Flem's apogee and fall are chroni-

Dust jacket for Richard Wright's 1940 novel about the life of a young black man in Chicago

cled in *The Mansion,* published in 1959. The title refers not to the governor's mansion but to Flem's antebellum home in Jefferson, its rooms outfitted by Sears and Roebuck.

Richard Wright. *Native Son.* New York & London: Harper, 1940.

Wright's novel about the life of black Southerners out of the South was published after the start of World War II, which was characterized by even more inhumanity than the first world war. Conceptually, *Native Son* was worthy of a Theodore Dreiser, whose 1925 novel *An American Tragedy* it resembles in some respects, but it showed that race, not class, was the obstacle for African Americans, wherever they lived in the country.[20] As Alferdteen Harrison has written in her introduction to *Black Exodus* (1991), *Native Son* is also "steeped in the world of the Great Migration," that sometimes purposeful, too often forced displacement of African Americans north or northeast.[21] The protagonist, Bigger Thomas, whose given name is meant to resonate with a common racial epithet, responds to the wretched conditions of urban poverty in Chicago by trying to escape from his own culture. His introduction to the white world, however, brings his ruin. Not as surreal as *Their Eyes Were Watching God, Native Son* nonetheless achieves by its fierce and unflinching naturalism something of the same effects of modernist distortion. Bigger becomes a driver for a wealthy white family. After driving the daughter and her boyfriend around town while they get drunk, he carries the daughter to her bedroom. When the mother, who is blind (literally and figuratively), appears at the bedroom door, he covers the girl's face with a pillow to silence her and inadvertently suffocates her. He dismembers the body, which he feeds into the family's furnace to hide his crime, causing a rain of gray ash outside the house. Convicted of his crime, unlike Dreiser's Clyde Griffiths in *An American Tragedy,* Bigger appears to come to an understanding of the social forces that have created the net in which he is caught, smiling a "faint, bitter, dry smile" before he is taken to be executed.[22] Like Faulkner, Wright had discovered that Fyodor Dostoyevsky's fiction provided a good model for the depiction of racial crises in America and for showing the blundering human sources of a descent into evil and agony such as the one Bigger undergoes.

In her biography of Wright, the African American novelist Margaret Walker observes that the "spectacular success of *Native Son* was unlike anything black or white America had seen of a black writer," though "Wright's relatives in Mississippi told him not to come home or he would be lynched,"[23] ironically a threat also made to Wolfe for his portrayal of people and events in Asheville in *Look Homeward, Angel.* Like many Southerners, Wright felt that the kind of writing he wished to do supplanted a sentimental literature, in his case that of earlier African American authors who had portrayed humility, primness, and even servility in their characters or had emphasized the pitiful in a way that made "bankers' daughters weep" and feel better for doing so, something he even charged himself with doing in his first book, *Uncle Tom's Children.*[24] Like Wolfe's and Faulkner's, Wright's work was edited at the insistence of his publisher, in this case to remove passages considered obscene. The excised passages have been restored to the text of *Native Son* in *Early Works* (1991), the first volume in the two-volume Library of America edition of Wright's works.

James Agee and Walker Evans. *Let Us Now Praise Famous Men.* Boston: Houghton Mifflin, 1941.

Let Us Now Praise Famous Men, with text by Agee and photographs by Evans, is a meditation on the rural poor of the South. Its sentimentality about poverty, though meant to show pity and concern, is just as nostalgic as William Alexander Percy's uncritical depiction of the static social order of the Mississippi Delta plantations in *Lanterns on the Levee,* published the same year. *Let Us Now Praise Famous Men* began as a journalistic assignment for Evans—who took many of the most arresting photographs that documented the Great Depression—and Agee. *Fortune* magazine, a property of the company that published *Time* and *Life,* was the sponsor, and the editors wanted a simple story, with pictures, about sharecroppers in Alabama. Agee, who grew up in Knoxville, Tennessee, became fascinated with the families he and Walker met when they went on the assignment, and he spent the next five years working on the book.

The result, in Agee's words in the introduction to the book, was a text meant to be read aloud, accompanied by photographs that were not merely illustrative, as in a journalistic piece. *Let Us Now Praise Famous Men* is as lyrical as *Lanterns on the Levee,* with a preamble in Agee's voice in which he struggles with his medium and his subject out loud: "If I could do it, I'd do no writing at all here. It would be photographs; the rest would be fragments of cloth, bits of cotton, lumps of earth, records of speech, pieces of wood and iron, phials of odors, plates of food and of excrement."[25] Instead, he was forced to put words to his vision of poor sharecroppers in Alabama: "In the square pine room at the back the bodies of the man of thirty and of his wife and of their children lay on shallow mattresses on their iron beds and on the rigid floor, and they were sleeping, and the dog lay asleep in the hallway."[26] The rhythms of the Bible seem apparent, and the observer's privileged peek into this place, and his care, are expressed in a quiet prose that suggests tip-toeing. Further on, Agee becomes frantically apologetic. Addressing Mrs. Ricketts, one of the subjects of the study, he says,

> You realized what the poor foolishness of your husband had let you all in for, shout-ing to you all to come out, children sent skinning barefooted and slaver-mouthed down the road and the path to corral the others, the Woods and the Gudgers, all to stand there on the porch as you were in the average sorrow of your working dirt and get your pictures made; and to you it was as if you and your children and your hus-band and these others were stood there naked in front of the cold absorption of the camera in all your shame and pitiableness to be pried into. . . .[27]

This Faulknerian sentence continues unstopped for pages, revealing Agee's debt to the chronicler of Mississippi.

Let Us Now Praise Famous Men was to be the first of three volumes with the working title "Three Tenant Families," but the whole project was never realized. Agee, who died in 1955, had a successful if too brief career as a movie reviewer and screenwriter. He also wrote two novels, *The Morning Watch* (1951) and the posthumously published *A Death in the Family* (1957). A piece written but not used in *A Death in the Family* shows Agee's stylistic debt to Wolfe:

> Those who have gone before, backward beyond remembrance and beyond the beginning of imagination, backward among the emergent easts, and the blind, pre-scient ravenings of the youngest sea, those children of the sun, I mean, who brought forth those, who wove, spread the human net, and who brought forth me; they are fallen backward into their graves like blown wheat and are folded under like babies in blankets, and they are all melted upon the mute enduring earth like leaves, like wet snow.[28]

One of his biographers has argued that Agee "vehemently refuses to view the farmer as either a member of the 'Underprivileged' or a ready-made symbol of the Depression" because his "people are not rep-resentative men and women, but avatars and legatees of 'famous men.' They are the chosen ones and a breed apart. . . . Inheritors of a moral heroism."[29] This is a fair statement about the best restitutions of human value to marginalized members of society made by Southern artists—

Welty, Wright, Cabell, Green, Tate, Faulkner, and many others. In the everyday, even in its frequent wretchedness and viciousness, they saw acts and personas that were "avatars and legatees" of the biblical heroes and heroines, the goddesses and the gods of myth, the struggling children of fairy tale, the pith and marrow of humanity, and they spoke them.

Wilbur J. Cash. *The Mind of the South.* New York: Knopf, 1941.

Cash, a newspaperman in Charlotte, North Carolina, had pondered his native region for several years, writing a short essay titled "The Mind of the South" for Mencken's *The American Mercury* that was published in the October 1929 issue, about the time of the stock-market crash. Cash's completion of his ideas in the 1941 book of the same title focused mainly on the South he knew, the Piedmont region of North Carolina, although he wrote as if the myths he wanted to discredit were Pan-Southern—and in some respects they were. Among the myths attacked in *The Mind of the South* is the legend of a widespread aristocratic and cultured planter society whose members lived in columned mansions. Cash was well aware that there were many Souths. In the book he observes that anyone could see the enormous diversity of the South

> simply by riding along any of the great new motor roads which spread across it—through brisk towns with tall white buildings in Nebraska Gothic; through smart suburbs, with their faces newly washed; through industrial and Negro slums, medieval in dirt and squalor and wretchedness, in all but redeeming beauty; past sleepy old hamlets with wide fields and black men singing their sad songs in the cotton, past log cabin and high grave houses, past hill and swamp and plain.[30]

Cash's hope, however, unlike that of Wolfe, was not to capture all the physical and human variety but to identify the "mind" of the South, a mind, as he wrote,

> continuous with the past . . . its primary form . . . determined not nearly so much by industry as by the purely agricultural conditions of that past. So far from being modernized in many ways it has actually always marched away, as to this day it continues to do, from the present toward the past. . . . [T]o get at its nature we shall have first of all to examine the question of exactly what the Old South was really like.[31]

What Cash found when he conducted this investigation was that many old myths hampered the modern South, for though the region was proud, "brave, honorable by its lights, courteous, personally generous, loyal, swift to act, often too swift, but signally effective, sometimes terrible, in its action," it had in the modern era fallen away from some of its virtues:

THE "TRADITION-DIRECTED" SOUTH

"What is suggested by all the devotion to the Lost Cause and the deference to its veterans is that the South prior to the First World War was, in relation to the remainder of the United States, a tradition-directed society, in the terminology of David Riesman's *The Lonely Crowd.* It had high growth potential both in terms of population and of production. It had a high degree of conformity dictated by family, caste, and historical circumstance. It received few of the immigrants who were pouring into the other areas of the United States. It was a Solid South—united, much more so than during the War itself, by devotion to a Confederate past, the Democratic Party, the Protestant Church, and a fierce antipathy toward the freed Negro. It depended upon myth, legend, and song for most of its cultural coherence, upon a literature of moonlight and magnolias for the remainder."

Lewis Lawson

From "Twentieth-Century Southern Fiction," in his *Another Generation: Southern Fiction Since World War II* (Jackson: University Press of Mississippi, 1983), pp. 4-5.

Violence, intolerance, aversion and suspicion toward new ideas, an incapacity for analysis, an inclination to act from feeling rather than from thought, an exaggerated individualism and a too narrow concept of social responsibility, attachment to fiction and false values, above all too great attachment to racial values and a tendency to justify cruelty and injustice in the name of those values, sentimentality and a lack of realism—these have been its characteristic vices in the past. And, despite changes for the better, they remain its characteristic vices today.[32]

How Cash explores these virtues and vices, in more than four hundred pages, still makes fascinating reading, even if his historical interpretation is somewhat impressionistic; the book continues to invite debate. Like Quentin Compson in Faulkner's *The Sound and the Fury* and *Absalom, Absalom!*, Cash was, in the words of critic David Hackett Fischer, "devoted to the South but critical of its folkways."[33] Also like Quentin, Cash committed suicide as an aftermath to his meditation on the South.

William Alexander Percy. *Lanterns on the Levee: Recollections of a Planter's Son.* New York: Knopf, 1941.

William Alexander "Will" Percy died not long after he finished *Lanterns on the Levee,* but not, like Cash, by his own hand. Completing the memoir while he was ill became an act of determination for him. Not for nothing did the young cousin whom he helped raise, Walker Percy, name the central figure of his novels *The Last Gentleman* (1966) and *The Second Coming* (1980) "Will Barrett." A suicide would not have been unusual for the Percy family, which had a melancholy streak so strong that from the eighteenth century on, a male Percy in each generation but one had killed himself.[34] In fact, Will Percy's first cousin, Walker Percy's father, succumbed to this recurrent family malady. But the family had another streak, too, a stubborn honor that persisted into an age when such a posture seemed like an anomaly; this honor is partly what *Lanterns on the Levee* is about. Like Tate's poem "Ode to the Confederate Dead," Will Percy's book hearkens back to a time when good men's lives were simpler, because unequivocal, and their actions were direct and counted for something. Walker Percy has a funny passage about this decline of certainty in *The Message in the Bottle* (1975), his first collection of essays, in which he notes that such certainty is now possible only in the movies, where a cowboy who doesn't carry a pistol can still chill a mob by borrowing a weapon and demonstrating uncanny marksmanship. If someone were to try duplicating this feat in real life, he would surely fail.[35]

The tone of *Lanterns on the Levee* is autumnal nostalgia, and doubtless not just because Will Percy's life was fading as he wrote the book. His experiences in World War I had changed him irrevocably, more than the culture he came from ever knew, and the advent of World War II probably pleased him even less than did the rise of the "redneck" politicians who defeated his father in his reelection bid for the U.S. Senate. Percy begins by noting that reminiscence "arises not so much . . . from the number of years you may happen to have accumulated as from the number of those who meant most to you in life who have gone on the long journey. They were the bulwarks, the bright spires, the strong places. When they have gone, you are a little tired, you rest on your oars. . . ." He adds, "I will indulge a heart beginning to be fretful by repeating to it the stories it knows and loves of my own country and my own people. A pilgrim's script—one man's field-notes of a land not far but quite unknown."[36]

As an historian of the Percy family, Bertram Wyatt-Brown, has written, "With a wry humor and an elegant style, *Lanterns on the Levee* offered a tragic vision of past and failure . . . the exposition of an 'elegiac wisdom'" found in many works of the period, including Faulkner's *The Sound and the Fury*.[37] One charm of Percy's book is its language. About his being sent to college at the University of the South because it was "near and healthy," he writes, "I was fifteen plus one month, in short trousers, small, weakly, self-reliant, and ignorant as an egg."[38] After the great flood of the Mississippi River in 1927, Percy commanded relief efforts in the Delta. His account of this disaster is as richly written as Faulkner's description of the flood in the "Old Man" sections of his novel *The Wild Palms* (1939).[39] In Percy's account,

> It was cold and a steady rain fell, freezing the workers and softening the levee. The greatest flood in the history of the Mississippi was roaring south between levees that trembled when you walked on them. The workers knew the fight was well-nigh hopeless, but there was nothing else to do but fight. They knew that if they lost, terror and desolation and death would spread over the hundred miles of thickly populated country from Cleveland to Vicksburg, over the fifty miles from Greenville to Greenwood. . . . [W]hile the five thousand Negroes with croker sacks over their heads and hundred-pound sandbags on their shoulders trotted in long converging lines to the threatened point, the river pushed, and the

great dike dissolved under their feet. The terrible wall of water like an imbecile blind Titan strode triumphantly into our country. The greatest flood in American history was upon us. We did not see our lands again for four months.

If the Lord was trying to cement us with disaster, He used a heavy trowel that night.[40]

If Percy thought God could cement the peoples of the South, it would have been as they were at the time—the African Americans doing hard labor; the white bosses yelling; the gentry deciding to stay at home on the night of the flood, like Percy, reading the proofs of a book of his poems; the white sharecroppers lurking desperately in their flimsy cabins; and all the women more or less invisible behind the scenes. As Fred Hobson has noted, Percy's "unqualified defense of the planter class, his defense of sharecropping, his traditional attitude toward the Negro would find little support among liberal Southerners, no matter how highly they regarded the man himself."[41] Still, the elegiac tone, the irony and wit, and the stoicism of a man convinced that he would go into any battle—and to death—alone with his thoughts are riveting. Percy ends the book, like the speaker in Tate's "Ode to the Confederate Dead," in a cemetery, giving an account of the graves there, similar to what Edgar Lee Masters did in his *Spoon River Anthology* (1915). But, unlike in Masters's book, in which the former inhabitants of Spoon River speak from their graves, Percy's voice is the only one to be heard:

They lie there under the grass in the evening light so helplessly, my townsmen, a tiny outpost of the lost tribe of our star. Understanding breaks over my heart and I know that the wickedness and the failures of men are nothing and their valor and pathos and effort everything. Circumscribed and unendowed, ailing in body, derided and beguiled, how well they have done! They have sipped happiness and gulped pain, they have sought God and never found Him, they have found love and never kept him—yet they kept on, they never gave up, they rarely complained. Among these handfuls of misguided dust I am proud to be a man and assuaged for my own defects . . . one tiny life with darkness before and after, and it at best a riddle and a wonder.[42]

Eudora Welty. *A Curtain of Green*. Garden City, N.Y.: Doubleday, Doran, 1941.

A contemporary of Wright and an admirer of Faulkner, Welty put her short-story-writing career into full gear in the late 1930s, especially when she received the encouragement of Katherine Anne Porter, who was then married to one of the men who edited *The Southern Review* in Baton Rouge. Porter wrote an admiring introduction to *A Curtain of Green*, Welty's first collection of stories, a volume so large her editors must have believed she would write a great deal more. The seventeen stories of *A Curtain of Green* include many that have become classics of both the Southern

Renaissance and the short-story genre as well, such as "Lily Daw and the Three Ladies," "A Piece of News," "Petrified Man," "Why I Live at the P. O.," "The Hitch-Hikers," "Death of a Traveling Salesman," "Powerhouse," and "A Worn Path." The humor, poignance, deft characterization, and subtlety of Welty's stories lift the best of them to the level of poetry, and consequently they are sometimes as compressed and difficult as great poetry for the casual reader who seeks only action. "Death of a Traveling Salesman," one of Welty's earliest magazine publications, records the last hours of a man named R. J. Bowman, who long ago gave up some kind of rooted life, probably in the country, to travel for a firm that manufactures shoes. Getting over an illness and on the road again too soon, he becomes lost on a remote road, nearly drives his car over a precipice, and walks to a country cabin to seek aid in extricating his automobile. His initial judgment about the woman he sees in the cabin—that she is lonely and lives in austerity—proves wrong: she has a husband and is expecting a baby; they are good, charitable people who help him. But for Bowman the revela-

Eudora Welty in 1955

tion of the couple's domesticity and kindness comes too late. In the sudden realization of all he has missed by living a life on the road, he feels shame, then desperation, and finally fright. His heart begins to fail him as he has, in a different sense, failed his heart: "He sank in fright onto the road, his bags falling about him. He felt as if all this had happened before. He covered his heart with both hands to keep anyone from hearing the noise it made."[43] But nobody hears it.

"Powerhouse" is a virtuoso portrayal of a concert by a noted jazz band led by a fast-talking pianist modeled after the entertainer Fats Waller, but the story's purpose is to dramatize the difference between white and black in a Southern city. "A Worn Path" gives mythic stature to an elderly black woman, Phoenix Jackson, who undertakes an annual quest to the city for medicine. "The Hitch-Hikers" is about another commercial traveler, a man whose coming is much anticipated in the Delta towns where he makes calls. Like the traveling salesman Bowman, Tom Harris, who sells office supplies, misses much of the significance of the life he sees. When two hitchhikers he picks up quarrel over stealing his car, and one kills the other in the process, his response is mystification; he simply arranges to have the car cleaned so that he can continue his business. The poignance of the event is caught only by a little African American boy who asks Harris, "Does you want the box?" "The what?" he replies, at first unaware that the child is asking about the guitar one of the hitchhikers was carrying. "The po' kilt man's gittar," the boy says movingly. "Even the policemans didn't want it." The salesman hands it over, and, one can imagine, a Delta bluesman is born to wail of human feeling, contingency, loss, and love in ways that Harris will never comprehend.

Welty always infused her stories with motion, myth, legend, folklore, and ancient story. "Death of a Traveling Salesman" resonates with John Bunyan's *Pilgrim's Progress* (1678). "A Worn Path" suggests quest journeys of many kinds, and "The Hitch-Hikers" recalls the ancient Greek myth of Orpheus, among other things. Her next book after *A Curtain of Green* was a small novel, *The Robber Bridegroom* (1942), that she later called "a fairy tale of the Natchez Trace," linking the Brothers Grimm with the wickedly funny backwoods tales of the Old Southwestern frontier in a way compatible with Faulkner's linking the same tall-tale tradition with Native American myth and Bible stories in *Go Down, Moses*.

Faulkner. *Go Down, Moses*. New York: Random House, 1942.

For *Go Down, Moses* Faulkner adapted two sets of previously written stories. Some of them had, like the Snopes stories, been published while the author scrambled unsuccessfully to avoid screenwriting work in Hollywood by writing for mass-circulation magazines. One set of stories concerns Lucas Beauchamp and his family. He is a dignified, independent, but difficult African American man of considerable age who is much venerated on the small plantation where he lives as an uncharacteristically successful sharecropper. The stories about Lucas, his wife, Mollie, and their daughter Nat resemble Hurston's short stories, which were appearing in magazines at the same time as Faulkner's. But beneath the surface humor, Lucas's somber recollections of his past disclose a more philosophical and heroic tale. He reveals his relationships with the white owners and managers of the plantation where he lives. They are actually his direct blood relations, a matter about which he has pride, but their shared lives have not always been easy. The simplest version of the relationship is that Lucas is the grandson of the founder of the plantation,

Lucius Quintus Carothers McCaslin (referred to as "L.Q.C."). In his own view, Lucas is a better man, a better farmer, and more proud of his McCaslin heritage than the current owner of the plantation, Roth Edmonds, a great-great grandson of the founder but, unlike Lucas, descended from a female McCaslin. Thus, in Lucas's patriarchal view, Roth is a diminished McCaslin. Lucas's view suggests the treatment of women in the South, a theme that Faulkner investigates morally throughout the novel.

Another cycle of stories in *Go Down, Moses* sets up a contrast between the McCaslin plantation and the increasingly distant big woods of the Mississippi Valley river bottoms, where bear, deer, cat, and other game have abounded. The central figure in these stories is Ike McCaslin, also a grandson of L.Q.C. McCaslin. Ike's story is quite different from Lucas's, and not merely because of race; in fact, Lucas's

FAULKNER'S MODERNISM

"Perhaps no other major American writer would struggle as hard as Faulkner did to become a Modernist, fighting to overcome the claims of family and region. His career would be spent gathering up the fragments of myth and culture that had been bequeathed to him in order to recast them into a workable identity that could withstand the new conditions of twentieth-century life and perhaps off the possibility of heroic action."

Daniel J. Singal

From *William Faulkner: The Making of a Modernist* (Chapel Hill: University of North Carolina Press, 1997), p. 20.

life, for all its circumscription, is richer, fuller, and more successful than Ike's. The many biblical allusions in the novel—from the title to such character names as Isaac—underscore the point that Southerners were more like the patriarchs of the Old Testament than the Greeks and Romans for whom they named their children (L.Q.C. McCaslin had twin sons named Theophilus and Amodeus). The book plays variations on the themes of patriarchy, filial responsibility, lost birthrights, pairs of male children tempted or forced by circumstances to take different paths, sacrifice, flight, bondage, and freedom.

Though he has been married, Ike has no children, does not farm, and has refused ownership of land that, by right, is supposed to be his. His reasons for this refusal appear to be many, as he tries at various times to explain to kinsmen or to himself why he has repudiated the family farm. The apparent key is shame, brought on by his realization that his grandfather sired a daughter by a slave and then sired another child by this daughter. Lucas is the son of that second child, Terrel (called "Tomey's Turl"), and thus is both grandson and great-grandson of L.Q.C. McCaslin. Ironically, the family history that causes Ike great shame and cultural paralysis is taken by Lucas as a sign of cultural and personal power. Though he has also struggled to prevent any repetition of such events, Lucas has deliberately claimed his own birthright. Ike has almost nothing to do with Lucas simply

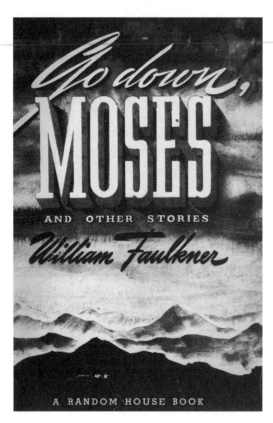

Dust jacket for William Faulkner's 1942 collection of interconnected stories

because Ike has not taken over the farm and because Lucas does not join him in the annual hunts. The loss is Ike's, a loss for which he is not able to compensate with his apparent devotion to the wilderness, where he also fails, finally, as a truly spiritual hunter.

Lucas's marriage is a model for the African American community, though the reader learns that it has often been tested. Ike's marriage was a childless truce between himself and his short-lived wife. Lucas does not hunt since the black man is not allowed a man's role in the hunt. Ike does not farm because the land, in his view, is tainted with the arrogance of those who believed they could own it and own the people who worked it for them.

Faulkner's dramatic blending of the Beauchamp and McCaslin cycles of stories has a paradoxical conclusion. The sins of the fathers, as the Bible says, are visited upon the third and fourth generations. Ike's misplaced shame does nothing to stop the cycle of exploitation that, in his view, curses the South. A Beauchamp-McCaslin descendant, who has been run off the plantation for breaking into a building where the history of the place is told, is executed for murder in Chicago, himself a victim of that exile and anger that, as Wright's *Native Son* illustrates, perversely creates the young black criminal of the city.[44]

NOTES

1. Wendy Steiner, "The Diversity of American Fiction," in *Columbia Literary History of the United States,* edited by Emory Elliott and others (New York: Columbia University Press, 1988), p. 854.

2. Robert Stepto, "Afro-American Literature," in *Columbia Literary History of the United States,* p. 797.

3. Cecilia Tichi, "Women Writers and the New Woman," in *Columbia Literary History of the United States,* p. 603.

4. Local opportunities for writers were, of course, equally limited, except that publishing was at least an accessible national phenomenon. During the rise of Southern letters in the 1920s it was necessary, as it always had been, that Southern books be published out-

side the South—mainly in New York and Chicago. Even worse, only the largest Southern cities boasted bookstores where Southern books could be bought directly by Southerners. Public libraries in the South were likewise neither plentiful nor well funded, and in any case they were often managed by genteel librarians who did not necessarily welcome modernist literature of any stripe, including that by Southerners. Certainly, they tried to prevent the young and impressionable from reading anything socially or sexually suggestive. In *One Writer's Beginnings* (1984) Welty, for example, remembers the stringent rules of her local librarian. As late as the 1940s, lending libraries in drugstores and in private homes were often the only places a Southern reader could find recent and controversial work by Southern writers.

5. Margaret Mitchell, review of *Soldiers' Pay;* reprinted in *Margaret Mitchell, Reporter: Journalism by the Author of Gone with the Wind,* edited by Patrick Allen (Athens, Ga.: Hill Street Press, 2000), pp. 325–326.

6. Allen Tate, "Narcissus as Narcissus," in his *Essays of Four Decades* (Chicago: Swallow Press, 1968), pp. 596–597, 598.

7. William Faulkner, "Classroom Statements at the University of Mississippi," in *Lion in the Garden: Interviews with William Faulkner, 1926–1962,* edited by James B. Meriwether and Michael Millgate (New York: Random House, 1968), p. 58.

8. Thomas Wolfe, *O Lost: A Story of the Buried Life,* text established by Arlyn and Matthew J. Bruccoli (Columbia: University of South Carolina Press, 2000). The editors have restored passages that Maxwell Perkins, Wolfe's editor at Scribners, removed for the publication of *Look Homeward, Angel.*

9. Faulkner, "Interview with Jean Stein vanden Heuvel," in *Lion in the Garden,* p. 255.

10. Michael Millgate, *The Achievement of William Faulkner* (New York: Random House, 1966), p. 103.

11. "Introduction: A Statement of Principles," in Donald Davidson and others, *I'll Take My Stand: The South and the Agrarian Tradition* (New York: Harper, 1962), p. xix.

12. Ibid., p. xxx.

13. Wayne Mixon, *The People's Writer: Erskine Caldwell and the South* (Charlottesville & London: University Press of Virginia, 1995), pp. 43, 44.

14. Ibid., p. 48.

15. Margaret Mitchell, *Gone with the Wind* (New York: Macmillan, 1936), p. 1037.

16. Even seemingly proletarian figures such as Erskine Caldwell received good instruction early at home. Many other writers of the Southern Renaissance attended excellent small-town schools and went on to modest universities, where it took only a few highly informed professors to make a great difference in their points of view: the Fugitives at Vanderbilt, Wolfe and Green at the University of North Carolina, and Faulkner at the University of Mississippi.

17. "Hurston, Zora Neale," in *The Oxford Companion to American Literature,* edited by James D. Hart, fifth edition (New York & Oxford: Oxford University Press, 1983), p. 356.

18. Edward L. Ayers and Bradley C. Mittendorf, eds., *The Oxford Book of the American South* (New York & Oxford: Oxford University Press, 1997), p. 297.

19. Elaine Showalter, "Women Writers between the Wars," in *Columbia Literary History of the United States,* p. 839.

20. The context of Wright's novel among other works by African American writers during the period is handled well in Lee Greene's "Black Novelists and Novels, 1930–1950," in *The*

History of Southern Literature, edited by Louis D. Rubin and others (Baton Rouge: Louisiana State University Press, 1985), p. 389.

21. Alferdteen Harrison, introduction to *Black Exodus: The Great Migration from the American South,* edited by Harrison (Jackson: University Press of Mississippi, 1991), p. xv.

22. Richard Wright, *Native Son* (New York: Harper, 1940), p. 359.

23. Margaret Walker, *Richard Wright, Daemonic Genius: A Portrait of the Man, a Critical Look at His Work* (New York: Warner, 1988), p. 149.

24. Arnold Rampersad, "Too Honest for His Own Time," in *The Critical Response to Richard Wright,* edited by Robert J. Butler (Westport, Conn. & London: Greenwood Press, 1995), p. 163.

25. James Agee and Walker Evans, *Let Us Now Praise Famous Men* (Boston: Houghton Mifflin, 1941), p. 13.

26. Ibid., p. 19.

27. Ibid., p. 363.

28. Agee, "Now as Awareness," in *Agee: His Life Remembered,* edited by Ross Spears and Jude Cassidy, narrative by Robert Coles (New York: Holt, Rinehart & Winston, 1985), pp. 179–180.

29. Alan Spiegel, *James Agee and the Legend of Himself* (Columbia: University of Missouri Press, 1998), p. 142.

30. Wilbur J. Cash, *The Mind of the South* (New York: Vintage, 1960), pp. vii–viii.

31. Ibid., p. x.

32. Ibid., p. 440.

33. David Hackett Fischer, "Two Minds of the South: Ideas of Southern History in W. J. Cash and James McBride Dabbs," in *W. J. Cash and the Minds of the South,* edited by Paul D. Escott (Baton Rouge: Louisiana State University Press, 1992), p. 145.

34. Bertram Wyatt-Brown, *The House of Percy: Honor, Melancholy, and Imagination in a Southern Family* (New York & Oxford: Oxford University Press, 1994), p. 13.

35. Walker Percy, "The Man on the Train," in his *The Message in the Bottle* (New York: Farrar, Straus & Giroux, 1975), p. 94.

36. William Alexander Percy, *Lanterns on the Levee* (New York: Knopf, 1975), pp. [i–ii].

37. Wyatt-Brown, *The House of Percy,* pp. 4–5.

38. Percy, *Lanterns on the Levee,* p. 92.

39. *The Wild Palms,* a title Faulkner's editor gave to the novel, is now available in a corrected text with the author's original title, *If I Forget Thee, Jerusalem* (New York: Vintage, 1995).

40. Percy, *Lanterns on the Levee,* pp. 247–248.

41. Fred Hobson, *Tell About the South: The Southern Rage to Explain* (Baton Rouge: Louisiana State University Press, 1983), p. 277.

42. Percy, *Lanterns on the Levee,* p. 348.

43. Eudora Welty, "Death of a Traveling Salesman," in *The Collected Stories of Eudora Welty* (New York: Random House, 1983), p. 130.

44. This theme in Wright's work is pointed out in Walker's *Richard Wright, Daemonic Genius,* p. 150.

CRITICAL RESPONSE TO THE SOUTHERN RENAISSANCE

INTRODUCTION

In occasional essays written from the mid 1930s on, the poet Allen Tate, who participated in many aspects of the Southern Renaissance, debated with himself and others about the development of Southern literature. His first idea was that such a literature could not develop, especially in the modern world, without a radical change in Southern society: one would need serious magazines, publishing houses, a literate community of readers, and a profession of letters by which individuals could make a living. In 1935 Tate observed that whatever one thought of Southern history and culture, "the Southern tradition has left no cultural landmark so conspicuous that the people may be reminded by it constantly of what they are. We lack a tradition in the arts; more to the point, we lack a literary tradition. We lack even a literature."[1] It was as if he were repeating, in a milder and more bemused form, the charge leveled against the South by H. L. Mencken in 1920: that it was the Sahara Desert of the beaux arts. Yet, Tate himself was a key figure in a renovation—not just a revival—of the writing profession among Southerners, from his participation as a student in faculty-directed poetry sessions at Vanderbilt University in the 1920s to his role in organizing the Agrarian symposium *I'll Take My Stand* in 1930 and his broad acquaintance with significant and productive literary figures from Charleston to Richmond.

But once the Southern Renaissance had taken a sufficiently large portion of the nation's, and the world's, attention as a literary phenomenon, Tate acknowledged it, though not without giving the matter his own spin. In "A Southern Mode of the Imagination" (1959) he wrote that "the period now somewhat misleadingly called the Southern Renaissance . . . was more precisely a birth, not a rebirth. . . . None of us . . . thirty-five years ago, was conscious of playing any part at all" in a new movement, he observed, and he found that the "essays and books about us that have begun to appear give me a little less than the shock of recognition," especially when they attributed causes and influences to one person or another.[2]

H. L. Mencken with the Georgia novelist Frances Newman in Atlanta, 1926

But come the books—and essays—did, so that the critical effort expended on the Southern Renaissance is extensive and still growing. The existent and ongoing critical literature on modern Southern literature alone—that is, on the writers and writing associated with the prime period of the Southern Renaissance—is dauntingly vast. Early in the field came collections of essays edited by Louis D. Rubin Jr., who has remained a major discussant and popularizer of writers from the South, and Robert D. Jacobs. Their *Southern Renascence: The Literature of the Modern South* (1953) and *South: Modern Southern Literature in Its Cultural Setting* (1961) helped to establish the subject as a singular field of endeavor for academic critics. Also early in the field were books about the Fugitives. Tate's "A Southern Mode of the Imagination" mentions John M. Bradbury's *The Fugitives: A Critical Account* (1958), and Bradbury followed up this book in 1963 with a broad general study titled *Renaissance in the South: A Critical History of the Literature, 1920–1960.*

Once the floodgates were open, the flow of writing about this and earlier periods of literature in the South experienced a renaissance of its own. Jay B. Hubbell's *The South in American Literature, 1607–1900* (1954) was a landmark study, many years in the making, of Southern literature prior to the renaissance period. As William Faulkner and other Southern writers have taught, however, when the present changes, the past changes, and Hubbell's painstaking and sympathetic study of earlier southern writing might well be rewritten now in the light of how the generation between the two world wars changed the perception of the Old South's institutions and values. An attempt to encompass the whole field of Southern literature, *The History of Southern Literature,* was published in 1985, under the general editorship of Rubin, with nearly two hundred pages devoted to the period of the Southern Renaissance. This volume was a kind of culmination of other scholarly projects initiated and often led by Rubin that have had the result of making Southern literature a bona fide field of study. In 1969 he edited *A Bibliographical Guide to the Study of Southern Literature,* a volume that features lengthy bibliographies and bibliographical essays, beginning with general works on the South and on Southern literature. There are also bibliographies on each of the periods of Southern writing and on scholarship and criticism of individual Southern writers. Faulkner's significance to this enterprise is underscored by a note at the head of the bibliography for the Southern Renaissance: "It should be added that although Faulkner items *per se* are excluded from this list, there is a considerable body of literature (listed elsewhere in this volume) on Faulkner and the South and on the influence, direct and indirect, of Faulkner on other Southern writers which should not be ignored by anyone interested in the Southern Renaissance."[3]

Rubin's bibliography has been supplemented annually by checklists of scholarship and criticism on Southern writing—with a section on the Southern Renaissance—in *Mississippi Quarterly: The Journal of Southern Culture,* published by the Department of English at Mississippi State University. A project to collect these supplements into a volume like the 1969 bibliography is under way. *Southern Writers: A Biographical Dictionary* (1979) includes brief biographical accounts and guides to criticism of many writers of the Southern Renaissance—including some figures not covered in the present volume because of limitations of space. Additional guidance to individual writers can be found in the annual reviews of scholarship on American literature found in *American Literary Scholarship: An Annual,* sponsored by the American Literature Section of the Modern Language Association and published by Duke University Press. Other sources include the *Dictionary of Literary Biography* and the *Columbia Literary History of the United States* (1988). There are also classroom text anthologies devoted exclusively to Southern literature, such as *The Oxford Book of the American South* (1997), *The Literature of the American South* (1998), and *The South in Perspective: An Anthology of Southern Literature* (2001).[4]

Anthologized and historicized, the subject of the Southern Renaissance has attained the kind of solidity that invites postmodern doubt or reconfiguration. Michael O'Brien's *The Idea of the American South, 1920–1941* (1979), Daniel Joseph Singal's *The War Within: From Victorian to Modernist Thought in the South, 1919–1945* (1982), Fred Hobson's *Tell About the South: The Southern Rage to Explain* (1983), Richard Gray's *Writing the South: Ideas of an American Region* (1986), and Michael Kreyling's *Inventing Southern Literature* (1998) represent different approaches to a reconsideration of the causes and results; the sources, ideas, and themes; and the psychology and politics that lie behind the culture of writing in and about the South. Many of these critics psychoanalyze those interpreters of the South contemporary with the Southern Renaissance. Doubtless a new generation of scholars and critics will come along to psychoanalyze them, suggesting why they took their particular combative or appreciative stances toward Southern literature.

THE CROSS-CULTURAL RESPONSE TO THE SOUTHERN RENAISSANCE

Several questions arise upon consideration of how other world cultures, or even other American regional cultures, have responded to the

Southern Renaissance. In "The New Provincialism" (1945) Tate raises an interesting consideration regarding whether a whole nation can ever be a pure region and whether a "nationalist" literature can ever absolutely represent a nation, especially a nation's distinct regions. He suggests that some critics seem to want, or predict, an international literature, and he argues that the idea is as absurd at the international level as it is at the national. What he calls "mere regionalism," he makes plain, "is not enough. For this picturesque regionalism of local color is a by-product of nationalism. And it is not informed enough to support a mature literature. But neither is nationalism."[5]

Tate goes on to say that "no literature can be mature without the regional consciousness; it can only be senile. . . . For without regionalism, without locality in the sense of local continuity in tradition and belief, we shall not get a whole literature."[6] The point he raises is resolved in a perceptive observation by the contemporary Southern poet, fiction writer, and essayist Wendell Berry of Kentucky. The best regionalism, Berry explains, is not sentimental or chauvinist; the surest way to lose it, in fact, is to reduce it to political or social stereotypes:

> There is, for instance, a "regionalism" based upon pride, which behaves like nationalism. And there is a "regionalism" based upon condescension, which specializes in the quaint and the eccentric and the picturesque, and which behaves in general like an exploitive industry. These varieties, and their kindred, have in common a dependence on false mythology that tends to generalize and stereotype the life of a region. That is to say it tends to impose false literary or cultural generalizations upon false geographical generalizations.[7]

The best regionalism, Berry argues, is "local life aware of itself" that "substitutes for the myths and stereotypes of a region a particular knowledge of the life of the *place* one lives in and intends to *continue* to live in. . . . The motive of such regionalism is the awareness that local life is intricately dependent, for its quality but also for its continuance, upon local knowledge."[8]

This assessment of regionalism is a key to how other cultures have, at their best, taken an interest in the Southern Renaissance and its writers. Authors from all over the world—first in Western Europe, then Latin America, Japan, Eastern Europe, and elsewhere—found that reading the works of many Southern Renaissance writers revealed to them the distinct (and, of course, different) regional cultures in which they had grown up in their own countries. On a broad scale, writers in places that had recently experienced the shift from a largely agrarian economy to a modern economy based on industrial organization—where, as in the American South, even agriculture became more and more organized on such principles—saw in modern Southern literature reflections of their own place.

Writers in places ravaged by war—defeated countries, obviously, but also those that had been occupied before emerging victorious, such as France—found inspiration and familiarity in modern Southern reflections on the period of the Civil War. Writers and readers in countries with racial and economic stratification—countries with colonial empires or a relatively imprisoned peasant class—found aspects of their own history and present conditions in writing of the Southern Renaissance. The potential impact of a great literature is, of course, limitless, as the impact of nineteenth-century Russian and French literature on Southern writers, for example, proves in a different way. The attention paid to writers of the Southern Renaissance by readers in other parts of the world confirms that the critical imaginations of the best Southern writers of the 1920s and beyond have indeed traveled the world with great impact.

CRITICAL SELECTIONS

A sampling of writing about the Southern Renaissance or relevant to discussion of the subject follows.

In 1917 Mencken published a short essay in the *New York Evening Mail*, "The Sahara of the Bozart," in which he roundly denounced the entire region of the South for an appalling lack of culture in any form. He later collected many of his earlier newspaper and magazine pieces in a series of volumes appropriately (and honestly) titled *Prejudices*. In the second volume of this series, published in 1920, Mencken included an expanded and improved version of "The Sahara of the Bozart," which attracted widespread attention North and South and provoked a variety of responses. The 1920 version of the essay is reproduced here.

H. L. Mencken, "The Sahara of the Bozart," in his *Prejudices: Second Series* (New York: Knopf, 1920), pp. 136–154.

> Alas, for the South! Her books have grown fewer—
> She never was much given to literature.

> In the lamented J. Gordon Coogler, author of these elegaic [sic] lines, there was the insight of a true poet. He was the last bard of Dixie, at least in the legitimate line. Down there a poet is now almost as rare as an oboe-player, a dry-point etcher or a metaphysician. It is, indeed, amazing to contemplate so vast a vacuity. One thinks of the interstellar spaces, of the colossal reaches of the now mythical ether. Nearly the whole of Europe could be lost in that stupendous region of fat farms, shoddy cities and paralyzed cerebrums: one could throw in France, Germany and Italy, and still have room for the British Isles. And yet, for all its size and all its wealth and all the "progress" it babbles of, it is almost as sterile, artistically, intellectually, culturally, as the Sahara Desert. There are single acres in Europe that house more first-rate men than all the states south of the Potomac; there are probably single square miles in America. If the whole of the late Confederacy were to be engulfed by a tidal wave tomorrow, the effect upon the civilized minority of

men in the world would be but little greater than that of a flood on the Yang-tse-kiang. It would be impossible in all history to match so complete a drying-up of a civilization.

I say a civilization because that is what, in the old days, the South had, despite the Baptist and Methodist barbarism that reigns down there now. More, it was a civilization of manifold excellences—perhaps the best that the Western Hemisphere has ever seen—undoubtedly the best that These States have ever seen. Down to the middle of the last century, and even beyond, the main hatchery of ideas on this side of the water was across the Potomac bridges. The New England shopkeepers and theologians never really developed a civilization; all they ever developed was a government. They were, at their best, tawdry and tacky fellows, oafish in manner and devoid of imagination; one searches the books in vain for mention of a salient Yankee gentleman; as well look for a Welsh gentleman. But in the south there were men of delicate fancy, urbane instinct and aristocratic manner—in brief, superior men—in brief, gentry. To politics, their chief diversion, they brought active and original minds. It was there that nearly all the political theories we still cherish and suffer under came to birth. It was there that the crude dogmatism of New England was refined and humanized. It was there, above all, that some attention was given to the art of living—that life got beyond and above the state of a mere infliction and became an exhilarating experience. A certain noble spaciousness was in the ancient southern scheme of things. The Ur-Confederate had leisure. He liked to toy with ideas. He was hospitable and tolerant. He had the vague thing that we call culture.

But consider the condition of his late empire today. The picture gives one the creeps. It is as if the Civil War stamped out every last bearer of the torch, and left only a mob of peasants on the field. One thinks of Asia Minor, resigned to Armenians, Greeks and wild swine, of Poland abandoned to the Poles. In all that gargantuan paradise of the fourth-rate there is not a single picture gallery worth going into, or a single orchestra capable of playing the nine symphonies of Beethoven, or a single opera-house, or a single theater devoted to decent plays, or a single public monument (built since the war) that is worth looking at, or a single workshop devoted to the making of beautiful things. Once you have counted Robert Loveman (an Ohioan by birth) and John McClure (an Oklahoman) you will not find a single southern poet above the rank of a neighborhood rhymester. Once you have counted James Branch Cabell (a lingering survivor of the *ancien regime*: a scarlet dragonfly imbedded in opaque amber) you will not find a single southern prose writer who can actually write. And once you have—but when you come to critics, musical com-

SOUTHERN CULTURE

"[Mencken] may not have approved of the southern civilization, culture, or literature that he observed, but they had effectively satisfied southern needs for fifty years. In thousands of towns and villages much of southern civil life revolved around the statue of the Confederate soldier, eyes vigilant under his kepi or slouch hat, still facing north, like the one that dominates the last scene of Faulkner's *The Sound and the Fury*. Confederate veterans dominated southern politics from the end of Reconstruction until the First World War. Since the Protestant South viewed Christmas and Easter as Popish celebrations, Thanksgiving as a New England luxury, and the Fourth of July as a Negro holiday, the most solemn ritual was Confederate Monument Day or Confederate Memorial Day, when, one observer notes, 'the whole population of a town turns out in procession, headed by the Ladies Memorial Association, and decorates the graves.'"

Lewis Lawson

From "Twentieth-Century Southern Fiction," in his *Another Generation: Southern Fiction Since World War II* (Jackson: University Press of Mississippi, 1983), p. 4.

posers, painters, sculptors, architects and the like, you will have to give it up, for there is not even a bad one between the Potomac mud-flats and the Gulf. Nor an historian. Nor a sociologist. Nor a philosopher. Nor a theologian. Nor a scientist. In all these fields the south is an awe-inspiring blank—a brother to Portugal, Serbia and Esthonia.

Consider, for example, the present estate and dignity of Virginia—in the great days indubitably the premier American state, the mother of Presidents and statesmen, the home of the first American university worthy of the name, the *arbiter elegantiarum* of the western world. Well, observe Virginia to-day. It is years since a first-rate man, save only Cabell, has come out of it. The old aristocracy went down the red gullet of war; the poor white trash are now in the saddle. Politics in Virginia are cheap, ignorant, parochial, idiotic; there is scarcely a man in office above the rank of a professional job-seeker; the political doctrine that prevails is made up of hand-me-downs from the bumpkinry of the Middle West— Bryanism, Prohibition, vice crusading, all that sort of filthy claptrap; the administration of the law is turned over to professors of Puritanism and espionage; a Washington or a Jefferson, dumped there by some act of God, would be denounced as a scoundrel and jailed overnight. Elegance, *esprit,* culture? Virginia has no art, no literature, no philosophy, no mind or aspiration of her own. Her education has sunk to the Baptist seminary level; not a single contribution to human knowledge has come out of her colleges in twenty-five years; she spends less than half upon her common schools, *per capita,* than any northern state spends. In brief, an intellectual Gobi or Lapland. Urbanity, *politesse,* chivalry? Go to! It was in Virginia that they invented the device of searching for contraband whisky in women's underwear. . . . There remains, at the top, a ghost of the old aristocracy, a bit wistful and infinitely charming. But it has lost all its old leadership to fabulous monsters from the lower depths; it is submerged in an industrial plutocracy that is ignorant and ignominious. The mind of the state, as it is revealed to the nation, is pathetically naive and inconsequential. It no longer reacts with energy and elasticity to great problems. It has fallen to the bombastic trivialities of the camp-meeting and the chautauqua. Its foremost exponent—if so flabby a thing may be said to have an exponent—is a stateman [sic] whose name is synonymous with empty words, broken pledges and false pretenses. One could no more imagine a Lee or a Washington in the Virginia of to-day than one could imagine a Huxley in Nicaragua.

I choose the Old Dominion, not because I disdain it, but precisely because I esteem it. It is, by long odds, the most civilized of the southern states, now as always. It has sent a host of creditable sons northward; the stream kept running into our own time. Virginians, even the worst of them, show the effects of a great tradition. They hold themselves above other southerners, and with sound pretension. If one turns to such a commonwealth as Georgia the picture becomes far darker. There the liberated lower orders of whites have borrowed the worst commercial bounderism of the Yankee and superimposed it upon a culture that, at bottom, is but little removed from savagery. Georgia is at once the home of the cotton-mill sweater and of the most noisy and vapid sort of chamber of commerce, of the Methodist parson turned Savonarola and of the lynching bee. A self-respecting European, going there to live, would not only find intellectual stimulation utterly lacking; he would actually feel a certain insecurity, as if the scene were the Balkans or the China Coast. The Leo Frank affair was no isolated phenomenon. It fitted into its frame very snugly. It was a natural expression of Georgian notions of truth and justice. There is a state with more than half the area of Italy and more population than either Denmark or Norway, and yet in thirty years it has not produced a single idea. Once upon a time a Georgian printed a couple of books that attracted notice, but immediately it turned out that he was little more than an amanuensis for the local blacks—that his works were really the products, not of white Georgia, but of black Georgia. Writing afterward *as* a white man, he swiftly subsided into the fifth rank. And he is not only the glory of the literature of Georgia; he is, almost literally, the whole of the literature of Georgia—nay, of the entire art of Georgia.

Virginia is the best of the south to-day, and Georgia is perhaps the worst. The one is simply senile; the other is crass, gross, vulgar, and obnoxious. Between lies a vast plain of mediocrity, stupidity, lethargy, almost of dead silence. In the north, of course, there is also grossness, crassness, vulgarity. The north, in its way, is also stupid and obnoxious. But nowhere in the north is there such complete sterility, so depressing a lack of all civilized gesture and aspiration. One would find it difficult to unearth a second-rate city between Ohio and the Pacific that isn't struggling to establish an orchestra, or setting up a little theater, or going in for an art gallery, or making some other effort to get into touch with civilization. These efforts often fail, and sometimes they succeed rather absurdly, but under them there is at least an impulse that deserves respect, and that is the impulse to seek beauty and to experiment with ideas, and so to give the life of every day a certain dignity and purpose. You will find no such impulses in the south. There are no committees down there cadging subscriptions for orchestras; if a string quartet is ever heard there, the news of it has never come out; an opera troupe, when it roves the land, is a nine days' wonder. The little theater movement has swept the whole country, enormously augmenting the public interest in sound plays, giving new dramatists their chance, forcing reforms upon the commercial theater. Everywhere else the wave rolls high—but along the line of the Potomac it breaks upon a rock-bound shore. There is no little theater beyond. There is no gallery of pictures. No artist ever gives exhibitions. No one talks of such things. No one seems to be interested in such things.

As for the cause of this unanimous torpor and doltishness, this curious and almost pathological estrangement from everything makes for a civilized culture, I have hinted at it already, and now state it again. The south has simply been drained of all its best blood. The vast blood-letting of the Civil War half exterminated and wholly paralyzed the old aristocracy, and so left the land to the harsh mercies of the poor white trash, now its masters. The war, of course, was not a complete massacre. It spared a decent number of first-rate southerners—perhaps even some of the very best. Moreover, other countries, notably France and Germany, have survived far more staggering butcheries, and even showed marked progress thereafter. But the war not only cost a great many valuable lives; it also brought bankruptcy, demoralization and despair in its train—and so the majority of first-rate southerners that were left, broken in spirit and unable to live under the new dispensation, cleared out. A few went to South America, to Egypt, to the Far East. Most came north. They were fecund; their progeny is widely dispersed, to the great benefit of the north. A southerner of good blood almost always does well in the north. He finds, even in the big cities, surroundings fit for a man of condition. His peculiar qualities have a high social value, and are esteemed. He is welcomed by the codfish aristocracy as one palpably superior. But in the south he throws up his hands. It is impossible for him to stoop to the common level. He cannot brawl in politics with the grandsons of his grandfather's tenants. He is unable to share their fierce jealousy of the emerging black—the cornerstone of all their public thinking. He is anaesthetic to their theological and political enthusiasms. He finds himself an alien at their feasts of soul. And so he withdraws into his tower, and is heard of no more. Cabell is almost a perfect example. His eyes, for years, were turned toward the past; he became a professor of the grotesque genealogizing that decaying aristocracies affect; it was only by a sort of accident that he discovered himself to be an artist. The south is unaware of the fact to this day; it regards Woodrow Wilson and Col. John Temple Graves as much finer stylists, and Frank L. Stanton as an infinitely greater poet. If it has heard, which I doubt, that Cabell has been hoofed by the Comstocks, it unquestionably views that assault as a deserved rebuke to a fellow who indulges a lewd passion for fancy writing, and is a covert enemy to the Only True Christianity.

What is needed down there, before the vexatious public problems of the region may be intelligently approached, is a survey of the population by competent ethnologists and anthropologists. The immigrants of the north have been studied at great length, and any one who is interested may now apply to the Bureau of Ethnology for elaborate data as to their relative capacity for education, and the changes that they undergo under American *Kultur.* But the older stocks of the south, and particularly the emancipated and dominant poor white trash, have never been investigated scientifically, and most of the current generalizations about them are probably wrong. For example, the generalization that they are purely Anglo-Saxon in blood. This I doubt very seriously. The chief strain down there, I believe, is Celtic rather than Saxon, particularly in the hill country. French blood, too, shows itself here and there, and so does Spanish, and so does German. The last-named entered from the northward, by way of the limestone belt just east of the Alleghenies. Again, it is very likely that in some parts of the south a good many of the plebeian whites have more than a trace of negro blood. Interbreeding under concubinage produced some very light half-breeds at an early day, and no doubt appreciable numbers of them went over into the white race by the simple process of changing their abode. Not long ago I read a curious article by an intelligent negro, in which he stated that it is easy for a very light negro to pass as a white in the south on account of the fact that large numbers of southerners accepted as white have distinctly negroid features. Thus it becomes a delicate and dangerous matter for a train conductor or a hotel-keeper to challenge a suspect. But the Celtic strain is far more obvious than any of these others. It not only makes itself more visible in physical stigmata—*e.g.*, leanness and dark coloring— but also in mental traits. For example, the religious thought of Wales. There is the same naive belief in an anthropomorphic Creator but little removed, in manner and desire, from an evangelical bishop; there is the same submission to an ignorant and impudent sacerdotal tyranny, and there is the same sharp contrast between doctrinal orthodoxy and private ethics. Read Caradoc Evans' ironical picture of the Welsh Wesleyans in his preface to "My Neighbors," and you will be instantly reminded of the Georgia and Carolina Methodists. The most booming sort of piety, in the south, is not incompatible with the theory that lynching is a benign institution. Two generations ago it was not incompatible with an ardent belief in slavery.

It is highly probable that some of the worst blood of western Europe flows in the veins of the southern poor whites, now poor no longer. The original strains, according to every honest historian, were extremely corrupt. Philip Alexander Bruce (a Virginian of the old gentry) says in his "Industrial History of Virginia in the Seventeenth Century" that the first native-born generation was largely illegitimate. "One of the most common offenses against morality committed in the lower ranks of life in Virginia during the seventeenth century," he says, "was bastardy." The mothers of these bastards, he continues, were chiefly indentured servants, and "had belonged to the lowest class in their native country." Fanny Kemble Butler, writing of the Georgia poor whites of a century later, described them as "the most degraded race of human beings claiming an Anglo-Saxon origin that can be found on the face of the earth—filthy, lazy, ignorant, brutal, proud, penniless savages." The Sunday-school and the chautauqua, of course, have appreciably mellowed the descendants of these "savages," and their economic progress and rise to political power have done perhaps even more, but the marks of their origin are still unpleasantly plentiful. Every now and then they produce a political leader who puts their secret notions of the true, the good and the beautiful into plain words, to the amazement and scandal of the rest of the country. That amazement is turned into downright incredulity when news comes that his platform has got him high office, and that he is trying to execute it.

In the great days of the south the line between the gentry and the poor whites was very sharply drawn. There was absolutely no intermarriage. So far as I know there is not a single instance in history of a southerner of the upper class marrying one of the bondwomen described by Mr. Bruce. In other societies characterized by class distinctions of that sort it is common for the lower class to be improved by extra-legal crosses. That is to say, the men of the upper class take women of the lower class as mistresses, and out of such unions spring the extraordinary plebeians who rise sharply from the common level, and so propagate the delusion that all other plebeians would do the same thing if they had the chance— in brief, the delusion that class distinctions are merely economic and conventional, and not congenital and genuine. But in the south the men of the upper classes sought their mistresses among the blacks, and after a few generations there was so much white blood in the black women that they were considerably more attractive than the unhealthy and bedraggled women of the poor whites. This preference continued into our own time. A southerner of good family once told me in all seriousness that he had reached his majority before it ever occurred to him that a white woman might make quite as agreeable a mistress as the octaroons [sic] of his jejune fancy. If the thing has changed of late, it is not the fault of the southern white man, but of the southern mulatto women. The more sightly yellow girls of the region, with improving economic opportunities, have gained self-respect, and so they are no longer as willing to enter into concubinage as their grand-dams were.

As a result of this preference of the southern gentry for mulatto mistresses there was created a series of mixed strains containing the best white blood of the south, and perhaps the whole country. As another result the poor whites went unfertilized from above, and so missed the improvement that so constantly shows itself in the peasant stocks of other countries. It is a commonplace that nearly all negroes who rise above the general are of mixed blood, usually with the white predominating. I know a great many negroes, and it would be hard for me to think of an exception. What is too often forgotten is that this white blood is not the blood of the poor white but that of the old gentry. The mulatto girls of the early days despised the poor whites as creatures distinctly inferior to negroes, and it was thus almost unheard of for such a girl to enter into relations with a man of that submerged class. This aversion was based upon a sound instinct. The southern mulatto of to-day is a proof of it. Like all other half-breeds he is an unhappy man, with disquieting tendencies toward anti-social habits of thought, but he is intrinsically a better animal than the pure-breed descendant of the old poor whites, and he not infrequently demonstrates it. It is not by accident that the negroes of the south are making faster progress, economically and culturally, than the masses of the whites. It is not by accident that the only visible aesthetic activity in the south is wholly in their hands. No southern composer has ever written music so good as that of half a dozen white-black composers who might be named. Even in politics, the negro reveals a curious superiority. Despite the fact that the race question has been the main political concern of the southern whites for two generations, to the practical exclusion of everything else, they have contributed nothing to its discussion that has impressed the rest of the world so deeply and so favorably as three or four books by southern negroes.

Entering upon such themes, of course, one must resign one's self to a vast misunderstanding and abuse. The south has not only lost its old capacity for producing ideas; it has also taken on the worst intolerance of ignorance and stupidity. Its prevailing mental attitude for several decades past has been that of its own hedge ecclesiastics. All who dissent from its orthodox doctrines are scoundrels. All who presume to discuss its ways realistically are damned. I have had, in my day, several experiences in point. Once, after I had published an article on some phase of the eternal race question, a leading southern newspaper replied by printing a column of denunciation of my father, then dead nearly twenty years—a philippic placarding him as an ignorant foreigner of dubious origin, inhabiting "the Baltimore ghetto" and speaking a dialect recalling that of Weber & Fields—two thousand words of incandescent nonsense, utterly false and beside the point, but exactly meeting the latter-day southern notion of effective controversy. Another time, I published a short discourse on lynching, arguing that the sport was popular in the south because the backward culture of the region denied the populace more seemly recreations. Among such recreations I mentioned those afforded by brass bands, symphony orchestras, boxing matches, amateur athletic contests, shoot-the-chutes, roof gardens, horse races, and so on. In reply another great southern journal denounced me as a man "of wineshop temperament, brass-jewelry tastes and pornographic predilections." In other words, brass bands, in the south, are classed with brass jewelry, and both are snares of the devil! To advocate setting up symphony orchestras is pornography! . . . Alas, when the touchy southerner attempts a greater urbanity, the result is often even worse. Some time ago a colleague of mine printed an article deploring the arrested cultural development of Georgia. In reply he received a number of protests from patriotic Georgians, and all of them solemnly listed the glories of the state. I indulge in a few specimens:

> Who has not heard of Asa G. Candler, whose name is synonymous with Coca-Cola, a Georgia product?

> The first Sunday-school in the world was opened in Savannah.

> Who does not recall with pleasure the writing of . . . Frank L. Stanton, Georgia's brilliant poet?

> Georgia was the first state to organize a Boys' Corn Club in the South—Newton county, 1904.

> The first to suggest a common United Daughters of the Confederacy badge was Mrs. Raynes, of Georgia.

> The first to suggest a state historian of the United Daughters of the Confederacy was Mrs. C. Helen Plane (Macon convention, 1896).

> The first to suggest putting to music Heber's "From Greenland's Icy Mountains" was Mrs. F. R. Goulding, of Savannah.

And so on, and so on. These proud boasts came, remember, not from obscure private persons, but from "Leading Georgians"—in one case, the state historian. Curious sidelights upon the ex-Confederate mind! Another comes from a stray copy of a negro paper. It describes an ordinance lately passed by the city council of Douglas, Ga., forbidding any trousers presser, on penalty of forfeiting a $500 bond, to engage in "pressing for both white and colored." This in a town, says the negro paper, where practically all of the white inhabitants have "their food prepared by colored hands," "their babies cared for by colored hands," and "the clothes which they wear right next to their skins washed in houses where negroes live"—houses in which the said clothes "remain for as long as a week at a time." But if you marvel at the absurdity, keep it dark! A casual word, and the united press of the south will be upon your trail, denouncing you bitterly as a scoundrelly Yankee, a Bolshevik Jew, an agent of the Wilhelmstrasse. . . .

Obviously, it is impossible for intelligence to flourish in such an atmosphere. Free inquiry is blocked by the idiotic certainties of ignorant men. The arts, save in lower reaches of the gospel hymn, the phonograph and the chautauqua harangue, are all held in suspicion. The tone of public opinion is set by an upstart class but lately emerged from industrial slavery into commercial enterprise—the class of "hustling" business men, of "live wires," of commercial club luminaries, of "drive" managers, of forward-lookers and right-thinkers—in brief, of third-rate southerners inoculated with all the worst traits of the Yankee sharper. One observes the curious effects of an old tradition of truculence upon a population now merely pushful and impudent, of an old tradition of chivalry upon a population now quite without imagination. The repose is gone. The old romanticism is gone. The philistinism of the new type of town-boomer southerner is not only indifferent to the ideals of the old south; it is positively antagonistic to them. That philistinism regards human life, not as an agreeable adventure, but as a mere trial of rectitude of efficiency. It is overwhelmingly utilitarian and moral. It is inconceivably hollow and obnoxious. What remains of the ancient tradition is simply a certain charming civility in private intercourse—often broken down, alas, by the hot rages of Puritanism, but still generally visible. The southerner, at his worst, is never quite the surly cad that the Yankee is. His sensitiveness may betray him into occasional bad manners, but in the main he is a pleasant fellow—hospitable, polite, good-humored, even jovial. . . . But a bit absurd. . . . A bit pathetic.

Wilbur J. Cash was, like Mencken, a journalist, primarily a newspaperman in Charlotte, North Carolina. His 1929 meditation on the "mind of the South," which was published in Mencken's intellectual journal *The American Mercury,* differs from "The Sahara of the Bozart" in that it digs deeply into the character of Southern consciousness and explores how the thinking common to the region sustained a social system with many tragic tensions. Cash's essay later evolved into a book-length work with the same title that was published in 1941.

W. J. Cash, "The Mind of the South," *American Mercury,* 17 (October 1929): 185–192.

One hears much in these days of the New South. The land of the storied rebel becomes industrialized; it casts up a new aristocracy of money-bags which in turn spawns a new *noblesse;* scoriac ferments spout and thunder toward an upheaval and overturn of all the old social, political, and intellectual values and an outgushing of divine fire in the arts—these are the things one hears about. There *is* a new South, to be sure. It is a chicken-pox of factories on the Watch-Us-Grow maps; it is a kaleidoscopic chromo of stacks and chimneys on the club-car window as the train rolls southward from Washington to New Orleans. But I question that it is much more. For the mind of that heroic region, I opine, is still basically and essentially the mind of the Old South. It is a mind, that is to say, of the soil rather than of the mills—a mind, indeed, which, as yet, is almost wholly unadjusted to the new industry.

Its salient characteristic is a magnificent incapacity for the real, a Brobdingnagian talent for the fantastic. The very legend of the Old South, for example, is warp and woof of the Southern mind. The "plantation" which prevailed outside the tidewater and delta regions was actually no more than a farm; its owner was, properly, neither a planter nor an aristocrat, but a backwoods farmer; yet the pretension to aristocracy was universal. Every farmhouse became a Big House, every farm a baronial estate, every master of scant red acres and a few mangy blacks a feudal lord. The haughty pride of these one-gallus squires of the uplands was scarcely matched by that of the F. F. V.'s of the estuary of the James. Their pride and their legend, handed down to their descendants, are today the basis of all social life in the South.

Such romancing was a natural outgrowth of the old Southern life. Harsh contact with toil was almost wholly lacking, as well for the poor whites as for the grand dukes. The growing of cotton involves only two or three months of labor a year, so even the slaves spent most of their lives on their backsides, as their progeny do to this day. The paternal care accorded the blacks and the white trash insured them against want. Leisure conspired with the languorous climate to the spinning of dreams. Unpleasant realities were singularly rare, and those which existed, as, for example, slavery, lent themselves to pleasant glorification. Thus fact gave way to amiable fiction.

Wilbur J. Cash in 1936. His 1929 essay "The Mind of the South" was the germ of a book-length work with the same title, published in 1941.

It is not without a certain aptness, then, that the Southerner's chosen drink is called moonshine. Everywhere he turns away from reality to a gaudy world of his own making. He declines to conceive of himself as the mad king's "poor, bare, forked animal"; in his own eyes, he is eternally a noble and heroic fellow. He has always displayed a passion for going to war. He pants after Causes and ravening monsters—witness his perpetual sweat about the nigger. (No matter whether the black boy is or is not a menace, he serves admirably as a dragon for the Southerner to belabor with all the showiness of a paladin out of a novel by Dr. Thomas Dixon. The lyncher, in his own sight, is a Roland or an Oliver, magnificently hurling down the glove in behalf of embattled Chastity.)

Even Rotary flourishes primarily as a Cause, as another opportunity for the Southerner to puff and prance and be a noble hotspur. His political heroes are, typically, florid magnificoes, with great manes and clownish ways—the Bleases and the Heflins. (It is said sometimes, I know, that they are exalted only by the rascals and the dolts, but, on a basis of observation, I make bold to believe that, while all decent Southerners vote against them, most do so with secret regret and only for the same reason that they condemn lynching, to wit: that they are self-conscious before the frown of the world, that they are patriots to the South.)

When the Southerner has read at all, he has read only Scott or Dumas or Dickens. His own books have been completely divorced from the real. He bawls loudly for Law Enforcement in the teeth of his own ingenious flouting of the Fourteenth and Fifteenth Amendments. He boasts of the purity of his Anglo-Saxon blood—and, *sub rosa*, winks at miscegenation. Yet, he is never—consciously, at least—a hypocrite. He is a Tartarin, not a Tartuffe. Whatever pleases him he counts as real. Whatever does not please him he holds as non-existent.

II

How this characteristic reacts with industrialism is strikingly shown by the case of the cotton-mill strikes in the Carolinas. Of the dozen-odd strikes which flared up a few months ago, not one now remains. All failed. New ones, to be sure, are springing up as a result of the unionization campaign which Thomas F. McMahon, president of the United Textile Workers of America, is waging in the region. But the U. T. W. A. failed in similar campaigns in 1920 and in 1923 and, in the light of recent history, I see no reason to believe that the present drive is likely to be any more successful.

Yet the peons of the mills unquestionably have genuine grievances, *in the absolute*. Wages rarely top $20. The average is from $11 to $14, with the minimum as low as $6. The ten-hour or eleven-hour day reigns. It is true that, as most of the mills own their own villages, houses are furnished the workers at nominal rentals. But save in the cases of Cramerton, N.C., the Cone villages at Greensboro, and a few other such model communities, the houses afforded are hardly more than pig-sties. The squalid, the ugly, and the drab are the hallmarks of the Southern mill town. Emaciated men and women and stunted children are everywhere in evidence.

But the southerner sees and understands nothing of this. Force his attention to the facts and he will, to be sure, appear for the nonce to take cognizance of them, will even be troubled, for he is not inhuman. But seek to remind him tomorrow of the things you have shown him today and you will discover no evidence that he recalls them at all; his talk will be entirely of the Cone villages and Cramerton and he will assume in all discussions of the merits of the case that these model kraals are typical of the estate of the mill-billy. The whole cast of his mind inhibits retention and contemplation of the hard facts, and he honestly believes that Cramerton is typical, that the top wage is the average wage. That is to say, he can honestly see only the pleasant thing. That is why, quite apart from antinomian considerations, the Southern newspapers almost unanimously

THE EXAMPLE OF THE SOUTH

"[T]he South as examplar [*sic*] for the rest of the world? That is a far more difficult matter to deal with, and I must confess that I shrink from judgment of the complex and often inconsistent eulogizing vision of their native land that the writers [of the South] present. In honesty, however, I feel I should make three objections: first, that to hold up a society for the admiration of the rest of the world (and of itself) is inevitably to deny its many-sidedness, a dangerous denial; second, that the 'pastness' of the past is something that must be acknowledged; the past can certainly fertilize the present, and in the end that is perhaps all the Agrarians desired. But their tone often suggests a desire to reinstate the past, something that no one has ever been able to do. And third, it can surely not be denied that what they say may have been true for the white Southerners, but for the black it was a different story, and there are many people, including most blacks (and myself), for whom even the most benevolent paternalism is an insufferable notion."

Paul Binding

From *Separate Country: A Literary Journey through the American South* (New York & London: Paddington Press, 1979), pp. 96–97.

denounced the accurate stories of the strikes printed by the New York *World* and the Baltimore *Sun* as baseless fabrications, inspired purely by sectional malice.

North Carolina furnished an interesting case study in this phase of the Southern mind when, at Gastonia, thugs, combed from the ruffians of two States and made sheriff's deputies, were loosed on a parade of inoffensive strikers, and dotards and women were mercilessly clubbed. A rumbling of protest shook the State. The Greensboro *Daily News* and the Raleigh *News and Observer* went so far as to denounce the business editorially. Whereupon—but that was all. Confronted by the damned facts, North Carolina gaped for a moment, then hastily brushed the offensive object into the ashcan, poured itself an extra-long drink, and went back to the pleasant business of golf-gab or mule-swapping.

If I have made incidental mention of violence, let it not be inferred that, in general, the strikes have been crushed by the blackjack. It is a significant fact that only at mills owned and operated by Yankees, or, in the case of Elizabethton, Tenn., by Germans, has violence been in evidence. The native baron simply closes his mill and sits back to wait for nature to take its course. He understands, that is, that the strikes may be trusted to go to pieces in the mind of the striker himself.

That mind is, in every essential respect, merely the ancient mind of the South. It is distinctly of the soil. For the peon, in origin, is usually a mountain-peasant, a hill-billy of the valleys and coves of the Appalachian ridge. He is leisured, lazy, shiftless. He is moony, sharing the common Southern passion for the lush and the baroque. He yammers his head off for Heflin and Blease, not because they promise him better working and living conditions—they don't—but because Heflin is his captain in the War against the Pope, because Bleases led him in that grand gesture for Human Freedom, that Storming of the Bastille—the flinging open of the gates of the South Carolina penitentiary. He crowds such swashbuckling and witless brotherhoods as the Klan, the Junior Order, the Patriotic Order Sons of America, and the American Legion. He is passionately interested in the shouting of souls "coming through" at a tent-revival, in the thrilling of his spine to "Washed in the Blood" at the Baptist synagogue, in a passing medicine show, and in the next installment of "Tiger Love" at the Little Gem. But in such hypothetical propositions as his need of a bathtub, in such prosaic problems as his economic status, he is interested but vaguely if at all.

In brief, he is totally blind to the realities of his condition. Though for a quarter of a century he has been in contact with industry, and has daily rubbed elbows with a standard of living higher than his own, his standards remain precisely those of a hill-billy. He holds it to be against God to take a bath at any other time than Saturday night. Often enough, indeed, he sews himself into his underwear at Hallowe'en, not to emerge again until the robin wings the northern way. Scorning the efforts of Y. M. C. A. secretaries to lure him into shower-baths, he continues, with a fine loyalty to tradition, to perform his ablutions in the tin tub which does duty on Monday as the family laundry.

So with everything. He is not displeased with his mill-shanty—for the reason that it is, at its worst, a far better house than the cabins of his original mountain home. And he has little real understanding that his wages are meagre. In his native hill society, money was an almost unknown commodity and the possession of ten dollars stamped a man as hog-rich; hence, privately and in the sub-conscious depths of him, he is inclined to regard a wage of that much a week as affluence. He is still at heart a mountain lout, lolling among his hounds or puttering about a moonshine-still while his women hoe the corn. He has no genuine conviction of wrong. His grievances exist only in the absolute. There is not one among them for which he is really willing to fight. And that is the prime reason why all Southern strikes fail.

III

Moreover, the mind of the Southerner is an intensely individualistic mind. There again, it strikes back to the Old South, to the soil. The South is the historic champion of States' Rights. It holds Locke's "indefeasibility of private rights" as axiomatic. Its economic philosophy is that of Adam Smith, recognizing no limitations on the pursuit of self-interest by the individual, and counting unbridled private enterprise as not only the natural order but also the source of all public good. *Laissez-faire* is its watchword.

The Southerner is without inkling of the fact that, admirably adapted as such a philosophy was to the simple, agricultural society of the Jeffersonian era, it is inadequate for dealing with the industrial problems of today. He has never heard of the doctrine of the social function of industry and would not understand it if he had. He cannot see that industrialism inevitably consolidates power into the hands of a steadily decreasing few, and enables them, unchecked, to grab the lion's share of the product of another man's labor; he cannot see that the worker in a machine age is not an individual at all but an atom among atoms—that he is no longer, and cannot possibly be, a free agent. Under the Southern view, even a cotton-mill is an individual. If a peon cares to work for the wage it chooses to pay, very well; if he doesn't, let him exercise a freeman's privilege and quit. But for him to combine with his fellows and seek to tie up the operation of the mill until his wages are raised—that, as the South sees it, is exactly as if a lone farm-hand, displeased with his pay, took post with a shotgun to bar his employer from tilling his field.

The lint-head of the mills, indeed, is the best individualist of them all, and for this there is excellent reason. Often enough he owns a farm, his ancestral portion in the hills—rocks, pinebrush, and abrupt slopes, but still a farm, well adapted to moonshining. If he is landless, there are hundreds of proprietors eager to secure him as tenant, an estate in which he will not have to work more than three months out of twelve. As a result, there is a constant flow back and forth between the soil and the mills. Thus the Southern peon is not, in fact, and *as an individual,* as irrevocably bound to the wheel of industry as his Northern brother, since he may always escape to churldom. The equally valid fact that, because only a handful can escape at any given time, the mass of his fellows are held irretrievably in bondage is lost upon him. He is always, in his own eyes, a man apart. He exhibits the grasping jealousy for petty personal advantage, the refusal to yield one jot or tittle for the common good, characteristic of the peasant. If, by a miracle, he is ambitious, his aspirations run, not to improving his own status by improving that of the class to which, in reality, he is bound, but to gaudy visions of himself as a member of the master class, as superintendent or even president of the mills. His fellows may be damned.

Another excellent reason, then, for the failure of Southern strikes is the impossibility of holding in organization the individualized yokel mind. The peon, to be sure, will join the union, but that is only because he is a romantic loon. He will join anything, be it a passing circus, a lynching-bee, or the Church of Latter Day Saints. He will even join the Bolsheviks (as at Gastonia, where the strikers were organized by the National Textile Workers' Union), though he is congenitally incapable of comprehending the basic notion of communism. The labor-organizers, with their sniffling pictures of his dismal estate, furnish him with a Cause for which he can strut and pose and, generally, be a magnificent galoot. And the prospect of striking involves visions of hell popping, the militia, parades, fist-fights and boozy harangues—just such a Roman holiday as he dotes on. By all means, he'll join the union!

But when flour runs low in the barrel, when monotonous waiting succeeds the opening Ku Klux festivities, when fresh clodhoppers, lured by the delights of movie-houses and ice-cream joints, begin to pour in and seize the vacant jobs in the mills, and when a strike-breaker drops around to the back door to say that, while the boss is goddam sore, he is willing to give everybody just one more chance, well, the lint-head, who has no deep-seated sense of wrong, who all along has rather suspected that the business he is embarked on is indistinguishable from road-agentry, and who decidedly likes the ego-warming backslap of the boss, does the natural thing for a romantic and sidesteps reality—does the natural thing for an individualist and goes back to work.

IV

Finally, the mind of the South begins and ends with God, John Calvin's God—the anthropomorphic Jehovah of the Old Testament. It is the *a priori* mind which reigned everywhere before the advent of Darwin and Wallace. The earth is God's stage. Life is God's drama, with every man cast for his rôle by the Omnipotent Hand. All exists for a Purpose—that set forth in the Shorter Catechism. The Southerner, without, of course, having looked within the damned pages of Voltaire, is an ardent disciple of the Preceptor Pangloss: "It is demonstrable . . . that things cannot be otherwise than they are; for all being created for an end, all is necessary for the best end. Observe that the nose has been formed to bear spectacles—thus we have spectacles." Whatever exists is ordered. Even Satan, who is forever thrusting a spoke into the rhythm of things, is, in reality, ordained for the Purpose. But that in nowise relieves those who accept his counsels or serve his ends; their damnation is also necessary to the greater glory of God.

Under this view of things, it plainly becomes blasphemy for the mill-billy to complain. Did God desire him to live in a house with plumbing, did He wish him to have better wages, it is quite clear that He would have arranged it. With that doctrine, the peon is in thorough accord. He literally holds it to be a violation of God's Plan for him to have a bath save on Saturday night. Could he have a clear-seeing conviction of his wrongs, could he strip himself of his petty individualism, he would nevertheless, I believe, hesitate under the sorrowing eyes of his pastor, wilt, and, borne up by the promised joys of the poor and torments of the rich in the Life to Come, go humbly back to his post in the mills. If you doubt it, consider the authentic case of the mill-billy parents who refused to let a North Carolina surgeon remove cataracts from the eyes of their blind daughter on the ground that if God had wanted her to see He would have given her good eyes at birth. The peon is always a Christian.

The South does not maintain, of course, that, even in a closed, ordered world, change is impossible, but such change must always proceed from God. In the case of the lint-head, for example, it could come about in two ways. God could directly instruct the barons, who are such consecrated men that they pay the salaries not only of their uptown pastors but of the peon's shepherds as well, to give the peon better wages and a bathtub, in which case He, of course, would be promptly obeyed. It is clear that He has not yet resorted to this method, which, indeed, must be described as somewhat extraordinary. The more usual way would be for Him to communicate His wishes to His immediate servants, the Holy men. These holy men hold audience with Him several times daily, so that the South is in constant touch with His plans. At this writing, the uptown pastors seem agreed that God is insistent that there must be less ranging after vain things like porcelain baths and more concerns with the Higher Life. With this report that of the peon's shepherds coincides perfectly.

The liaison thus maintained between God and the South through His intelligence men is the explanation of many things—for instance, the paradox that our States' Rights, individualistic, *laissez-faire* hero is the chief champion of Prohibition. Many explanations for that have been offered, but it seems to me to be pretty evident that the Noble Experiment arose in the South primarily from the fact that the college of canons went into a huddle with God and emerged with the news that He wanted a Law. The gallant Confederate, of course, was and is not, in fact, dry. But if God wanted a Law—well, He got it. That is why the South will tolerate no monkey-business with the Volstead Act. It is God's Law. And therein, indeed, is stated the South's whole attitude towards morals. Adultery, thievery, horse-racing, cockfighting, whatnot, are wrong not because they react unfavorably on human society but because they are forbidden by God, either in the Bible or in the dictums of the chosen vessels of His Will. Individual transgressions of most of these laws may, to be sure, be glossed over by an extra dollar on the collection plate on Sunday, but to oppose the laws themselves is to oppose God. Blasphemy is the first crime in the Southern calendar.

It follows, from both his romanticism and his theology, that the Southerner is ungiven to reflection. Thinking involves unpleasant realities, unsavory conclusions; and, happily, there is no need for it, since, as everything is arranged by God, there is nothing to think about. The South, with more leisure than New England, has yet produced no Emerson nor even a Thoreau. Though the British friars shrieked and tore their garments as lustily when Darwin advanced the doctrine of evolution in 1859 as did their Southern brethren when such Catalines as Dr. W. L. Poteat, of North Carolina, bore it below the Potomac forty years afterward, yet all England accepted it within two decades, while the South, in significant contrast, is no more reconciled to it today than in 1900. All that matter of the origin of man was settled very long ago—set down in Genesis by God Himself. To question it is to blaspheme. All ideas not approved by the Bible and the *shamans* are both despised and ignored. And, indeed, a thinker in the South is regarded quite logically as an enemy of the people, who, for the common weal, ought to be put down summarily—for, to think at all, it is necessary to repudiate the whole Southern scheme of things, to go outside God's ordered drama and contrive with Satan for the overthrow of Heaven.

All problems are settled categorically. Maxim and rule are enough. Precedent is inviolable. And nice distinctions are, of course, impossible. A nigger, for example, is either a vile clown or an amiable Uncle Tom. If he insists on upsetting things by being something else, he passes, like Elijah, in a chariot of fire, and is wafted to his reward on wings of kerosene. (The Southerner, faced with any reality which refuses to fit into his rose-colored, pigeon-holed world, quietly abolishes it. Lynching is not only a romantic gesture but a protective one as well.) The more serious and intelligent of the cotton-mill operatives, unlike their peers in most industrial hives, are never found pondering Prince Kropotkin, Karl Marx, or even Upton Sinclair. Their minds run rather to the problem of convincing sinful souls of the merits of total immersion. Their own case is disposed of by maxims: "The poor we have with us always," "Servants, obey your masters" and "God's in His Heaven; all's right with the world."

It is this lack of thoughtfulness which accounts for the fact that the mind of the South is almost impervious to change, that, for a quarter of a century, it has successfully resisted the steadily increasing pressure of industrialism, blithely adopting the Kiwanis moonshine—all those frothy things it found compatible—but continuing, in the main, to move through the old rhythms. I have paid much attention herein to the cotton-mill peon because it seems obvious to me that if change is to come about in the Southern mind, it must arise from him, for he is in most direct contact with industry and it is in his status that the inadequacy of the old formula is most clearly evident. Everywhere revision of values and adjustment of the agricultural mind to industrialism have been brought about by the revolts of the laboring classes, since it is the natural tendency of the upper classes to assume that *quand le Roi avait bu, la Pologne etait ivre,* and to ask: "When all goes so well, why trouble to change?"

But the Southern peon is scarcely touched by Industrialism. He accepts; he does not question and challenge. His desultory revolts have not arisen from his own convictions but from the urging of professional agitators. Even the recent spontaneous walkouts in South Carolina were inspired, not by protest against wages and living conditions, but by collision between the peon's native shiftlessness and so-called efficiency system introduced in Yankee-owned mills; they prove nothing save that he declines to become industrialized.

V

But if the much-proclaimed industrialization of the South is merely a matter of externals, the remaining ingredients of the New South formula are scarcely more than wind. The money-bags do exist, certainly—a handful of parvenus. But they have begotten no new cultural *noblesse,* nor are they likely to. Sworn enemies of the arts, of all ideas dating after 1400, and of common decency, they have imported the senseless Yankee dogma of work for work's sake, and seek rather to destroy than to increase that leisure which must be the basis of any culture. All their contributions to educational institutions, of which the Duke gift is the outstanding example, have been motivated by a desire to perpetuate the old order, not to create an enlightened new one. As for the prognostications of social, political, and intellectual revolution, the prophecies of the outpouring of heavenly fire—they, like the great Woof-Woof in Kansas, arise from nowhere; like the earth, they are hung upon nothing—unless, indeed it be the cabalistic imaginations of those occult professors who write books called "The New South" or "The Rising South" or "The Advancing South."

There to be sure, is the breaking of the Solid South, the swinging of traditionally Democratic States into the Republican column last Fall. But that was proof, not that the mind of the South had changed, but that it was unchanged. Satan had seized the Democratic party, and the oriflamme of God, as was witnessed by all the holy men, had passed to the keeping of the Republicans. The Southerner merely chose to remain loyal to the All Highest. The sadly moth-eaten Cause of White Supremacy was laid aside for two shiny and extraordinarily juicy new ones—the plot of the Pope (Satan's cousin) and the scarcely less electric plot of the Rum Ring. Save among cotton-mill barons and a few Babbitts, the Hoover *élan* and Republican principles—whatever, and if, they may be—had nothing to do with the matter. As I write, the De Priest incident seems to have miraculously refurbished and revivified the bogey of the Ethiop—and the Southern Democratic bosses are engaged in identifying themselves with the War on the Pope by bellowing for Raskob's scalp and openly threatening to repudiate the national party if Great Moral Ideas are again defied. Whichever party best combines causes and monsters and clinches its claim to the banner of God will win. Party labels may or may not be changed. In any case, I believe, the mind of the South will remain the same.

There are, too, of course, Mr. James Branch Cabell, Mr. DuBose Heyward, Mrs. Julia Peterkin—a little group of capable craftsmen who have abandoned the pistols and coffee-lilacs and roses-sweetness and light formulae of Southern littérateurs to cope with reality. It is true also that the South swells with pride in them. But—I have myself watched a lone copy of "The Cream of the Jest" gather flyspecks for two years in a bookshop not two hundred miles south of Monument avenue. For, gloss it over as one will, it is undeniably true that Mr. Cabell's persons do things forbidden by the Bible, that Poictesme, as compared with the satrapies of Bishops Cannon, Mouzon, *et al.*, is in sin, and that (O base infidelity!) he fails to view these matters with becoming indignation. Of late days, I have heard often the plaint that "Mamba's Daughters" is both pointless and untrue to the Southern Negro, which last is to say that Mr. Heyward's portrayals fit neither the Uncle Tom formula nor that of the vaudeville buffoon. And Mrs. Peterkin's "Scarlet Sister Mary" is barred from the library at Gaffney, in her native State of South Carolina, as an immoral book. The gloomy fact is that, however much patriotic pride the Southerner may take in the fame of these people, he is bewildered and infuriated by their works.

Lastly, there are such diverse factors—to mention a few out of many—as Odum's *Social Forces* and Koch's Playmakers at the University of North Carolina, Poteat's teaching of evolution in face of the stake, to young Baptists at Wake Forest College for the past thirty years, and the Commission for Inter-racial Coöperation, which aims to foster a more reasonable attitude toward the Negro. It would be foolish to say that they have had no civilizing influence. But it is insanity to claim that they have had any definite effect on the mass of Southerners, to assert that there is any prospect of their engendering, at an early date, a revolution of thought in the South. The men who are responsible for these things, like the artists I have discussed, are not, in any true sense, of the Southern mind. All of them are of that level of intelligence which is above and outside any group mind. They are isolated phenomena, thrown up, not because of conditions in the South, but in spite of them.

Eventually, of course, must come change. Perhaps, indeed, the beginning of it is already at hand. For, undeniably, there is a stir, a rustling upon the land, a vague, formless, intangible thing which may or may not be the adumbration of coming upheaval. Tomorrow—the day after—eventually—the cotton-mill peon will acquire the labor outlook and explosion will follow. In the long run the mind of the South will be remade. Will that bring on the millennium which the prophets profess to see as already in the offing? Will Atlanta become another Periclean

South Carolina novelist DuBose Heyward, author of *Porgy* (1925). He adapted the novel for the stage in 1927; the play version was the basis for the 1935 jazz opera *Porgy and Bess*, with music by George Gershwin and lyrics by Ira Gershwin and Heyward.

Athens, Richmond a new Augustan Rome? I don't know, certainly, but I glance at the cotton-mill barons, the only product of readjustment yet in evidence, and take the liberty of doubting it. I suspect that the South will merely repeat the dismal history of Yankeedom, that we shall have the hog apotheosized—and nothing else. I suspect that we shall merely exchange the Confederate for that dreadful fellow, the go-getter, Colonel Carter for Mr. Lowell Schmaltz, the Hon. John LaFarge Beauregard for George F. Babbitt. I suspect, in other words, that the last case will be infinitely worse that the first.

Cleanth Brooks wrote nearly two-dozen books on literature and literary theory, and with Robert Penn Warren he edited anthologies that influenced two or three generations of students and teachers in the practice of formalist criticism. Though Brooks taught for decades at Yale University, he maintained a lifelong fascination with and affection for the South. He wrote many essays on Southern literature and culture, including three critical books on Faulkner, employing brilliant flourishes of rhetoric to lead his readers toward his own vision of the region and its literary expression.

Cleanth Brooks, "What Deep South Literature Needs," *Saturday Review of Literature* (19 September 1942); reprinted in *Defining Southern Literature: Perspectives and Assessments, 1831–1952,* edited by John E. Bassett (Madison & Teaneck, N.J.: Fairleigh Dickinson University Press / London: Associated University Presses, 1997), pp. 423–429.

Eudora Welty's fine first book of short stories, "A Curtain of Green," was reviewed a few months ago under the title "The Gothic South." The title and the review itself impressed me with the lack of understanding which the writer of the Deep South has to face. I do not mean lack of sympathy, necessarily, or lack of interest. I do not even mean to insist that the characterization of the present South as Gothic may not shed some illumination, though I do not think that it does. Moreover, it is quite possible that Miss Bogan's comparison of Eudora Welty to Gogol, and the analogies which she draws between the Southern scene and the Russian are quite legitimate, and may serve to suggest to her readers, by allowing them to move from the known to the unknown, something of the character of the strange land which borders the Gulf.

Miss Bogan goes on to say: "the inhabitants of a big house (either mad, drunk, or senile), the idiots and ageless peasant women, the eccentric . . . all these could come out of some broken-down medieval scene. . . ." Doubtless they could, and, if one is allowed some liberty in defining "medieval," doubtless they have. I have no disposition to quarrel with the text of Miss Bogan's review. What I am interested in is the obvious effort to comprehend the strange. As Miss Bogan herself says: "so much of the work of writers from the American South has puzzled critics." Much of it does clearly puzzle them. There is an honest lack of understanding of the section itself, and as a consequence, a lack of understanding of the attitude of the Southern author toward his material.

It is for this reason that the Southern author who essays the fantastic may discover to his amusement or alarm that he is a savage realist mercilessly exposing a land of Yahoos, or he may be quite as much surprised to discover that his serious consideration of a topic is a willful exploitation of the unreal and romantic. Of course, this state of affairs is not merely to be accounted for by the country's intense interest in and ignorance of the South. It is in part the result of the decay of our ability to read, and of our current confusions about the nature of literature.

But, for whatever reasons, the Deep South is peculiarly cursed with those twin evils of modern literature: sociologism and romantic escapism. The writer is forced into one category or the other, willy-nilly. Some years ago, in *The New Republic,* Mr. Hamilton Basso attempted to separate the sheep from the goats, that is, the progressive writers from the traditionalists. A good deal of squeezing and stretching was necessary to make the division work. That Mr. Basso, a novelist of some ability himself, should try to set up this distinction is convincing testimony in itself of the extent to which it dominates our minds: the Southern writer *must* be either whitewashing the magnolia blossom or urging us to some particular reform.

Of course there are writers who are ready-measured for the Procrustean bed, or rather, writers who cynically measure themselves for it—by studying the market and giving the public what it thinks it wants. They dish up local color to order, or write the exposés or defenses. This local color literature is probably at its worst when it attempts to reproduce, for a *Ladies' Home Journal* audience, imitations of "Gone with the Wind." It is probably seen at its best when it abandons the form of fiction altogether and attempts frankly, like Marjorie Kinnan Rawlings's recent "Cross Creek," to give an account, written with some charm and sympathy, of the habits of the natives.

The Southern literary critic Cleanth Brooks in his early forties

It is not surprising, of course, that in Southern literature the peculiarities of the South should come in for a great deal of attention, whether they are viewed as welcome additions to the cultural variety of the country, or as quaint and picturesque aberrations of, or abominable deviations from, the national norm. The point of importance is how the specifically Southern elements are used by the writer and how they affect his attitude toward his work.

If, as we have already suggested, the exploitation of local color tends to break out of the pattern of fiction altogether, taking the form of a travel book or an autobiography, so perhaps the attempt to make exposés or defenses, in its frankest and most honest form, also tends to desert the form of fiction. I am thinking of two recent instances, William Alexander Percy's "Lanterns on the Levee" and William Bradford Huie's "Mud on the Stars."

It is interesting, by the way, to notice the effect which a reading of "Lanterns on the Levee" often exerts on people whose ideology demands that Percy be really

FORMING A CRITICAL STANDARD

"The greatest enemies of any literary movement are those who carry adulation in criticism to an excess. Southern literature has, until recently, found itself handicapped through a deplorable lack of any discriminating standards by which to judge it. However unified the fundamental interests of this country may be, the South—as well as any other section—has had a growth peculiarly its own. We would not deny the individuality of New England, even though that individuality be recognized as an element only in the evolution of the nation. So it is with the South—a section wherein the social forces have conserved a distinct type of people upon its soil—one which, temperamentally as well as geographically, claims for itself a difference from its neighbors which is deeper than dialects or superficial prejudices, and which is coincident with the life that fostered it."

Montrose J. Moses

From the introduction to his *The Literature of the South* (New York: Crowell, 1910); reprinted in *Defining Southern Literature: Perspectives and Assessments, 1831–1952,* edited by John E. Bassett (Madison & Teaneck, N.J.: Fairleigh Dickinson University Press / London: Associated University Presses, 1997), p. 274–275.

a sort of Southern *Junker,* and to hear them express surprise that there might be another side to many "Southern" problems about which they had comfortably made up their minds. "Lanterns on the Levee" is a very uneven book, and undoubtedly it has been the charm of a personality rather than the cogency of an argument which has won it a favorable audience. In contrast to Percy's book, "Mud on the Stars" would represent the New South rather than the Old, but it too finds its interest, in spite of its sub-title, "A Novel," in an analysis of some of the forces at play on a young Southerner of this generation. If its title suggests a contradiction of "Lanterns on the Levee," the contradiction is far from absolute. The criticism of the Southern tradition which it undertakes amounts not so much to a denial of the tradition as a modification of it.

The reason why self-conscious analyses and criticisms of the South tend to fall outside the pattern of fiction ought to be easy enough to see. Poetry, drama, and fiction at their best dramatize issues rather than argue toward solutions—they build up dramatic tensions rather than "making a case for" a particular program. If we insist that literature give a program, under penalty of being damned as irresponsible or complacent if it fails to, we shall misconstrue its purposes and probably end up by misreading it.

The harm done, of course, varies with the seriousness of the writer's intention and the general nature of the intention. For example, Dr. Thaddeus St. Martin's "Madame Toussaint's Wedding Day," which is a charming enough bit of genre writing, will suffer little distortion; nor will the "Old Man Adam" stories of Roark Bradford (though one can see this material begin to get out of hand in "The Green Pastures" when Marc Connolly attempts a more serious ending than the material itself can bear).

Very great harm may be done, however, in the case of, say, Caldwell and Faulkner, who are frequently bracketed together to the detriment of both authors and to the confusion of ourselves. Mr. Faulkner, if I understand him properly, is interested in tragedy, and, at his best, attains it. Mr. Caldwell, on the other hand, who possesses a real ability to use folk materials for comic effect, has frequently been pushed into propaganda for various causes with a resulting confusion of his attitude towards his material. It is not a question of talent: both men possess talent; and it is not a question of their failures. The failures of either are likely to produce the sense of mere violent, anarchic disorder. The matter of real importance is that Mr. Faulkner's readers frequently misunderstand his purpose, and that Mr. Caldwell frequently misunderstands his own purpose.

I should say that in the case of Caldwell, what comes through is a sense of terrific vitality, animal vitality, carried to the point of gusty burlesque. Caldwell deals with it most successfully, one feels, when, while preserving an artist's sympathy for it, he yet tacitly establishes some sort of esthetic distance between it and himself by treating it in terms of the grotesque. His human sympathy for his material, a sympathy which tends to translate itself into a program for the People, does credit to him as a citizen and as a man, but on occasion confuses him as an artist. Faulkner takes this vitality into account in his work, too—his novels certainly testify to its presence. But there is an attempt to define it and analyze it, to make distinctions: it may be the meaningless animal tenacity and persistence of a Snopes, or the powerful influence of the land exerted on the human beings who attempt to hold it or are held by it, or the stubborn rear-guard action fought by a Miss Emily Grierson or a Colonel Sartoris to maintain some kind of integrity under the pressure of a collapsing social pattern. But Faulkner's attitude is anything but a gleeful exultation at the collapse of a way of life; and he is not indulging in a sardonic and cynical description of decay nor is he propagandizing for a particular program which will make all shiny, sanitary, and aseptic.

To take one other instance of the pressure exerted on the reader of Southern literature or on the Southern author himself: I would suggest that a writer like Grace Lumpkin may be more serious and may be actually getting into an exposition of what the South is, through some of her quieter stories about life in a Southern small town—say, "The Treasure"—than in her earlier "propaganda novels." The point I would make is not that the Southern writer should be debarred from the violent or the horrible, and certainly not from a serious treatment of his material; but rather that he has to avoid formulas of any kind, even those formulas which will tend to insure that he will "face conditions realistically and urge people to do something about them."

I began this note with the observation that the writer of the Deep South faced particular difficulties because of national ignorance of his section, and because of a widespread confusion as to what the proper job of the artist is. But it would be idle to suggest that he does not possess some very real advantages. One of these I have already suggested: the vitality of the common folk of his region, and his own closeness to them. I do not mean merely that there are a great many picturesque types at his disposal for him to exploit as odd and interesting to his metropolitan audience, though this will be a temptation to which the weaker writer will succumb. I mean rather that the basic human problems about which literature has revolved present themselves in forms which can be seen sharply and apprehended dramatically. For the weaker writer, of course, it will be merely the picturesque poverty of the Negroes and poor whites, or the opportunity for sensationalism which violent and simply motivated human action offers. But for the more serious artist the fact that the problem of motivation is not muffled, but emerges concretely and overtly, offers perhaps a special stimulus and a special problem. There is a second advantage that the Southern author possesses: the contrast, on so many levels, between the pattern of life in his own section and the national pattern is so sharp that he is driven back upon an inspection of the meaning of his society and the significance of the regional pattern which is by implication, if not explicitly, called in question.

Perhaps comparisons with other provincial areas may be illuminating here. The Southerner is very apt to find himself in the position, say, of the eighteenth century Scot in the period after the union with England had brought Scotland sharply into the English consciousness. He is apt to find that his native region has for the national mind a strange ambivalent quality: it is the home of romance, of wild Highland clans, the last stubborn home of a lost cause; and on the other hand, it is the land of flea-bitten poverty, poor, bigoted, and behind the times. Or, to take another instance, since the specific Scottish parallels are not important: the Southerner may find himself in the position of the Irish writer of a generation ago. Again, his country is a land of romance on the one hand, and poverty and bigotry on the other; moreover it is a land producing a great deal of literature and yet reading very little literature. (William Butler Yeats wrote one of his friends that for twenty-five years he had none of his books sent to Dublin for review, knowing that a provincial press secretly ashamed of Ireland and anxious to ape London, would have had nothing of significance to say of them. For much the same reason, a Southern writer, particularly one who is attempting to redefine the Southern tradition, might ask his New York publisher to disregard the book reviewers of some of the large Southern cities.)

I should not like to force these parallels too far, but they may suggest the special advantages and disadvantages which a very definite provincial status confers, and further, that the disadvantages of provincialism, by the way, are double edged: it is quite as disastrous for the writer to be swayed too much by what New York likes, as to be pridefully contemptuous of anything except what he feels will flatter the prejudices of his own section.

I have tried to give some reasons for revising the pattern within which various practising writers of the Deep South are usually placed. But I have too little confidence in the revised pattern to wish to force the writers of the Deep South into it, even though I believe it provides a more meaningful set of categories than that generally given. For any set of categories involves over-simplifications. Even in "Gone with the Wind," as patly as it fits into the pigeonhole labelled "local color and the romantic past," one may discern an attempt at a kind of interpretation and a kind of evaluation of the tradition. And whatever one thinks of its defects of structure or of style, there is certainly a narrative drive which deserves its meed of praise. Again, the blurb thoughtfully added by the publishers to the dust jacket of Pat O'Donnell's "Green Margins" would seem to "place" the book definitely in the category of writings which purvey quaintness to the bored metropolis (this book, the publishers tell us, deals with literary materials never previously exploited, the delta country below New Orleans). But O'Donnell's book, though far from a great novel, deserves something better than this. Indeed, the most hopeful thing about present literature in the Deep South is the amount of resistance which novelists and short story writers have put up against the pressures exerted on them by publishers, reviewers, and the national clichés which dominate thinking on the whole subject of their region.

Perhaps the healthiest aspect of all is the effort of the writers to find a form for their material. This is particularly significant among the younger writers. It is too much, perhaps, to expect to see the larger manifestations of form yet; but, on the level of style, what one finds in the work of Mary King (of Texas, now living in New Orleans), particularly in her short stories; of Peter Taylor (of west Tennessee, now in the army); and of Eudora Welty—to take only a few instances—is most promising. Eudora Welty's work is remarkable for the variety of styles which she has mastered.

One should expect this concern for form to show most powerfully in poetry, and there, to be sure, the literature of the Deep South is weak. Except for the brilliant and powerful poetry of Robert Penn Warren (who no longer lives in the Deep South and whose work properly is to be connected with the Upper South) there are no first rate poets to be claimed. One can point, however, among the seasoned writers, to Katherine Anne Porter, who has reduced her material to form, not only line by line, but in terms of her larger whole—a writer whose work has been so thoroughly shaped and controlled that the casual reader tends to miss the fact that her work, too, contains the violent and even sensational (see "Noon Wine"), but the violent ordered and freed from any sense of strain for the sensational.

I should like in this connection to bring these notes to a close with a further comment on William Faulkner. In Faulkner the attempt at a style, as has been pointed out from time to time, gets out of control and obtrudes itself on the work as a literary self-consciousness. At his best, however, (and I believe that his last book, "Go Down Moses" [*sic*], is among his best), the style tends to become an adjunct to the larger form, a form in which a real sense of the historical pattern, a real concern for moral values, and a real interest in the land and its people, coalesce into a work which is not the less important for all the fact that it carries no liberal slogans and propagandizes for no immediate program.

To sum up, the Deep South presents a picture of a section producing a vigorous and powerful literature, a more able literature one feels the section deserves. I suggest that what it needs is not better writers but more intelligent readers, both at home and abroad, and a group of critics and reviewers more sensitive and more intelligent than it presently has.

Daniel Singal is a cultural historian who has, like many in his profession, taken a powerful interest in the literary culture of the South. He has written extensively on Faulkner. The following essay comes from a book that examines—some would say psychoanalyzes—two groups of Southerners from the early twentieth century, one conservative and literary, the other liberal and engaged in social research.

Daniel Joseph Singal, "Coda," in his *The War Within: From Victorian to Modernist Thought in the South, 1919–1945* (Chapel Hill: University of North Carolina Press, 1982), pp. 373–377.

For any who still doubted it, the triumph of southern Modernism was demonstrated in 1941 with the publication of Wilbur J. Cash's *The Mind of the South*. Surely the great significance of that work lay in the knockout blow it delivered to the Cavalier myth. Gathering the insights of the new generation of southern writers, Cash presented the Old South as a frontier society dominated by the "hard, energetic, horse-trading type of man" who attempted to disguise his crudeness by posing as an aristocrat. For Cash, the post-Reconstruction South was even more cutthroat and individualistic. Indeed, ugliness, conflict, and brutality abounded in his portrait. Relying heavily on his understanding of Freud, Cash posited a near-schizophrenic split within the southern psyche, between a voracious hedonism and an equally powerful Puritan guilt, a split that led to all sorts of pathological behavior from miscegenation to lynching. The final impression left was not that of civilized society, but rather of one governed, to use Cash's own phrase, by a "savage ideal." *The Mind of the South*, in short, represented a complete reversal of the vision of the region's history once offered by New South writers—it read like a compendium of those aspects of the South they had deliberately screened out.[1]

What was remarkable was the rapidity with which this distinctly unflattering description of the region found general acceptance, not only in the North but among southern intellectuals as well. Save for Donald Davidson's harsh attack in

Donald Davidson, a member of the Nashville-based group of writers and critics known as the Fugitives

the *Southern Review* and one other unfavorable notice, no dissenting voices were raised against Cash's work. On the contrary, the book became an instant classic, thereby testifying to the firm hold the Modernist viewpoint had gained among the South's educated elite. What would have been regarded as an unpublishable scandal a quarter century earlier was now largely accepted as a conventional truth.[2]

In fact, it is probably not unfair to say that Cash's South of conflict and depravity was, ironically, coming to enjoy the mythological status that had once characterized the innocent and genteel South of the nineteenth century. From Erskine Caldwell to Tennessee Williams, from C. Vann Woodward to Marshall Frady, southern authors carried the critical spirit to its logical extreme, until Americans living outside the region formed a picture of southern society as one immense Tobacco Road. In doing this writers were simply following one of the basic dynamics of Modernist culture, with its rebellion against the practice of deliberate evasion. Cash himself was shrewd enough to recognize that the debunking he and others were engaged in represented a "sort of reverse embodiment of the old sentimentality." There should be no surprise in this: cultures typically take their shape in reaction to the culture being rejected, and their excesses often arise by way of correcting the excesses of their predecessors. Beyond doubt the false optimism and complacent self-deception of Victorianism needed correction, and that is precisely what the new generation accomplished.[3]

Perhaps the clearest articulation of these tendencies in the 1940s appeared in the writings of Lillian Smith, who, more than anyone else, brought the issues of race and segregation into the open. With her, the assault against the Victorian ethos reached maturity. Her account of the psychic forces sustaining segregation identified the Victorian dichotomy, with its separation of mind and body, as the chief culprit:

> Not only Negroes but everything dark, dangerous, evil must be pushed to the rim of one's life. Signs put over doors in the world outside and over minds seemed natural enough to children like us, for signs had already been put over forbidden areas of our body. The banning of people and books and ideas did not appear more shocking than the banning of our wishes which we learned early to send to the Dark-town of our unconscious.

Smith's entire crusade was pitched against this compartmentalization that her inherited culture had depended upon. Her goal was to establish a new culture based upon the opening of "doors" and the recapture of previously forbidden human energies. For her, "integration" meant more than a racial strategy; it meant the effort to restore man's "wholeness" in the deepest Modernist sense.[4]

Yet the striking thing is that, as bold as these pronouncements sounded in the late 1940s, today they have about them the ring of the commonplace. At the time Lillian Smith wrote, the Supreme Court's historic decision on school desegregation was still more than five years away, and the ensuing civil rights movement was beyond the imagination of most southerners. Now the so-called Second Reconstruction appears to be over; legal segregation has been banished, and the cultural battle Smith waged has largely been won. As a result, her description of southerners as repressed, violent, and perverted strikes readers of the 1980s as extravagant and overdramatic, much as Cash's critique of the South does. Her contention that blacks possess a unique culture that permits them a "marvelous love of life and play, a physical grace and rhythm and a psychosexual vigor," is now greeted with suspicion. Above all, her prescriptions for psychic health and liberation, radical as they seemed at first, evince a certain stilted quality for the present-day reader. We have long since passed this stage of the cultural debate, with the result that Smith's insights have become stale.[5]

Perhaps the fact that the main battle was over, that the transition to Modernist culture was essentially completed among southern writers, helps account for the noticeable drop in the intensity of intellectual activity in the region

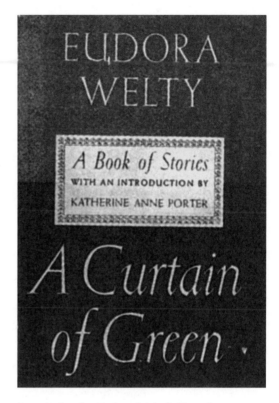

Dust jacket for Eudora Welty's first short-story collection, published in 1941

since the 1950s One almost senses that southerners had little new to say about their society. Those sociologists who focused on the region continued the work of the Odum school, but their work, however competent, was not original or exciting. A high level of craftsmanship also distinguished southern journalism, with many newspapers earning Pulitzer Prizes during the civil rights struggle. However, from the standpoint of intellectual content their editorials in most instances repeated the themes set forth by the Regionalists. And in literature the shadows of Faulkner, Tate, and Warren loomed mightily over their successors: the Modernist mode had become a tradition. Tragedy, paradox, heroic endurance—those flashes of literary fire that had lit up the southern landscape during the interwar era—all became the staples of the new established mythology.[6]

By the 1960s, a few writers, among them William Styron, Eudora Welty, and Walker Percy, were beginning to reexamine the new mythology or at least were carrying its inner logic to the point where some of its contradictions stood revealed. In *The Last Gentleman,* for example, Percy created a character who attempts to carry out the Modernist search for meaning and integrity only to find the world gone totally mad. Like Warren's Jack Burden, Will Barrett is engaged on a quest that is fundamentally religious, though he has rejected any formal ties to a church. Rather, he seeks to plunge himself into everyday reality, opening himself up fully to experience in order to discover his true identity. Barrett's problem, though, is that his Modernist perceptivity has become so keen, his ability to see through appearances so great, that the world seems constantly to slip away from him. In this dilemma he instinctively tries to recapture what he can of his heroic Cavalier heritage. On one occasion he goes so far as to blow up a plaque on the Princeton campus commemorating the Union dead. Unfortunately for Barrett's purposes the plaque was hidden behind shrubbery, and no one discovers his deed. On returning to his hometown in Mississippi he finds himself in the midst of a racial confrontation and recalls the brave acts of his forebears in keeping racial peace. But this time all the characters involved in the confrontation are busy playing theatrical roles that have little connection to the moral issues at stake. Indeed, all of life becomes a theater for Barrett, a theater of the absurd. He reflects, "there [are] no clear issues anymore. Arguments are spoiled. Clownishness always intervenes."[7]

In his search for a route back to the heroic, Barrett attaches himself to Sutter Vaught, a failed young physician from Alabama, whose quest for existential meaning has taken him to the New Mexico desert. By stripping his existence down to a bare minimum, by reducing it to little more than the pleasures of the flesh, Vaught has endeavored to find a core to life that is both authentic and durable. "I accept the current genital condition of human relations," he explains, "and try to go beyond it. I may sniff like a dog but then I try to be human rather than masquerade as human and sniff like a dog. I am a sincere, humble, and even moral pornographer." What attracts Barrett is precisely this commitment of Sutter's to achieve heroism within a Modernist frame of values. Sutter has gone into the desert alone, suffered his personal Gethsemane, yet somehow survived. Unlike the heroic Cavalier, however, Sutter cannot share his vision with anyone; he can civilize no one, not even himself. All he can (or will) do for Barrett is pose questions:

> Which is the best course for a man: to live like a Swede, vote for the candidate of your choice, be a good fellow, healthy and generous, do a bit of science as if the world made sense, enjoy a beer and a good piece (not a bad life!). Or: to live as a Christian among Christians in Alabama? Or to die like an honest man?

Neither Barrett nor Sutter can answer these questions, and *The Last Gentleman* ends appropriately in total ambiguity, leaving no hint of how the two will resolve their lives.[8]

This was the quandary to which Modernist culture had brought southern writers by the mid-1960s. If one followed its mode of perception consistently and looked relentlessly beneath "appearances," one was lost in a world of paradox and moral relativism. Returning to the apparent stability of the nineteenth century was not an option: we are reminded of this by the plight of Barrett's father, a man of imposing self-certainty who blasts his head off with a shotgun, thus revealing the impasse of concealed agony the Victorians had come to. The twentieth century had at least brought these tensions into the open. Yet the price for liberation has been high, and perhaps it is now time for a liberation from liberation itself. Having freed the individual from the old moral code and reinstated the animal part of his being, Modernist culture may have reached its furthest limits. A new source of guidance has to be found. Surely the South, with its acute sense of loss of the old certainties, will have a role to play in that quest.

NOTES TO SINGAL

1. W. J. Cash, *The Mind of the South* (New York: Knopf, 1941), pp. 153, 60, 197, 327.

2. C. Vann Woodward, *American Counterpoint: Slavery and Racism in the North-South Dialogue* (Boston: Little, Brown, 1971), pp. 261–263; Richard King, *A Southern Renaissance: The Cultural Awakening of the American South, 1930–1955* (New York & Oxford: Oxford University Press, 1980), pp. 146–150; Donald Davidson, "Mr. Cash and the Proto-Dorian South," *Southern Review,* 7 (Summer 1941): 1–20.

3. Cash, *The Mind of the South,* p. 387.

4. Lillian Smith, *Killers of the Dream* (New York: Norton, 1949), pp. 75–76, 98, 210.

5. Ibid., 99–100.

6. The one new direction in the recent sociological study of the South can be found in John Shelton Reed, *The Enduring South,* a work that treats "southern-ness" as an independent variable and attempts to measure its strength and characteristics using public opinion surveys. One hopes that more work will be done along these lines.

7. Walker Percy, *The Last Gentleman* (New York: Farrar, Straus & Giroux, 1966), pp. 267–268, 313–314, 318–326, 55, 234.

8. Ibid., pp. 281–379.

Thomas L. McHaney has devoted most of his career to studying Faulkner's works. An interest in Faulkner's creative life and the culture of reading in which he developed has led McHaney into the study of cultural and intellectual history, particularly the culture of modernism as it affected those alert to its presence in the South. The present essay originated as a presentation at a conference reevaluating the modern perception of Southern culture.

Thomas L. McHaney, "Literary Modernism: The South Goes Modern and Keeps on Going," in *Southern Literature in Transition: Heritage and Promise,* edited by Philip Castille and William Osborne (Memphis: Memphis State University Press, 1983), pp. 43–53.

It is doubtful that Modernism, like Ellen Glasgow's realism, crossed the Potomac going north long before anyone noticed. But Modernism was in southern soil early enough; and the literary movement usually called the Southern Renascence was, in reality, a southern branch office of the midwestern division of the North American franchise of that international movement in the arts that flourished in Paris, London, Milan, Munich, and other capitals during the second and third decades of the twentieth century. The southern movement, Lewis Simpson has argued, "has been fully joined in the wider literary and artistic opposition to *modernity.*"[1] I would like to discuss this at some length in order to counter the recent lamentations about the end of southern literature, my point being that the Southern Renascence, as unique phenomenon, never existed and therefore as such cannot really end.

Southern experience during the period in question was essentially isomorphic with the experience of the rest of the western world, and it is not surprising, given minds of sufficient talent and will, that southern literature corresponds in many respects to the literature of the larger movement. In a way, the Modern Movement is ironically named, for it was, as Lewis Simpson says, united in its opposition to *modernity*. *Modern* derives from *modo,* "just now," by analogy to the word *hodiernus,* from *hodiea,* "today." It appears first, appropriately, during the Renaissance, another transcontinental movement, and without it we would have had to find a different name for the Quarrel Between the Ancients and the Moderns, a quarrel that we seem engaged upon again in our own time, where the Moderns are, by now of course, the Ancients, and the "now" generation, said to be incapable of matching its forebears, is identified as the Moderns. Modern is simply that which is up to the moment, but the Modern Movement, as we know, is both reactionary and radical, conservative and revolutionary, packaging its puritanism in the latest fashions. The modernists were both the *avante-garde* and the guards of the *derrière,* usually in one and the same person. The Modern Movement is a conservative movement using revolutionary techniques, everything about it implying tension, mediation, paradox.

In *Ulysses, The Waste Land, and Modernism,* Stanley Sultan defines "modernism" simply as that period in twentieth-century letters that felt the impact of the two seminal books of his title. Both works, we know, perform that mediation between past and present that Eliot identified as the "mythical method" in his famous review of Joyce's novel. More generally, Harry Levin has argued that the modernists felt both "belated and up-to-date simultaneously," that they worked "experimental transformations into traditional continuities."[2] Writing about the southerners, Richard James Calhoun expresses a view that explains why it is easy to recognize them as Moderns. They derive their power, he suggests, from a "tension" that existed because of their desire to be unsentimental southerners and, at the same instant, to be technically modern. So far so good, but he goes on to claim that their

> differences from previous Southern writers lay in their dual perspective revealed in their themes and their techniques—on the one hand, their not being completely modern in that they did not feel as fully . . . the historical and metaphysical discontinuities of the most modern writer, while on the other hand they repudiated those traditions and conventions of their Southern past that had mitigated against a significant literature.[3]

I would say that the case was just the opposite. These writers were able to make a significant literature of their traditions and conventions precisely because they felt the historical and metaphysical discontinuities. The error in Calhoun's remarks is that he does not see the southerners as "completely modern." This error, or something like it, is what has prevented many southern scholars from perceiving the so-called Southern Renascence as less than unique. Combined with a natural chauvinism, this view has created a lively trade under the banner "Southern Renascence" and has caused the more recent lamentations for or jeremiads against contemporary southern writing.

Perhaps it is true, as Louis Rubin observes, that this was the "first generation of young southerners since early in the nineteenth century to be brought into direct contact and confrontation with the vanguard of the most advanced thought and feeling of their times."[4] Were they, in this regard, really unique? They were part of a national literary generation, all of whom had grown up under certain cultural and familial pieties, whether they were raised in Oak Park, St. Paul, Reading,

Cambridge, or a southern community. They had uncommon perception, all of them, and no one who perceives his own time and place acutely can fail to find discontinuities. They were, in fact, all part of a general "culture of alienation," as Lewis Simpson calls it. Walker Percy's version of what occurred to bring about the modern age and this culture of alienation is a useful one. The age that began about 300 years ago with the dawn of science is over, he says, and along with it, the ways it offered us to explain ourselves. The view that sustained man was

> a viable belief in the sense that it ani-
> mated the culture and gave life its
> meaning . . . something men lived by,
> even when they fell short of it . . . the
> belief that man was created in the
> image of God with an immortal soul,
> that he occupied a place in nature
> somewhere between the beasts and
> the angels.

What has survived and carries current significance in our culture, Percy continues, "are certain less precise legacies of this credo: the 'sacredness of the individual,' 'God is love,' the 'Prince of Peace,' 'the truth shall make you free,' etc." and "a kind of mish-mash view of man, a slap-up model put together of disparate bits and pieces" complemented by the ordinary man's commonsense view of the way science defines him: an organism among organisms.[5]

SOUTHERN MODERNISM: AN EARLY ASSESSMENT

"Except that there is to be found a fresh vitality in the best writing that comes out of the South today, its books defy classification. . . .

"William Faulkner of Mississippi, the author of 'Soldiers' Pay' and 'Mosquitoes,' knows as much about how to write the prose to which we give the convenient tag 'modern' as any habitué of the corner made by the crossing of the Boulevards Montparnasse and Raspail in Paris."

Herschel Brickell

From "The Literary Awakening in the South," Bookman, 76 (October 1927); reprinted in *Defining Southern Literature: Perspectives and Assessments, 1831-1952,* edited by John E. Bassett (Madison & Teaneck, N.J.: Fairleigh Dickinson University Press / London: Associated University Presses, 1997), p. 209.

These definitions no longer work, Percy argues, and those who do not take the matter seriously "forfeit the means of understanding themselves." Those who do take the matter seriously suffer the symptoms of alienation, either wordlessly because they do not know what they feel or, like Percy, by searching for new meanings.

The Modern generation surely felt these discontinuities and engaged in the search for new meaning. The difference between pure alienation and the mood of art, as Percy has written, is the difference between living unconsciously in "the way things are" and knowing how to say "the way things are." Such consciousness appears to have characterized the artist since the Romantic Movement, however, as our classical American authors reveal. The question is, then, when we regard what has been said about both the uniqueness and the demise of southern writing in the twentieth century, whether or not the consciousness of discontinuities, the search for new meanings, and the general changing can actually ever cease. It seems foolish to think so. If something has ended, then, what exactly is it?

To go back a moment, we can say, first, that the attempt to isolate the so-called Southern Renascence from the Modern Movement gives a false sense of distinctly regional achievement to southern writing. Second, claims that the Renascence is over reflect only the consciousness that the Modern Movement is over, unstated confusion about what that means, and a failure to read the metaphors in contemporary southern work for the current discontinuities they reflect. I will

Barren Ground

By ELLEN GLASGOW

Printed in GARDEN CITY, NEW YORK, *at the* Country Life Press

DOUBLEDAY, PAGE & CO. 1925

Title page of Ellen Glasgow's novel about a woman who returns to her Virginia home after being betrayed by her lover and, through great effort, becomes a successful farmer

limit myself to some remarks about the Modern Movement and its reported end, hoping that others will be sufficiently interested to take another look at the potential of contemporary southern writing.

The southern writer has had for a long time some of those paradoxical advantages that C. Vann Woodward addresses in *The Burden of Southern History,* though one should not minimize the possibility that America in general, settled by dissidents and radical puritans at the dawn of the age of science, knew more than it was willing to admit publicly about antinomies, paradoxes, and discontinuities. The southern writer also has known for a long time what a scholar like Harry Levin may have discovered only in the 1960s: that despite the freedom of the language in contemporary literature, there is one organ that is rarely dwelt upon—the brain. Ellen Glasgow's observations about Richmond are germane:

> I have always done both my reading and my thinking alone. I have known intimately, in the South at least, few persons really interested in books more profound than "sweet stories." My oldest and closest friends, with the exception of James Cabell, still read as lightly as they speculate, and this description applies as accurately to the social order in which I was born. . . . Nevertheless, as I had discovered in New York and London, the social levels are very much the same everywhere.[6]

As a consequence of his or her own "inner emigration," the southern writer has not needed so much of that literal expatriation that Levin perceives in "What Was Modernism?" as one of the chief preconditions to becoming Modern. Our greatest figures—Glasgow, Faulkner, Welty—traveled significantly outside the South, but they returned to be "underfoot locally," having seen that the country of the mind is a far country indeed, to most people, and one might as well live where one finds the material and can still own a little property. Indeed, staying at home, one is perhaps in a better position to monitor the discontinuities. In the twenties and thirties, there were plenty of discontinuities. Southern society changed, and it has continued to change. But do you suppose it will ever be done changing? It all depends on where you look and who is doing the looking. Glasgow, in fact, could not discern in Faulkner's work a reality that she herself was recording in *The Sheltered Life.* Some of the generation between Faulkner and now cannot discern either the reality or the meaning in people like Cormac McCarthy and Harry Crews. This is not cause for alarm unless writers themselves begin to believe that their countries of the mind, their searches, and their metaphors are not important.

We are in the midst of a Quarrel Between the Ancients and the Moderns, as I have said. Even the defeatist term "Post-Modern" suggests it, something that might have been formulated by J. Alfred Prufrock himself. Prufrock, however, is gone, and one of the things wrong with recent discussions of the end of the Modern Movement is that they focus upon the end of the *beginning* of the Modern Movement without knowing exactly what to make of the fact that Prufrock matured into the persona of the *Four Quartets*. If you reply, "Isn't it pretty to think so?" you should be reminded that Jake Barnes, who was wrong about practically everything and had to leave the waters of San Sebastian, was supplanted by the Old Man of the Sea, and that the suicide Quentin Compson was reincarnated happily as Lucius Priest, whose life-restoring adventure also begins with the death of a grandparent. The gnosticism that is supposed to characterize Post-Modernism exists in the work of Eliot, Faulkner, and Hemingway from the beginning, and it existed in the writing of Melville, Hawthorne, and Poe. The Modern Movement found deep significance in the real, linked the contrarieties, fused the ambiguities, made the mirror and the lamp into a single tool, mediated between past and present, and tried to bridge the supposed vortex between reason and intuition. This impulse is still with us, constantly renewed, and it is that fact that gives me hope—whatever the status of the Modern Movement—that the literary South, like the rest of the literary world, will continue to exist because it will continue to, as I call it, go modern—that is, it will still come up through today to right now, aroused by the discontinuities and able to name them.

We are not exactly born modern. We are born blue and startled like our mothers and our grandparents before us. We become modern when a peculiar consciousness strikes us. The effect may be momentary or lasting; usually, to make an artist, the process must be continually renewed.

In his volume of essays upon language and thought, *The Message in the Bottle*, Walker Percy starts from a moment of *gnosis* of his own. Preoccupied with thoughts about the division between mind and reality and the nature of language—recall Ishmael's desire not simply to meet a horror but to speak it, in order to be on good terms with all the denizens of this world—Percy says he began thinking of the remarkable moment when Helen Keller took possession of the miracle of language-consciousness—words and their relation to things. The moment included an incredible burst of knowledge and also the sudden manifestation of an ethic, a consciousness of regret for some past deeds. Percy is never able to unravel the "Delta-factor," as he calls it, the mechanism by which the connections between mind and thing occur in the act of making language. Whatever it is, he writes, whether "I" or "self" or "some neurophysiological correlate thereof, I could not begin to say."

I cannot say what it is, either, but one realizes that something like this "Delta-factor" is at work not only in the moment of a child's discovery that the patterns of experienced language can be built upon, even retrospectively, but also in the act of making literary art. It is analogous to the condition of "going modern," whether one sees that as the perception of discontinuities and joining the culture of alienation, or simply as speaking, through the consciousness of distance, that which was formerly unspeakable—beauty or horror, love or hate, and other antinomies. Hence the need to find new words and the difficulty of fitting what one has to say to the language one has to say it with. It is not without significance that the Modern Movement has made the paradoxes of physics, biology, and psychology its own, for they lie at the heart of the matter, too, and continue to haunt us. The beginning of the Modern Movement is a revelation to which we have not even begun to apply ourselves because we have been so busy applying ourselves to the forces that set it into motion and the techniques that it discovered to express its vision.

Fiction—poetry, drama, or prose—comes into being in the gap between one's life and one's imagination. The paradoxical truth of fiction depends upon correspondence, upon how truly one finds a metaphor to express one's vision of man's life, and fame depends upon how generally one's metaphor is accepted by thoughtful and sensitive people. Because I believe that this is the way literary art works, I believe there will continue to be southern literary art, and I imagine some of it will be quite good. There is consensus out there waiting to be challenged. Walker Percy says we enter the culture of alienation when we recognize that we, too, have departed from the consensus view of man such as existed in "thirteenth century Europe or seventeenth century New England, or even in some rural Georgia communities today." But far below the great western theological consensus that he is talking about there are those limited systems into which all of us are born, which many of us discover to be equally invalid, sometimes in ways that produce art. Perhaps it is the loss of the great western consensus that gives us the vision to make this smaller leap, but I doubt it; I think the gap has been perceived ever since man had the luxury and the power of language. As George Santayana said:

> Nature, in framing the human soul . . . unlocked for the mind the doors to truth and to essence . . . partly by endowing the soul with far greater potentialities of sensation and invention than daily life is to call forth. Our minds are therefore naturally dissatisfied with their lot and speculatively directed upon an outspread universe in which our persons count for almost nothing.[7]

What is our compensation? The images that we have made with our hands and our minds. Writers exist to discover language that fills the interstices between the consciousness of reality's potential and reality itself. Call it alienation if you like, and do not minimize the misery that results when the process fails. But trust that in the mysterious interstitial caves of thought there will always be vessels to fill and nourishment to carry back to those few who require or desire it (the news from poems, we know, is hard to get), North, West, East, or South.

Not everyone will agree with me, of course. One of the scientists who is trying to teach language to chimpanzees is hesitant to transmit to them the concept of personal death for fear that the chimps "will deal with this knowledge as bizarrely as we have." He does not want them to have our experience of dread, which, "in the human case, has led to the invention of ritual, myth, and religion"[8]—and one might say, literature. One has to admire his hubris, if not his Godlike restraint. But the real conclusion one draws from this is that they have not gotten very far with their teaching of the chimps, who obviously have not learned to say to one another, "Well, what are we going to do tomorrow?" "What did we do today?" or "Why are we in here and they out there?"

Since we humans seem to be cursed with dread, and hence with ritual, myth, and, if not in all cases religion, literature, one might be tempted to predict what form the next "just-now" literature of the South will take. There will continue to be some use of the grotesque, doubtless, but that is neither the burden nor the triumph of southern writing. Flannery O'Connor's witty remarks to the contrary, southerners are not the last people left who know a freak when they see one, nor are they always able to make the distinction—especially when it comes to politics—while the ability to say what the grotesque means is still a function of art in general. We also know Flannery O'Connor's remark in answer to a question about what kind of novels will be written in the future. The ones that have not been written yet, she said. As Harry Levin said more prosaically, "'nowness' is a precondition for newness, for what Whitman had termed 'the unperform'd.'" But Ezra Pound's admonition to "make it new" is also as old as Confucius. The Modern Movement and the so-called Southern Renascence had no monopoly on innovation or renovation; they will always be "what the age demanded."

What does the present age demand of the southern writer? In the culture of alienation there are many mansions. The previous generation was much occupied with the myth of the fall of southern society, a useful myth and an excellent regional metaphor for a world condition. The serpent was not only in the southern garden; he whispered his knowledge of the discontinuities all around. Now the myth is a "Second Coming"—Walker Percy has already preempted the title—and the question is, What rude beast slouches toward Atlanta, Birmingham, Memphis, or New Orleans?

Is the beast so rude? Like Shiloh, Antietam, and Malvern Hill, the names Birmingham, Memphis, New Orleans, and Atlanta are not all happy memories, but they stand, in part, for courage, sacrifice, and pity as much as they do for skyscrapers, parking lots, and fast-food franchises. Things happened in these cities that defy death and humiliation and despoliation of the human spirit. When we see a necessary relation between these two types of battlefields—and, even better, when we recognize that, in all their glory, the events associated with these places also contain the seeds of man's folly and his false pieties—then we will have a new literature.

Edwin Mims predicted in 1920 that "scholarship, literature, and art" would come to flourish in the South—and this is continually coming true. Edwin Alderman once claimed that the southern mind had been the agent to train "the democratic Union for its ultimate victory over the alien system of thought created by southern life."[9] In a strange way, the South has always been the nation's uncreated conscience. It has had its problems, openly. Our national faults and glories have received some of their most vocal and intelligent expression in the South. The South has been dragged into the twentieth century, at last, and the bulldozers have made the approaches to our cities and towns identical with towns in Ohio and California. These things are no more unattractive, however, than the mill village, the town strung along both sides of the railroad tracks, the slovenly wilderness cut by gullies or littered with spilled cotton that did not make it to ramshackle gins and faded compresses in the center of towns devoted to football and nigger-baiting. The collective artifacts of humankind are revealing, proving that the twentieth-century city has no monopoly on greed, litter, poverty, bestiality, or the genteel enclaves from which come the loudest lamentations about the decline and fall of gentility. Having come late to industry, urbanization, science, and a full free expression of the humanities, the South has a better chance to yoke them, to become the conscience of the complex society, not crying from the ruined wall, as some suggest, but walking quietly, reasoning upon important things, in the cooling and clicking garden.

As to subjects, there is much in the South that one returns to, literally or in memory, with the feeling that it is as yet unsung. Our main subjects, however, are ourselves. The concept of the Southern Renascence has had the pernicious effect of convincing some writers, as well as some scholars, that our subject is the Myth of the South, yet both these terms—Southern Renascence and Myth of the South—have reached the status of a "fallacy of misplaced concreteness," the mistaking of the abstraction for the real. What we have is our experience, and, to paraphrase Flannery O'Connor once again, no one who has survived childhood is likely to run out of material to write about. What we must make of our experience is metaphor, and for that we have a world of events and things spread out before us, history and the present age and, always, the changes. The South has gone modern, and it keeps on going.

NOTES TO McHANEY

1. Lewis Simpson, *The Dispossessed Garden: Pastoral and History in Southern Literature* (Athens: University of Georgia Press, 1975), pp. 65–66.

2. Harry Levin, "What Was Modernism?" in his *Refractions: Essays in Comparative Literature* (New York: Oxford University Press, 1966), p. 287.

3. Richard James Calhoun, "Southern Writing: The Unifying Strand," *Mississippi Quarterly,* 27 (Winter 1973–1974): 108.

4. Louis D. Rubin Jr., *The Writer in the South* (Athens: University of Georgia Press, 1972), p. 105.

5. Walker Percy, *The Message in the Bottle* (New York: Farrar, Straus & Giroux, 1975), pp. 18, 19.

6. Ellen Glasgow, *The Woman Within* (New York: Harcourt, Brace, 1954), p. 216.

7. George Santayana, "The Prestige of the Infinite," in his *Some Turns of Thought in Modern Philosophy* (Cambridge: Cambridge University Press, 1934), p. 120.

8. Quoted in Edward O. Wilson, *On Human Nature* (New York: Bantam, 1979), p. 28.

9. Edwin Mims, quoted in Rubin, *The Writer in the South,* pp. 98–99; Edwin Alderman, quoted in Robert Bush, "Dr. Alderman's Symposium on the South," *Mississippi Quarterly,* 27 (Winter 1973–1974): 16.

James H. Justus is the author of *The Achievement of Robert Penn Warren* (1981), among other works. In the following essay he addresses the continued vitality and variety of Southern narrative.

James H. Justus, foreword to *Southern Writers at Century's End,* edited by Jeffrey J. Folks and James A. Perkins (Lexington: University of Kentucky Press, 1997), pp. xi–xiii.

One of the minor issues in Southern studies that lost relevance about a decade ago—for which we should all be grateful—is whether or not the Southern Renascence ended in 1955. The Southern Renascence itself—which truly existed despite its inaccurate nomenclature—was premised on the assumption that writing from the South was distinctively different from that generated in other parts of the country. And one of the defining traits always listed, usually with the highest priority, was Southerners' heightened sense of place. And the revered text that ratified the critical consensus, the one that explicitly enunciated what critics had been implicitly assembling from the work of Faulkner, Porter, Wolfe, and others, was Eudora Welty's fine essay of 1956, "Place in Fiction." Never mind that this impeccably place-centered writer had called place one of the "lesser angels," and never mind that her examples were Flaubert, Mansfield, Brontë, and Hemingway along with Faulkner. "Place in Fiction" became the second most-quoted-from essay by the historians of Southern literature. (The first, Allen Tate's "The New Provincialism" of 1940, was the Rosetta Stone for "explaining" the remarkable efflorescence that began just after World War I, the "backward glance" that allowed modern Southern writers a perspective on their home region unavailable to their predecessors.)

One of the wry observations about the Southern Renascence, by both participants and scholars, was that there was a writer lurking in every Southern village, threatening to be discovered. In terms of practical criticism, however, the same eight or ten names claimed the spotlight, and, of these, Faulkner was, after World War II, the undisputed headliner. What is striking about the fiction of the last few decades is its diversity of setting, which merely reflects of course a more important phenomenon of this writing: the widely dispersed origins of its authors. There is as yet no voice as strong as Faulkner's among his successors, nor any imaginative geography equal to the unique fertility of Yoknapatawpha. But the storytelling cadences are distinctive and betray fewer anxieties about their unavoidable model than did Flannery O'Connor, Truman Capote, and their generation. And what may be lost in the tenacity and intensity of one mythic Southern county is commendably replaced by a refusal to elevate Southern place into something higher than a lesser angel. There are still a few haunted landscapes left over from the Southern modernists, but even they seem haunted by up-to-date ghosts raised by a stock car-and-insurance-and-VFW culture. There is little deference to be seen—either among themselves or for their predecessors—in the constructed worlds of Georgia (Hood, Walker), Kentucky (Mason), Tennessee (Drake, McCarthy, Marius), North Carolina (Chappell, Edgerton, Gibbons, Kenan, McLaurin, Pearson, Smith), South Carolina (Humphreys), Mississippi (Ford, Grisham, Hannah), or Louisiana (Burke, Dubus, Wilcox).

If traditionalists, in defining the particular slant of modern Southern fiction, insist upon the dominance of the organic community, its collective idiosyncrasies, its mores and morals, its dirty secrets and common report, its accrued wisdom and handed-down superstitions, its tolerance for reiterated stories for family archives, then the great period known as the Southern Renascence has passed. The Civil War in its fiction is finally over. The backward glance from a twentieth-century war that now compels Southern storytellers to reevalute their region is Vietnam.

Contemporary Southern fiction is frankly engaged with contemporary social problems, especially race relations and the struggle of the poor and marginal working class to wrest some meaning out of their lives beyond survival itself. Its familiar space for the italicizing of the problems tends to be a mobile home, not a ruined mansion. It is a fiction of social dislocation, dealing often with the frag-

A CULTURAL AWAKENING

"Every observant mind in the South to-day must be aware of what we may call, without too much enthusiasm, an awakening interest in ideas; and a few observant minds may have perceived in the rising generation an almost pathetic confusion of purpose. In the temper of youth we feel the quiver of expectancy and an eagerness to forsake the familiar paths and adventure into the wilderness."

Ellen Glasgow

From "The Novel in the South," *Harper's Monthly*, 143 (December 1928); reprinted in *Defining Southern Literature: Perspectives and Assessments, 1831–1952*, edited by John E. Bassett (Madison & Teaneck, N.J.: Fairleigh Dickinson University Press / London: Associated University Presses, 1997), p. 301.

mentation of family following divorce, with the psychologically wounded seeking healing rituals to overcome familial incoherence.

It is ironic that John Grisham—the very model of what one of my friends calls the new authopreneurs—should be the one writer who boldly overcame the anxiety that O'Connor expressed for her generation by setting up shop right on the tracks of the Dixie Special. But perhaps being unawed by Faulkner, even in the 1990s, requires an agenda in which Oxford is irrelevant as fortunate geography. "When you're writing suspense," Grisham confesses, "you can't spend a lot of time on persons, places, or settings." I suppose we should be grateful that most of his fellow Southerners don't write "suspense." For most of his writing generation, I find little diminution in interest from their predecessors in particularizing persons, places, and settings. Even that straddler of North and South, Anne Tyler, examines all the woeful effects of placelessness and dislocation without sacrificing any of the memorable incisiveness of her settings: they may be "impaired" or merely "remnant places" (in Leonard Lutwarck's terms), but they are the consequences of time spent imagining and inscribing them. Bobbie Ann Mason's Vietnamized Kentucky may be more an imaginative construct than it is Rand-McNally cartography—but, if so, her chronicles of rapid social change and its human costs are as firmly conceptualized and finely detailed as the more literalized characters and their ordeals in Tim McLaurin, whose interest, according to a friend, is in "a bunch of rednecks who fight and cut each other" in North Carolina.

By World War II, the common reader's response to Southern fiction already being celebrated by critics and academics was one based on the most natural need of the ordinary reader: that literature be inspirational, or at least consoling, in its depiction of the social scene. Serious Southern fiction was never that, of course. What garden-variety readers did not look for in the 1950s (or now, even in the impressive corner bookstore on the Oxford square) was a novel that engaged moral reality, especially if the conclusions of the authors happened to be darker than the most vocal pessimists of the Junior League. If some of the truisms of the Southern Renascence seem hopelessly dated in the writing of contemporary Southerners, the dark vision—Walker Percy said it was an old tradition oriented "toward tragedy"—is still darkly with us.

Richard Marius's narratives are as locally based as his great predecessors', but the old piety of place so common to the agrarian generation is no longer operable—his three novels are studded with transregional philosophical and religious questionings. The shaping Catholicism of James Lee Burke and Andre Dubus threads its way throughout their fiction. In Dubus, ordinary male-female relations are usually depicted in the context of Christian doctrine about the human relationship to God; the sacrament of the Eucharist and human sexuality are somehow equated in astonishing feats of analysis. The detective fiction of Burke is layered over with the older stories of the vulnerable hero battling his own internal demons without notable success; and because of external demons—Reaganism, American arrogance in foreign policy, corruption at all levels of government—a dour Cajun protagonist entertains no possibility for moral improvement in individuals and no melioristic vision for history, even the Southern variety.

It would be wrong to dismiss contemporary Southern novelists as homogenized mainstreamers in the national talent pool. Fictional settings no longer resonate with the liturgical undertones of the South as sacred place, but they are never merely invoked as necessary ingredients in the craft of fiction—following the writing-workshop rule that action must occur *somewhere*. Even Grisham's Memphis and New Orleans show that place is important to what happens because it is a lived-through, lived-in piece of geography before it is articulated as fictive scene.

Towns are seedier than they once were in earlier Southern fiction and the occasional cities have streets that are as mean as their Northern and Eastern counterparts. Kentucky coal mines and Vietnam veterans and Job Corps and labor strikes and ubiquitous trailer parks constitute a South more familiar to us from life situations than from books, but, thanks to the postmodern generation, they now are known as imagined venues as well.

NOTES

1. Allen Tate, "The Profession of Letters in the South," in his *Essays of Four Decades* (Chicago: Swallow Press, 1968), p. 320.

2. Tate, "A Southern Mode of the Imagination," in *Essays of Four Decades,* pp. 577, 579.

3. Richard J. Calhoun, "The Southern Renascence, 1925–1945," in *A Bibliographical Guide to the Study of Southern Literature,* edited by Louis D. Rubin Jr. (Baton Rouge: Louisiana State University Press, 1969), p. 48.

4. These anthologies follow a tradition. The head of the Department of English at Vanderbilt in the 1920s, Edwin Mims (with whom the Fugitives were sometimes in disagreement), co-edited with Bruce R. Payne of the Peabody College for Teachers in Nashville a 1910 "school" anthology, *Southern Prose and Poetry,* the contents of which are purely pre-Renaissance. Stark Young edited a textbook titled *Southern Treasury of Life and Literature* in 1937 that reflected a small amount of the new literature. Three modern Vanderbilt faculty members, Thomas Daniel Young, Richmond Croom Beatty, and Randall Stewart, teamed with Emory University professor Floyd Watkins to create an anthology first published in 1952 as *The Literature of the South* and revised for a 1968 reprint that was available for many years. An anthology published in 1970 under the editorship of Rubin and C. Hugh Holman of the University of North Carolina and Richard Beale Davis of the University of Tennessee, *Southern Writing, 1585–1920,* obviously does not cover writing of the Southern Renaissance.

5. Tate, "The New Provincialism," in *Essays of Four Decades,* p. 536.

6. Ibid.

7. Wendell Berry, "The Regional Motive," in his *A Continuous Harmony: Essays Cultural and Agricultural* (San Diego, New York & London: Harcourt Brace Jovanovich, 1972), pp. 63–64.

8. Ibid., p. 67.

THE SOUTHERN RENAISSANCE
AND OTHER MEDIA

MUSIC

JAZZ AND THE RISE OF LOUIS ARMSTRONG

Though the beginning date is in question, the musical and textual expression known as jazz began to go by that name in 1917. As one historian of jazz, Gunther Schuller, explains, "in purely musical terms the earliest jazz represents a primitive reduction of the complexity, richness, and perfection of its African and, for that matter, European antecedents."[1] This description, with only minor adjustment, might characterize the development of a new Southern literature in roughly the same period that jazz developed, a fusion of distinctly Southern and European antecedents in a new mode of frankness and with antipathy to the sentimental and the genteel.

The African American musicians who became the leading figures of jazz, Schuller recounts, had grown up in a musical climate dominated by genteel waltz music played in posh hotels and respectable concert venues. Even W. C. Handy, often called the father of the blues, succeeded mainly as a popular band leader and musical entrepreneur identified with a chain of bands that performed waltzes, ballads, cakewalk pieces, and decorous early ragtime for white audiences throughout the mid South. As Schuller observes, "the music played depended almost entirely on for whom it was played," whether for white society dances, traveling minstrel shows, New York novelty acts—all essentially decorous—or raucous backstreet honky-tonks.[2]

Growing out of a fusion of the rhythms and subjects of blues with brass-band marching music and the syncopated lilt of ragtime, jazz developed its most characteristic expression in the bars and bordellos of New Orleans and as dance music for an exclusively African American audience that was primarily of the working class. The coteries of musicians who picked up the frank and free new music from sitting in with other players were the equivalents, in a sense, of the groups of Southern

Louis Armstrong

writers who came together in cities or university towns to discuss the new literature coming out of Europe, New York, and Chicago, to imitate its qualities, and to read and comment on one another's writing. The small, independent, and often daring "little" magazines that these writers founded, or in which they sought to publish, had an important equivalent in the world of the jazz musicians: phonograph recordings that, beginning in about 1923, popularized, and to some degree formalized, jazz. As Schuller writes, however, "one cannot assume that the King Oliver of 1923, for example, was the same man and played the same music that first thrilled" his audience in the Storyville red-light district of New Orleans eight years earlier. Not only had the music evolved, but the opportunity for national "publication" on recordings doubtless enforced some self-censorship or revisionism similar to that experienced by most modernist writers when their work was accepted by major New York publishers. The music remained wild and freely expressive, though, and the lyrics frank to the level of the risqué.

Just as writers from various Southern cities and towns had different literary styles and subjects, so there was great variety among the forms of musical expression that evolved in different cities and regions of the South. This musical variety could also be found in the cities outside the South where African American musicians found opportunities for more rewarding and dignified lives: St. Louis, Kansas City, Chicago, Denver, San Francisco, and New York. This exodus, in fact, might be compared to the migration of those Southern writers who became college and university teachers outside the South, not always by simple choice but because many Southern universities were still politically compromised, economically limited, and cautious about, if not outright opposed to, a frank and critical literature.

Jazz is not only analogous to the literature of the Southern Renaissance, its development was also coincidental with the rise of that literature, and the music was both an influence upon the writing and frequently a source for at least some of it. William Faulkner's *Soldiers' Pay*, published in 1926, was written in New Orleans. At the center of the novel is a crucial scene set at a postwar dance, with Handy's jazz band from Memphis playing such then-suggestive songs as "Shake it and Break It" for a frenetic, youthful audience that excludes the more worldly but wounded and reserved men who fought in World War I. Many of the white writers of the Southern Renaissance were interested in "Negro" expression—Paul Green's plays, Julia Peterkin's novels, and Roark Bradford's folk epics and biblical parodies display this interest. Photographers documented life in the fields, cabins, juke joints, and small towns where

African Americans lived. Writers such as Faulkner made increasingly serious explorations of dramatic events set in motion by racial conflicts. The musical expression of these same concerns by talented African Americans should be considered an equal contribution to the Southern Renaissance.

Louis Armstrong is perhaps the musical equivalent of a writer like Faulkner—one who not only mastered his instrument and his medium but also carried it to levels not reached by others. Armstrong was born and raised in New Orleans, showed signs of being a prodigy by the time he was ten years old, and appeared on his first record in 1923, a watershed year for jazz recordings, playing trumpet with King Oliver's Creole Jazz Band. By 1925 he had his own band, Louis Armstrong's Hot Five, but he had also recorded with some of the greatest blues and jazz artists of his day, and he continued to do so. His early success thus coincided roughly with the rise of the Southern writers of the 1920s who founded new literary magazines to publish their own work and that of other like-minded writers. Schuller writes that "Armstrong's was a very special talent, and even in its earliest stages its innovative quality and originality shone through." He operated in a musical climate in New Orleans that had quite strict "canons" of play, a set of conventions so rigidly adhered to that "only the genius of a Louis Armstrong, erupting coincidentally with a major social revolution (brought on by the post-war industrial boom) . . . was able to break through these bonds." His achievement paralleled the revisionism of Faulkner and other Southern Renaissance writers who rebelled against both the generations before them and the society around them: "The New Orleans elders tried to preserve what was basically a nineteenth-century 'romantic' musical tradition in the face of enormous musical and stylistic changes. But one of their own was to cut those ties with finality. Through Louis Armstrong and his influence, jazz became a truly twentieth-century language. And it no longer belonged to New Orleans, but to the world."[3]

Armstrong, in fact, may have contributed to an influence on Faulkner through his participation in Bessie Smith's 1925 recording of

LOUIS ARMSTRONG'S PLAYING

"Armstrong emerged as the first inspirational genius of jazz in the 1920s, astonishing all who heard him with the effortlessly imaginative and lyrical quality of his improvisations. These were not necessarily of a complex nature, frequently keeping close to the thematic material, but showed a flexibility of tone and phrasing, an inherent sense of beat which could bring life to any ensemble he played in, and a general sense of freedom and self-expression that first revealed the potential of jazz and the importance of the individual soloist."

Peter Gammond

From *The Oxford Companion to Popular Music* (Oxford & New York: Oxford University Press, 1993), p. 21.

Handy's "St. Louis Blues." Faulkner took a line from the lyrics of the song for the title of a story about the Compson children of *The Sound and the Fury*, "That Evening Sun"—originally titled "That Evening Sun Go Down" when it was published in H. L. Mencken's *American Mercury* in March 1931.[4] The full line from the song—"I hate to see that evening sun go down"—bears comparison with the original working title of *The Sound and the Fury*, "Twilight." The cause of the singer's lament, "because that man of mine done left town" (that is, absence of a beloved person), is a major theme in Faulkner's novel, from the lament of Caddy Compson about the departure of her lover Dalton Ames to the obsessions of her brothers Benjy and Quentin. As an undated poster for an Armstrong concert advertised, the trumpeter, like Faulkner, was a "Master of Modernism."[5] In 1928 the novelist was writing his ground-breaking work of modernism, *The Sound and the Fury*. That same year Armstrong, in Schuller's description, "unleashed the spectacular cascading phrases of the introduction to *West End Blues* [and] established the general stylistic direction of jazz for several decades to come" and "also made clear that jazz could never again revert to being solely an entertainment or folk music" but "had the capacity to compete with the highest order of previously known musical expression."[6]

TEXAS STYLE AND WHITE FOLK MUSIC

An interesting question is why many Southern country musicians—heirs of the folk-song traditions that came into Appalachia and other areas with early settlers and evolved alongside occupations such as field work, cattle ranching, and railroading—wear cowboy hats and imitation Western clothes. The indispensable *Encyclopedia of Southern Culture* may have the answer in its fine brief chapter on Southern music, black and white: "The discovery of white folk music," writes the music historian Bill C. Malone, "came in the years before World War I," when the rapid progress of industrialization and urbanization caused many people to fear that rural music might be lost. Among the first such material to be collected and preserved appeared in John Lomax's *Cowboy Songs and Other Frontier Ballads* of 1910, at a time when the popularity of cowboy culture and the literary genre of the Western was at its peak, as seen in the work of writers such as Owen Wister and Zane Grey and the artwork of Frederic Remington and Charles Russell. Though cowboy culture was ethnically diverse and the songs had many sources, the popular imagination settled on a myth of white knights of the old West. A similarly mythic interpretation was given by the popular imagination to the ballads and folk songs of southern Appalachia, which were perceived as something frozen in amber, pure relics of a place where time had stood still. In fact, these folk songs were part of a highly varied, living tradition that included religious and dance music, as well as variations on folk materials brought by early settlers.

In 1923, when a Fort Worth, Texas, radio station created a "barn dance" format as a regular weekly feature, other radio stations followed, and the recording industry quickly caught up with the popularity of the best of local talent in gospel, string bands, fiddling, and such novelty acts as yodelers and "Hawaiian" ensembles. By the mid 1920s, Malone states, the country-music industry was established, and the most common term used to describe the music was "hillbilly." This epithet was played on for decades by toothless, jug-blowing comedians, who added humor and novelty to performances of derived, adapted, and specially written music imitating different kinds of white (and black) folk music. Like blues and jazz, the music underwent extensive changes due to commercialization, technology, and the touring that performers undertook to play for different audiences in a variety of venues.[7]

Within this rapidly changing musical tradition, however, there were and still are traces of authenticity and sources for writers. During the Southern Renaissance, traditional music inspired a new generation of local colorists to write novels and stories of the mountaineers. Even Faulkner was not immune, naming a character in his 1932 novel *Light in August* "Bobbie Allen," probably derived from the hard-hearted Barbara Allen of the English and Scottish folk ballads of the same name.

While it is true that country performers—like the poets, playwrights, and fiction writers of the Southern Renaissance and the legendary originators of jazz—were "torn between tradition and modernity," they also earned the chance to perfect their craft, develop their imaginations, and in many cases escape wretchedly impoverished or cruel pasts. Malone asserts that the most seminal performers in this early period of country music were Jimmie Rodgers from Mississippi and the Carter Family of Virginia, embodiments of another dramatic divide in the Southern experience, the rambling man singing songs of love and lonesomeness and the harmonious family duplicating in concerts the joys of parlor and church singing.[8]

RECORDINGS

Southern music is widely represented in the catalogue of recorded music, but a few boxed-set surveys of American folk music, country music, blues, and jazz provide a representative sampling with

JAZZ AND MODERNISM

"Only minimally aware of European teachings, often untrained and unable to read music, black musicians seem unlikely modernists. Yet they deserve inclusion in the category on their own merits: they were a conscious outgroup in a society demanding conformity, and they developed a new language to communicate among themselves. . . ."

Robert M. Crunden

From *American Salons: Encounters with European Modernism, 1885-1917* (New York & Oxford: Oxford University Press, 1993), p. 144.

which a student might begin to explore these rich fields. All of these musical genres have resonance with much of the literature of the Southern Renaissance.

The Blues. Washington, D.C.: Smithsonian Collection of Recordings, 1993. Four-CD boxed set with a booklet by W. K. McNeil.

Classic Country Music: A Smithsonian Collection. Washington, D.C.: Smithsonian Collection of Recordings, 1990. Four-CD boxed set with a booklet by Bill C. Malone.

Smithsonian Collection of Classic Jazz. Washington, D.C.: Smithsonian Collection of Recordings, 1987. Five-CD boxed set with a booklet by Martin Williams.

Folk Song America: A 20th Century Revival. Washington, D.C.: Smithsonian Collection of Recordings/Sony Music Special Products, 1991. Four-CD boxed set with booklet by Norm Cohen.

VISUAL ARTS
PAINTING AND FOLK ART

Though rich traditions of folk expression existed in the South in such areas as pottery, furniture- and tool-making, basketry, quilting, and weaving, the utilitarian nature of the objects made by artisans removed them from the category of "art" and often meant that they were used up instead of preserved. Painting as a form of art also existed in the South, in both naive and educated forms, but little attention was paid to it until the mid twentieth century. One might say that now there is a renaissance for Southern artists, as well as a renaissance of interest in the art made by Southerners in earlier periods, including the period 1919–1941. As with literature, drama, and poetry, a portion of what would or could have been considered Southern painting and plastic art during the period of the Southern Renaissance became, instead, connected with the Harlem Renaissance. A glance at work by such remarkable African American painters as Jacob Lawrence and Romare Bearden gives some idea of what could have happened in the South if the opportunity had existed for painters, black and white, to explore their culture in the same ways that novelists and poets explored it.

The paintings of Lawrence and Bearden, like the writing of Faulkner, Thomas Wolfe, and Eudora Welty, employ sophisticated reuse of folk images and traditions, modern legends, vernacular expression, jazz and blues, and memory within contexts made rich by connection with archetypes from classical, Renaissance, and modernist stories and images. Bearden, in fact, executed a whole series of striking lithographs in which he Africanized and vernacularized Homer's *Odyssey*, just as James Joyce matched Homer's epic to a tale set in Dublin. Lawrence's remarkable sixty paintings on the great migration of African Americans to the cities of the North and East rival in scope, image, coloration, and narrative power the novels of Faulkner and Wolfe. Naive painters such as Horace Pippin or Theora Hamblett recorded their distinctive impressions of everyday life and religious experience in ways that accord with the ironic and modernist methods of such poets as the Fugitives.

The following books represent a sampling of texts in which reproductions of painting and folk art from and about the South and relevant to the study of the Southern Renaissance may be found.

Bearden, Romare, and Harry Henderson. *A History of African-American Artists from 1792 to the Present*. New York: Pantheon, 1993.

Black, Patti Carr. *Art in Mississippi, 1729–1980*. Jackson: University Press of Mississippi, 1998.

Ferris, William. *Local Color: A Sense of Place in Folk Art*, foreword by Robert Penn Warren. New York: McGraw-Hill, 1982.

Howorth, Lisa, ed. *The South: A Treasury of Art and Literature*. New York: Hugh Lauter Levin Associates/Macmillan, 1993.

Livingston, Jane, and John Beardsley. *Black Folk Art in America, 1930–1980*. Jackson: University Press of Mississippi/Center for the Study of Southern Culture, 1982.

Morton, Robert. *Southern Antiques & Folk Art*. Birmingham, Ala.: Oxmoor House, 1976.

Painting in the South: 1564–1980. Richmond: Virginia Museum, 1983.

PHOTOGRAPHY

The photographic record of the South, especially those aspects of the South that so much influenced the writers of the Southern Renaissance, is voluminous. Photographs taken during the Great Depression as both propaganda and official record for New Deal recovery programs are gradually being recovered from archives in the Library of Congress and published, supplementing the already published pictures taken by some of the most famous photographers of the era. The following volumes provide a sampling.

Agee, James, and Walker Evans. *Let Us Now Praise Famous Men*. Boston: Houghton Mifflin, 1941.

Bourke-White, Margaret, and Erskine Caldwell. *You Have Seen Their Faces*. New York: Modern Age, 1937.

Dain, Martin. *Faulkner's County: Yoknapatawpha*. New York: Random House, 1964.

Glusker, Irwin, ed. *A Southern Album: Recollections of Some People and Places and Times Gone By,* narrative by Willie Morris. Birmingham, Ala.: Oxmoor House, 1975. Though a coffee-table book, this volume collects interesting historical photographs of people, places, pastimes, and celebrations dear to the hearts of even the most serious-minded writers of the Southern Renaissance.

Lange, Dorothea, and Paul Schuster Taylor. *An American Exodus: A Record of Human Erosion in the Thirties*. New Haven: Yale University Press, 1969.

Mason, Herman "Skip," Jr. *Going Against the Wind: A Pictorial History of African-Americans in Atlanta*. Atlanta: Longstreet Press, 1992.

McKenzie, Barbara. *Flannery O'Connor's Georgia,* foreword by Robert Coles. Athens: University of Georgia Press, 1980.

Morrow, Mark. *Images of the Southern Writer,* foreword by Erskine Caldwell. Athens: University of Georgia Press, 1985.

Natanson, Nicholas. *The Black Image in the New Deal: The Politics of FSA Photography*. Knoxville: University of Tennessee Press, 1992. A critique of how and why images of African Americans were used by Depression-era propagandists, this book serves also as a guide to a large number of photography books that came out of the Southern Renaissance (and Depression) era. Several images are reproduced.

Phillips, Sandra S., and John Szarkowski. *Wright Morris: Origin of a Species*. San Francisco: San Francisco Museum of Modern Art, 1992. This exhibition catalogue of photographs by the novelist and short-story writer Morris includes many striking images of the Depression-era South, including one of a ramshackle house teetering on the edge of an eroded gully in Faulkner's home county. Unlike photographs sponsored by the Farm Security Administration of the Works

Walker Evans photograph of an Alabama country store and gas station, 1936

Progress Administration (WPA) in Franklin Roosevelt's New Deal, Morris's images are documentary, not commentary.

Schulz, Constance B., ed. *A South Carolina Album, 1936–1948: Documentary Photography in the Palmetto State from the Farm Security Administration, Office of War Information, and Standard Oil of New Jersey.* Columbia: University of South Carolina Press, 1991. This book presents photographs of the rural countryside, buildings, and people of the period from the Depression until after World War II from various sources of official documentary photography. Though from only one Southern state and a brief span of time, the pictures are characteristic of other parts of the South in the era of the Southern Renaissance.

Spielman, David G. *Southern Writers,* text by William W. Starr, foreword by Fred Hobson. Columbia: University of South Carolina Press, 1997.

Welty, Eudora. *Eudora Welty: Photographs,* foreword by Reynolds Price. Jackson: University Press of Mississippi, 1989. Though Welty worked for a WPA project as a publicity agent, she was never an official photographer. Her snapshots were taken with a good camera and professional intent, though with a novice's eye, and record a variety of life in rural places and a few cities.

Welty. *One Time, One Place: Mississippi in the Depression,* revised edition, foreword by William Maxwell. Jackson: University Press of Mississippi, 1996.

DOCUMENTARY SOURCES

VIDEO RECORDINGS

Scores of excellent documentaries on individual Southern writers and on aspects of Southern music, folklife, storytelling, and culture are available in video format. Many of them are important to an understanding of the Southern Renaissance. Information about these videos can be found at the website Southfilm.com (http://www.southfilm.com), part of the Southern Culture Catalogue maintained by the Center for the Study of Southern Culture at the University of Mississippi. The following titles are of special interest.

The Southern Literary Renaissance. Produced by Manly, Inc., and the South Carolina Educational Television Network. Eminent Scholar/ Teacher Series. Detroit: Omnigraphics, 1988. Video recording of a lecture by Louis D. Rubin Jr., in which he discusses works by authors such as Faulkner, Wolfe, Welty, Warren, and Richard Wright.

Tell About the South: Voices in Black & White. Produced and directed by Ross Spears. Part 1, *Tell About the South;* part 2, *Prophets & Poets;* part 3, *Let Freedom Ring.* Charlottesville, Va.: James Agee Film Project, 1996–1999. *Tell About the South* is the most comprehensive documentary history of Southern literature yet produced as a motion picture. It begins in the first of three parts with a dramatic impersonation of Mencken reading "The Sahara of the Bozart" and a consideration of the Southern Renaissance period. The two succeeding movies take the story through the post–World War II period and through the Civil Rights movement.

AUDIO RECORDING

Louis D. Rubin Jr. *The Southern Renascence.* De Land, Fla.: Everett/ Edwards, 1976. Cassette recording of Rubin lecturing on a field of literary study he helped to pioneer.

THE WORLD WIDE WEB

Many useful sites on the World Wide Web are devoted to Southern literature, culture, and individual writers; several offer links to other informative sites. The following list is valuable in its own right, but it will lead the curious to additional information about the Southern Renaissance.

The American South Home Page. http://www.ibiblio.org/south. A project of the SunSITE-USA Workstation Development Group.

Center for the Study of Southern Culture Home Page. http://www.ole-miss.edu/depts/south. Site of the Center for the Study of Southern Culture at the University of Mississippi.

Documenting the American South. http://docsouth.unc.edu/index.html. A project of the Academic Affairs Library, University of North Carolina at Chapel Hill.

Mississippi Writers and Musicians. http://SHS.Starkville.K12.MS.US/mswm/MSWritersAndMusicians. Developed by staff and students at Starkville High School, Starkville, Mississippi. A comprehensive informational site about writers and musicians from Mississippi.

Society for the Study of Southern Literature. http://www-dept.usm.edu/~soq/sssl.html.

Southern Culture Resources. http://www.lib.ua.edu/smr/south1.htm. A project of the Bibliographic Instruction Department at Gorgas Library, University of Alabama.

Southern Literature and Culture on the Internet. http://www.vmi.edu/~english/southern.html. Site maintained by the Department of English and Fine Arts, Virginia Military Institute.

Virginia Center for Digital History. http://jefferson.village.virginia.edu/vcdh. Maintained by the Alderman Library, University of Virginia. One of the projects of this site, *The Valley of the Shadow* (http://jefferson.village.virginia.edu/vshadow2), is a remarkable documentary about two towns, one in Virginia that belonged to the Confederacy and one not far away in Pennsylvania that belonged to the Union, before, during, and after the Civil War. While not about writing or culture during the Southern Renaissance, this resource provides insight into the rich variety of lore on which writers of the 1920s and 1930s might have drawn for their own works about the Southern past.

NOTES

1. Gunther Schuller, *Early Jazz: Its Roots and Musical Development* (New York & Oxford: Oxford University Press, 1968), p. 63.

2. Ibid., p. 70.

3. Ibid., p. 88.

4. Hans Skei, *Reading Faulkner's Best Short Stories* (Columbia: University of South Carolina Press, 1999), p. 178.

5. The poster is reproduced on the cover of the booklet accompanying *Portrait of the Artist as a Young Man, 1923–1934* (New York: Columbia Legacy, 1994), a collection of Armstrong recordings sponsored by the Smithsonian Institution.

6. Schuller, *Early Jazz,* p. 89.

7. Bill C. Malone, "Music," in *Encyclopedia of Southern Culture,* edited by Charles Reagan Wilson and others (Chapel Hill: University of North Carolina Press, 1989), pp. 988–989.

8. Malone, "Country Music," in *Encyclopedia of Southern Culture,* p. 1004.

THE SOUTHERN RENAISSANCE AS STUDIED

OTHER WORKS AND WRITERS STUDIED WITH THE SOUTHERN RENAISSANCE

Southerners appear to have understood, or simply intuited, Marcel Proust's discovery that human beings are memory incarnate. Memory, oddly, is not static, fixed, and determined—it adjusts to new information all the time. When William Faulkner has a character in his 1951 novel, *Requiem for a Nun*, say, "The past is never dead. It's not even past," he is expressing such an idea, one that was behind the remarkable work of poets, novelists, and dramatists in the Southern states beginning in the 1920s. The writers of the Southern Renaissance are usefully studied in the context of Southern history, that which they had read when they were young, that which they had learned by the time they were established writers, and, if their lives were sufficiently long, the increasingly rewritten history that came into play as they reached their fifties, sixties, and beyond. It is no accident that several of the young poets who came out of Vanderbilt University in the 1920s engaged in historical and biographical research and composition. Although these Nashville writers came increasingly to oppose a group of more radical social thinkers in Chapel Hill, North Carolina—the sociologists at the University of North Carolina who worked with Howard Odum—the study of the Southern Renaissance benefits now from the investigations of the region set in motion by Odum and his colleagues.

Because the South changed—the assumptions and even the prejudices of its people changed, as did its legal and social codes—even its past changed, as Faulkner readily understood. The bibliography at the end of this volume lists many of the recent historical studies that in some respects validate the imaginations of many Southern writers, especially Faulkner, who took on Southern history more frequently than most of his contemporary Southern writers. The list of historical works provides several texts with which the literature of the Southern Renaissance may—and, in many cases, should—be read.

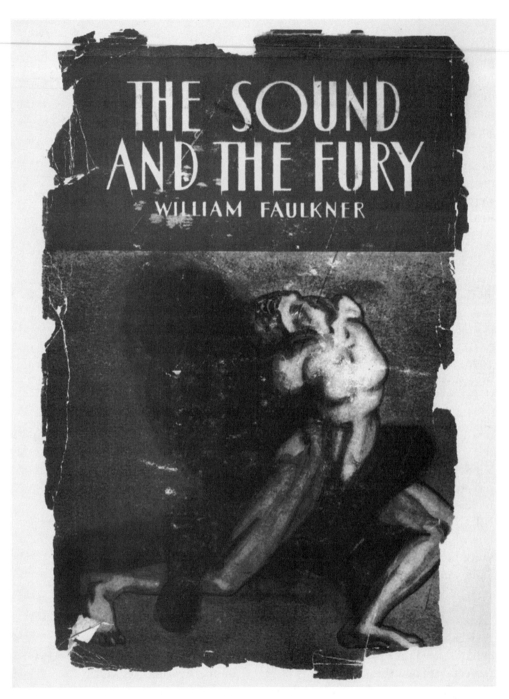

Dust jacket of the first edition of Faulkner's 1929 novel, in which he employed groundbreaking techniques of literary modernism while exploring the legacy of the Southern past in the tragic story of the Compson family

The surge of good writing in the South from the 1920s onward was not, however, a provincial phenomenon focused solely on local or regional history. It was contemporaneous with the noteworthy achievements of many other American writers—John Dos Passos, Ernest Hemingway, and Willa Cather, for example—who were inspired, in part, by experiments in narrative technique and structure from writers in Europe. Acutely important were the tides of new ideas in almost every field of humanistic endeavor that swept the Western world in the first two decades of the twentieth century, that interesting reaction to "modernity" that revolutionized the arts of music, painting, and writing. The Southern Renaissance and its writers are, therefore, both usefully studied in the context of the work of scientists from Charles Darwin to Albert Einstein and Sigmund Freud; composers from Claude Debussy to Igor Stravinsky and Arnold Schoenberg; painters from Claude Monet to Pablo Picasso, Georges Braque, and Henri Matisse; and writers from Charles Baudelaire to James Joyce, Virginia Woolf, T. S. Eliot, and Thomas Mann. Any serious author of the late nineteenth century or the first half of the twentieth century, European or American, is worthy of consideration alongside the writers of the Southern Renaissance, who in various ways went back to those who came before them and pushed forward toward those who came afterward. As a product of their later years as professors, Robert Penn Warren and his friend Cleanth Brooks teamed with the literary critic R. W. B. Lewis to write brilliant introductions to the selections in a two-volume anthology, *American Literature: The Makers and the Making* (1973), which they prepared for college use, in the process renewing their ties with the classic American authors.

Finally, the Southern Renaissance is perhaps most usefully studied in connection with the Harlem Renaissance, a roughly contemporaneous flourishing of poetry, drama, fiction, essay, and social criticism. If the racist codes and restrictions of the South had not existed, the black writers of the Harlem Renaissance might well have become the literary companions of those white authors who created their art in the harshly segregated Jim Crow South.

LESSONS OF THE PAST

"It is out of fashion in these days to look backward rather than forward. About the only American given to it is some unreconstructed Southerner, who persists in his regard for a certain terrain, a certain history, and a certain inherited way of living."

John Crowe Ransom

From "Reconstructed but Unregenerate," in *I'll Take My Stand: The South and the Agrarian Tradition* (1930), introduction by Louis D. Rubin Jr. (New York: Harper & Row, 1962), p. I.

RESOURCES FOR STUDY OF
THE SOUTHERN RENAISSANCE

STUDY QUESTIONS

1. Read H. L. Mencken's essay "The Sahara of the Bozart" and enumerate the many aspects of the arts he finds missing from the South. Discuss which points might have stung bright young Southerners the most. Think of a Southern persona to assume—a woman from New Orleans, an African American blues musician from the Mississippi Delta, a wealthy and well-educated lawyer from a major Southern city, and so forth—and write a reply to Mencken from that person's point of view.

2. Using a dictionary, find as many interpretations as possible for the magazine titles *The Fugitive* and *The Double Dealer*.

3. Define the term *renaissance* and discuss whether or not the term is appropriate to describe the flourishing of new writing in the South between 1919 and 1941.

4. List three to five essential characteristics of the Southern Renaissance and identify literary works that illustrate these characteristics.

5. Choose three hallmark works of the Southern Renaissance in different genres and identify common themes, character types, or styles. Then select one of these works and argue for or against the case that it is representative of the main emphases of the Southern Renaissance.

6. Research the words *agrarian* and *antebellum* and discuss how they are in some respects coded words that actually refer to some things that are not as pleasant as their literal meanings.

7. Ellen Glasgow declared that Southern writing at the time just before the Southern Renaissance began needed a dose of "blood and irony," but she disliked violence or sensationalism in literature. Look up the word *irony* and discuss what Glasgow might have meant by her recommendation.

8. Compare T. S. Eliot's "The Love Song of J. Alfred Prufrock" or *The Waste Land* with Allen Tate's "Ode to the Confederate Dead."

9. Find a short story by one of the writers of the Southern Renaissance, read it carefully with two or three other students, even reading it aloud, and discuss whether the subject matter and the language of the piece seem especially "Southern."

10. Find two poems (with the assistance of a teacher, if necessary), one by a writer of the Harlem Renaissance and another by an author of the Southern Renaissance, and compare the two for subject, themes, language, and meaning. Does one seem less Southern than the other? Why?

11. Three literary movements that preceded the Southern Renaissance had a great deal of importance for writers of the period: Southwestern or frontier humor (on the old Southern frontier, not that of the Wild West), local color, and realism. Look up these terms and write explanations of what each one means; discuss how each movement came to have significance for Southern writers of the 1920s and 1930s.

12. Using a biography of one of the writers of the Southern Renaissance, draw out information on the writer's childhood. Was this childhood typically "Southern"? Explain why. What aspects of the writer's childhood might be said to reappear in her or his mature writing?

13. Using a biography of a writer of the Southern Renaissance, draw out information about the writer's parents or grandparents. Did they influence or affect the writer? Explain how.

14. Find a short story by a writer of the Southern Renaissance that is especially detailed in the way it presents the story's setting—William Faulkner's "Barn Burning" and Eudora Welty's "A Worn Path" are good examples. What aspects of the presentation of the setting seem particularly Southern? What is the thematic function of place in the story?

15. The South is said to be a place where the strength of family is highly important; yet, many novels and stories of the Southern Renaissance depict serious faults and failures in family life. Read Faulkner's "A Rose for Emily" or "That Evening Sun," Welty's "Why I Live at the P. O.," or Katherine Anne Porter's "The Old Order" and write a report on the factors in the story that make the idealized version of the Southern family problematic.

16. Compare the opening chapters of two or more novels of the Southern Renaissance, for example, Zora Neale Hurston's *Their Eyes Were Watching God,* Thomas Wolfe's *Look Homeword, Angel,* and Faulkner's *Absalom, Absalom!* Is there anything similar about them? Judging by opening chapters, or even first pages, alone, what are the major themes and characters?

17. Find an early school history of a Southern state or a history of the South written before the 1960s and compare the treatments of dramatic historical episodes in one of these books with their treatment in state histories or general works of history written since the 1980s. Find a fictional treatment of the same incident or a similar incident. Compare the versions and discuss.

18. How did the "Great Migration" northward of Southern African Americans affect their lives, as well as the world they left behind? Write a report on some of the art, literature, and music inspired by this migration.

19. Research the early history of jazz in New Orleans and Chicago and write an essay relating its development to the Southern Renaissance.

20. Researching the history and nature of jazz, explain why Louis Armstrong can be called a "Master of Modernism" (as he was once described on a poster), a term that equates his achievement with that of Faulkner in a book such as *The Sound and the Fury.*

21. Choose a significant text written during the Southern Renaissance and discuss whether or not this book could have been written (or published) prior to the period 1919–1941.

22. Choose a work by a Southern writer who is active and popular at the present time and compare it to a similar work by a Southern author of the period 1919–1941. What are the differences in style and theme?

23. Choose a poem or story by a writer of the Southern Renaissance that may be compared and contrasted with a poem or story by Edgar Allan Poe. What are the differences in style and subject matter? How could Poe's piece be rewritten to make it more compatible with the kind of work done in the era of the Southern Renaissance?

24. Revive one of the early plays of Paul Green by doing a reading of it with several classmates.

25. Does dramatic writing of the Southern Renaissance period differ substantially from plays written in other regions of the United States at the same time? Perform research and write a report.

26. How does poetry of the Southern Renaissance differ from the poetry of such writers of the same era as Robert Frost, Marianne Moore, Wallace Stevens, or H.D. (Hilda Doolittle)? Write a report comparing a Southern poem with a poem from one of these writers from another region.

27. There was one female member of the Fugitive group, Laura Riding. Find examples of her poetry and write a report about her career. How was her career different from those of such writers as Tate, John Crowe Ransom, or Robert Penn Warren? In what ways is her poetry different from theirs?

28. Caroline Gordon, who was married to Tate, wrote successful fiction during the Southern Renaissance. Research her career and read some of her stories or one of her novels. Discuss her career as a writer of the Southern Renaissance.

29. Faulkner and Katherine Anne Porter both carried the Southern art of storytelling off the pages of fiction and into the re-creation of their own biographies. Write a report on the ways these two writers reinvented their own lives. Does this extraliterary invention have any bearing on their fiction?

30. Investigate the poetry of Donald Davidson or Ransom for signs of a purely Southern subject matter and write a report about this aspect of their work.

31. Though the Southern Renaissance is often regarded as a conservative and purely regional phenomenon, it was part of the international movement of literary modernism. Find some definitions of modernism and judge the writing of one or more writers of the Southern Renaissance by these definitions. Is it possible to demonstrate that these Southern writers were modernists? How?

GLOSSARY OF TERMS

Allegory. A narrative in which the characters, plot, and/or setting have both a literal and symbolic meaning.

Armistice. Generally, any suspension of hostilities between warring parties. "The Armistice" refers specifically to the 11 November 1918 settlement between Germany and the Allied powers that ended World War I.

Boll weevil. Insect that attacks the cotton plant. The boll weevil was a devastating force in Southern agriculture that migrated from Mexico and moved across the South through the 1920s, causing panic, migration of workers, and economic depression.

Cavalier. In the context of the Southern Renaissance, the term *Cavalier* referred to a legendary aristocracy of Virginia gentlemen popularized in such pre–Civil War novels as William Alexander Caruthers's *The Cavaliers of Virginia* (1834–1835).

Cubist. Refers to Cubism, an early-twentieth-century art style in which the abstract structure of the depicted object is highlighted by presenting it from various perspectives simultaneously or by breaking its form into fragments.

Decadence. Movement of late-nineteenth-century writers and artists in France and England who stressed artifice and unconventional subject matter in their work.

Depression, or **Great Depression.** Period of economic decline in the United States, Europe, and other industrial-ized parts of the world lasting from 1929 until 1939.

Expressionist. Refers to expressionism, an early-twentieth-century literary and artistic movement that emphasized the presentation of subjective emotions.

Federal Writers' Project. A program administered by the **Works Progress Administration** (see below) that hired unemployed writers, editors, and researchers to produce local histories, nature studies, and folklore compilations. The most significant achievement of the program was the completion of descriptive guides to every state in America.

Gothic. The descriptive term applied in literary studies to a type of novel first popularized in eighteenth-century England that featured exotic, medieval settings and mysterious, supernatural happenings. In the context of the literature of the Southern Renaissance, *Gothic* refers to writing characterized by an atmosphere of dread or terror, grotesque characters, and violent action.

Great Migration. The mass exodus of African Americans from the South to the North beginning around the time of World War I and lasting through the 1970s.

Imagists. A group of British and American writers who came to prominence in the 1910s and wrote poems that presented in direct, concrete terms the poet's response to some image or scene. Key members of the group were the Americans Ezra Pound and Amy Lowell.

Jazz Age. Term used to evoke the hedonistic lifestyle of American society in the 1920s, the decade when jazz music first rose to prominence.

Jim Crow Era. The period from 1877 to the 1950s when Southern states passed laws to enforce racial segregation.

Lost Cause. Term used in the defeated South to refer to the Civil War.

Modernism. Artistic and literary movement that began late in the nineteenth century and intensified at the time of World War I. It involved a deliberate break with earlier conventions of Western culture and art. Modernist writers such as James Joyce and T. S. Eliot made bold experiments in literary style and form that sought to reflect the seeming incoherence and disjointedness of modern life.

Naturalism. Related to **realism** (see below). Naturalism, which became influential in the late nineteenth century, was a literary style informed by the Darwinian view that the human race is merely another species of animal. Naturalist writers depicted characters at the mercy of instinctive drives and the pressures of their environment.

New Criticism. Critical approach to literature that began to be practiced in the 1920s. The term for the method was coined by John Crowe Ransom in his book *The New Criticism* (1941). Practitioners of New Criticism seek to examine the literary text by itself, without regard to information about the author's life or the culture in which he wrote. The chief exponents of this type of criticism were Cleanth Brooks and Robert Penn Warren.

New Deal. The set of public programs initiated by President Franklin D. Roosevelt in the 1930s to foster economic recovery during the Depression.

Prohibition. Period in American history from 1919 to 1933 when the manufacture, sale, and transportation of alcoholic beverages were prohibited by constitutional amendment.

Realism. The attempt in literature and art to depict life as it actually is, without idealization or sentimentality.

Reconstruction. Period from the end of the Civil War to 1877 when the governments of the states of the former Confederacy were reestablished and efforts were made to deal with the problems arising from their readmission to the United States.

Redeemers. Southerners who, during the period following Reconstruction, sought to disenfranchise freed blacks and restore the white-dominated social order that had prevailed before the Civil War.

Robber Barons. Late-nineteenth-century American capitalists who made their fortunes through exploitative practices.

Spanish Civil War. War (1936–1939) between the forces of the elected government of Spain, supported by the Soviet Union, and the conservative Nationalists (fascists), led by General Francisco Franco. Franco's Nationalists won the war.

Symbolists. A school of mid- to late-nineteenth-century French poets who conveyed emotion and themes in their work through heavily symbolic language. Notable members of the group were Charles Baudelaire, Paul Verlaine, and Arthur Rimbaud. Their work exerted a strong influence on modernist writers in Europe and America.

Works Progress Administration (WPA). One of Roosevelt's **New Deal** (see above) programs, established in 1935 to provide work for the unemployed.

SELECTED BIBLIOGRAPHY

REFERENCE WORKS

Bain, Robert, Joseph M. Flora, and Louis D. Rubin Jr., eds. *Southern Writers: A Biographical Dictionary*. Baton Rouge: Louisiana State University Press, 1979.

Cassidy, Frederic G., ed. *Dictionary of American Regional English*. Cambridge, Mass.: Belknap Press of Harvard University, 1985.

"Checklist of Scholarship in Southern Literature." *Mississippi Quarterly* (1968–). An annual supplement to *A Bibliographical Guide to the Study of Southern Literature* (1969), cited below.

Flora and Bain, eds. *Contemporary Fiction Writers of the South: A Bio-Bibliographical Sourcebook*. Westport, Conn.: Greenwood Press, 1993.

Flora and Bain, eds. *Contemporary Poets, Dramatists, Essayists, and Novelists of the South: A Bio-Bibliographical Sourcebook*. Westport, Conn.: Greenwood Press, 1994.

Flora and Bain, eds. *Fifty Southern Writers after 1900: A Bio-Bibliographical Sourcebook*. Westport, Conn.: Greenwood Press, 1987.

Foster, M. Marie Booth, ed. *Southern Black Creative Writers, 1829–1953: Biobibliographies*. Westport, Conn.: Greenwood Press, 1988.

Harkness, David James. *Literary Profiles of the Southern States: A Manual for Schools and Clubs*. Knoxville: Division of University Extension, University of Tennessee, 1953. A state-by-state account in narrative form of writers in the South, with hundreds of names, including many that are not included in John Bradbury's state-by-state list in his *Renaissance in the South: A Critical History of the Literature, 1920–1960* (1963), cited below.

Matuz, Roger, ed. *Contemporary Southern Writers*. Detroit: St. James Press, 1999. A biographical dictionary.

Pederson, Lee, ed. *Linguistic Atlas of the Gulf States*, 7 volumes. Athens: University of Georgia Press, 1986–1992.

Robinson, Ella. *A Guide to Literary Sites of the South*. Northport, Ala.: Vision Press, 1998.

Rubin, Louis D., Jr. *A Bibliographical Guide to the Study of Southern Literature*. Baton Rouge: Louisiana State University Press, 1969.

Snodgrass, Mary Ellen. *Encyclopedia of Southern Literature*. Santa Barbara, Cal.: ABC-CLIO, 1997.

Wilson, Charles Reagan and others, eds. *Encyclopedia of Southern Culture*. Chapel Hill: University of North Carolina Press, 1989.

THE SOUTHERN RENAISSANCE

Bradbury, John M. *Renaissance in the South: A Critical History of the Literature, 1920–1960*. Chapel Hill: University of North Carolina Press, 1963.

Gray, Richard. *The Literature of Memory: Modern Writers of the American South*. Baltimore & London: Johns Hopkins University Press, 1977.

King, Richard H. *A Southern Renaissance: The Cultural Awakening of the American South, 1930–1955*. New York & Oxford: Oxford University Press, 1980.

Mencken, H. L. "The Sahara of the Bozart." In his *Prejudices: Second Series*. New York: Knopf, 1920.

Rubin, Louis D., Jr., and Robert D. Jacobs, eds. *South: Modern Southern Literature in its Cultural Setting*. Garden City, N.Y.: Doubleday, 1961. A supplementary volume to the following one.

Rubin and Jacobs, eds. *Southern Renascence: The Literature of the Modern South*. Baltimore: Johns Hopkins University Press, 1953. The first book with a reference in the title to the Southern Renaissance and the first collection of essays on authors of the period considered under that rubric.

Singal, Daniel Joseph. *The War Within: From Victorian to Modernist Thought in the South, 1919–1945*. Chapel Hill: University of North Carolina Press, 1982. An historian's view of the dynamics that made, and existed within, the Southern Renaissance.

Sullivan, Walter. *A Requiem for the Renascence: The State of Fiction in the Modern South*. Mercer University Lamar Memorial Lectures, no. 18. Athens: University of Georgia Press, 1976.

THE FUGITIVES

Bradbury, John M. *The Fugitives: A Critical Account*. Chapel Hill: University of North Carolina Press, 1958.

Cowan, Louise. *The Fugitive Group: A Literary History*. Baton Rouge: Louisiana State University Press, 1959.

Davidson, Donald. *Southern Writers in the Modern World*. Eugenia Dorothy Blount Lamar Memorial Lectures, 1957. Athens: University of Georgia Press, 1958.

An account by a poet and teacher who was a member of the Fugitive group.

Fugitives: An Anthology of Verse. New York: Harcourt, Brace, 1928.

Karanikas, Alexander. *Tillers of a Myth: Southern Agrarians as Social and Literary Critics*. Madison: University of Wisconsin Press, 1966.

Stewart, John L. *The Burden of Time: The Fugitives and Agrarians*. Princeton: Princeton University Press, 1965.

INTERVIEWS WITH SOUTHERN WRITERS

Ever since 1958, when the critic Malcolm Cowley began collecting into single volumes the detailed interviews with American and international writers that had first been published in the literary magazine *The Paris Review*, similar collections of interviews with authors have appeared with increasing regularity. Writers of the Southern Renaissance are widely represented in this literature. For instance, the first collection of *Paris Review* interviews, *Writers at Work: The Paris Review Interviews* (1958), includes interviews with William Faulkner and Robert Penn Warren. Students can read authors' comments not only about the sources and practice of the writing life, but about their contemporaries and, where relevant, such phenomena as the Southern Renaissance itself. Several Southern writers are represented in the Literary Conversations Series published by the University Press of Mississippi, in volumes such as *Conversations with Eudora Welty* (1984), *Conversations with Erskine Caldwell* (1988), and *Conversations with William Faulkner* (1999).

SOUTHERN LITERATURE

Bassett, John E., ed. *Defining Southern Literature: Perspectives and Assessments, 1831–1952*. Madison & Teaneck, N.J.: Fairleigh Dickinson University Press / London: Associated University Presses, 1997. A collection of essays by various writers over the years that help to explain the heritage of the South before the Southern Renaissance and that comment specifically upon the period.

Brantley, Will. *Feminine Sense in Southern Memoir: Smith, Glasgow, Welty, Hellman, Porter, and Hurston*. Jackson: University Press of Mississippi, 1993.

Brown, Dorothy H., and Barbara C. Ewell, eds. *Louisiana Women Writers: New Essays and a Comprehensive Bibliography*. Baton Rouge: Louisiana State University Press, 1992.

Bryan, Violet Harrington. *The Myth of New Orleans in Literature: Dialogues of Race and Gender*. Knoxville: University of Tennessee Press, 1993.

Bryant, J. A., Jr. *Twentieth-Century Southern Literature*. Lexington: University of Kentucky Press, 1997.

Castille, Phillip, and William Osborne, eds. *Southern Literature in Transition: Heritage and Promise*. Memphis: Memphis State University Press, 1983.

Clark, Emily. *Ingenue Among the Lions: The Letters of Emily Clark to Joseph Hergesheimer*, edited, with an introduction, by Gerald Langford. Austin: University of Texas Press, 1965. Correspondence between the founder of the Richmond magazine *The Reviewer* and one of the writers whose works were published in it.

Clark. *Innocence Abroad*. New York: Knopf, 1931. In this volume Clark writes about the development of *The Reviewer* and the authors who published in it.

Cook, Sylvia Jenkins. *From Tobacco Road to Route 66: The Southern Poor White in Fiction*. Chapel Hill: The University of North Carolina Press, 1976.

Cutrer, Thomas W. *Parnassus on the Mississippi: The Southern Review and the Baton Rouge Literary Community, 1935–1942*. Baton Rouge: Louisiana State University Press, 1984.

Davenport, F. Garvin, Jr. *The Myth of Southern History: Historical Consciousness in Twentieth-Century Southern Literature*. Nashville: Vanderbilt University Press, 1970.

d'Haen, Theo, and Hans Bertens, eds. *"Writing" Nation and "Writing" Region in America*. Amsterdam: VU University Press, 1996.

Folks, Jeffrey J., and James A. Perkins, eds. *Southern Writers at Century's End*. Lexington: University of Kentucky Press, 1997. Accounts of fiction by twenty-two contemporary writers.

Fowler, Doreen, and Ann J. Abadie, eds. *Faulkner and the Southern Renaissance: Faulkner and Yoknapatawpha, 1981*. Jackson: University Press of Mississippi, 1982.

Gray, Richard. *Southern Aberrations: Writers of the American South and the Problems of Regionalism.* Baton Rouge: Louisiana State University Press, 2000.

Gray. *Writing the South: Ideas of an American Region.* Cambridge: Cambridge University Press, 1986.

Hobson, Fred. *The Southern Writer in the Postmodern World.* Mercer University Lamar Memorial Lectures, no. 33. Athens: University of Georgia Press, 1991.

Hobson. *Tell About the South: The Southern Rage to Explain.* Baton Rouge: Louisiana State University Press, 1983.

Hoffman, Frederick J. *The Art of Southern Fiction: A Study of Some Modern Novelists.* Carbondale: Southern Illinois University Press, 1967.

Holman, C. Hugh. *The Immoderate Past: The Southern Writer and History.* Lamar Lectures at Wesleyan College, 1976. Athens: University of Georgia Press, 1977.

Hönnighausen, Lothar, and Valeria Gennaro Lerda, eds. *Rewriting the South: History and Fiction.* Tübingen, Germany: Francke, 1993. Proceedings of a symposium on the South and Southern literature at the University of Bonn, Germany, demonstrating, like the volume edited by Lerda cited below, the increasing European interest not only in Southern literature but also in Southern history and culture.

Hubbell, Jay B. *The South in American Literature, 1607–1900.* Durham: Duke University Press, 1954.

Inge, M. Thomas. *Faulkner, Sut, and Other Southerners: Essays in Literary History.* West Cornwall, Conn.: Locust Hill Press, 1992.

Jones, Anne Goodwyn. *Tomorrow Is Another Day: The Woman Writer in the South, 1859–1936.* Baton Rouge: Louisiana State University Press, 1981.

Kennedy, Richard S., ed. *Literary New Orleans.* Baton Rouge: Louisiana State University Press, 1992. Essays on individual writers who sojourned in or made their careers in New Orleans, including William Faulkner and his circle.

Kennedy, ed. *Literary New Orleans in the Modern World.* Baton Rouge: Louisiana State University Press, 1998. More essays on the same topic.

Kreyling, Michael. *Inventing Southern Literature.* Jackson: University Press of Mississippi, 1998. A revisionist interpretation of the Southern Renaissance and how the literary history of the South has been made.

Lawson, Lewis A. *Another Generation: Southern Fiction Since World War II.* Jackson: University Press of Mississippi, 1984. Includes a lengthy list of post–World War II Southern novelists and essays by Lawson on several writers from this period.

Lerda, Valeria Gennaro, and Tjebbe Westendorp, eds. *The United States South: Regionalism and Identity.* Rome: Bulzoni, 1991. Proceedings of the First European Interdisciplinary Symposium of the Southern Studies Forum at the University of Genova, Italy. Like *Rewriting the South,* this publication is a sign of increasing European interest in Southern literature, history, and culture.

Manning, Carol S., ed. *The Female Tradition in Southern Literature: Essays on Southern Women Writers.* Champaign, Ill.: University of Illinois Press, 1993.

Pilkington, Tom. *State of Mind: Texas Literature and Culture.* College Station: Texas A & M University Press, 1998.

Romine, Scott. *The Narrative Forms of Southern Community.* Baton Rouge: Louisiana State University Press, 1999.

Rubin, Louis D., Jr. *The Faraway Country: Writers of the Modern South.* Seattle: University of Washington Press,

1963. Includes essays on Faulkner, Thomas Wolfe, Robert Penn Warren, Eudora Welty, and the poetry of the Agrarians.

Rubin. *The Mockingbird in the Gum Tree: A Literary Gallimaufry*. Baton Rouge: Louisiana State University Press, 1991.

Rubin. *The Writer in the South: Studies in Literary Community*. Mercer University Lamar Memorial Lectures, no. 15. Athens: University of Georgia Press, 1972.

Rubin, ed. *The American South: Portrait of a Culture*. Baton Rouge: Louisiana State University Press, 1980. Printed versions of broadcasts on the Voice of America radio network coordinated by Rubin. Topics include many aspects of Southern culture and literature, with a distinguished list of participants.

Rubin and others, eds. *The History of Southern Literature*. Baton Rouge: Louisiana State University Press, 1985.

Simpson, James Olney, and Jo Gulledge, eds. *The Southern Review and Modern Literature, 1935–1985*. Baton Rouge:

Louisiana State University Press, 1988.

Simpson, Lewis P. *The Dispossessed Garden: Pastoral and History in Southern Literature*. Athens: University of Georgia Press, 1975.

Skaggs, Merrill M. *The Folk of Southern Fiction*. Athens: University of Georgia Press, 1972.

Taft, Michael. *Blues Lyric Poetry: A Concordance*. 3 volumes. New York: Garland, 1984. An unusual resource for studying early blues and jazz lyrics based on transcriptions of songs recorded as early "race" records.

Walser, Richard. *Literary North Carolina: A Brief Historical Survey*. Raleigh, N.C.: State Department of Archives and History, 1970.

Wauchope, George Armstrong. *Literary South Carolina*. Columbia: University of South Carolina, 1923.

Young, Thomas Daniel. *The Past in the Present: A Thematic Study of Modern Southern Fiction*. Baton Rouge: Louisiana State University Press, 1981.

Young. *Tennessee Writers*. Knoxville: University of Tennessee Press, 1981.

SOUTHERN HISTORY

Many studies of Southern history have corroborated works by writers of the Southern Renaissance. Students of the period should look into one or two of the following books, at least, in order to compare the historian's research and craft with that of literary scholars, as well as with that of the Southern poets, novelists, short-story writers, and dramatists of the period 1919–1941.

Aiken, Charles S. *The Cotton Plantation South Since the Civil War*. Baltimore: Johns Hopkins University Press, 1998.

Alsberg, Henry G., and others, eds. *The American Guide: The South, The Southwest*. New York: Hastings House, 1949.

Ayers, Edward L. *The Promise of the New South: Life after Reconstruction*. New

York & Oxford: Oxford University Press, 1992.

Bartley, Numan V., ed. *The Evolution of Southern Culture*. Athens: University of Georgia Press, 1988.

Berry, Wendell. *A Continuous Harmony: Essays Cultural and Agricultural*. New York: Harcourt Brace Jovanovich, 1972. Berry, a novelist, poet, and former college professor who is also a working farmer, is at his best when commenting on the cultural ideas that have been important to writers of the Southern Renaissance. His essay "The Regional Motive" in this collection is an excellent restatement of what serious regional writing should undertake to accomplish.

Bertelson, David. *The Lazy South*. New York: Oxford University Press, 1967.

Bridenbaugh, Carl. *Myths and Realities: Societies of the Colonial South*. Baton Rouge: Louisiana State University Press, 1963.

Campbell, Edward D. C., Jr. *The Celluloid South: Hollywood and the Southern Myth*. Knoxville: University of Tennessee Press, 1981.

Cash, W. J. *The Mind of the South*. New York: Knopf, 1941.

Cobb, James C. *The Most Southern Place on Earth: The Mississippi Delta and the Roots of Regional Identity*. New York & Oxford: Oxford University Press, 1992.

Crunden, Robert M. "New Orleans." In his *American Salons: Encounters with European Modernism, 1885–1917*. New York & Oxford: Oxford University Press, 1993.

Daniel, Pete. *Standing at the Crossroads: Southern Life since 1900*. New York: Hill & Wang, 1986.

Degler, Carl N. *The Other South: Southern Dissenters in the Nineteenth Century*. New York: Harper & Row, 1974.

Degler. *Place Over Time: The Continuity of Southern Distinctiveness*. Baton Rouge: Louisiana State University Press, 1977.

Eaton, Clement. *The Mind of the Old South*. Baton Rouge: Louisiana State University Press, 1964.

Escott, Paul D., ed. *W. J. Cash and the Minds of the South*. Baton Rouge: Louisiana State University Press, 1992.

Floan, Howard R. *The South in Northern Eyes, 1831–1861*. Austin: University of Texas Press, 1958.

Flynt, J. Wayne. *Dixie's Forgotten People: The South's Poor Whites*. Bloomington: Indiana University Press, 1979.

Foner, Eric. *A Short History of Reconstruction*. New York: Harper & Row, 1988.

Franklin, John Hope. *The Militant South, 1800–1861*. Cambridge, Mass.: Belknap Press of Harvard University Press, 1956.

Gaines, Francis Pendleton. *The Southern Plantation: A Study in the Development and the Accuracy of a Tradition*. New York: Columbia University Press, 1924. Reprint, Gloucester, Mass.: Peter Smith, 1962.

Gaston, Paul M. *The New South Creed: A Study in Southern Mythmaking*. New York: Knopf, 1970.

Gerster, Patrick, and Nicholas Cords, eds. *Myth and Southern History*. 2 volumes. Chicago: Rand McNally, 1974.

Gispen, Kees, ed. *What Made the South Different?* Jackson: University Press of Mississippi, 1990.

Grantham, Dewey W. *The Democratic South*. Athens: University of Georgia Press, 1963.

Harrison, Alferdteen, ed. *Black Exodus: The Great Migration from the American South*. Jackson: University Press of Mississippi, 1991.

Hobson, Fred. *But Now I See: The White Southern Racial Conversion Narrative*. Baton Rouge: Louisiana State University Press, 1999.

Jordan, Winthrop D. *White Over Black: American Attitudes toward the Negro, 1550–1812*. Chapel Hill: Institute of Early American History and Culture (Williamsburg, Va.)/University of North Carolina Press, 1968.

Kirby, Jack Temple. *The Countercultural South*. Mercer University Lamar Memorial Lectures, no. 38. Athens: University of Georgia Press, 1995.

Kirby. *Media-Made Dixie: The South in the American Imagination*. Baton Rouge: Louisiana State University Press, 1978.

Kirby. *Rural Worlds Lost: The American South, 1920–1960*. Baton Rouge: Louisiana State University Press, 1987.

Levine, Lawrence W. *Black Culture and Black Consciousness: Afro-American Folk Thought from Slavery to Freedom*. New York: Oxford University Press, 1977.

McMillen, Neil R. *Dark Journey: Black Mississippians in the Age of Jim Crow*. Urbana & Chicago: University of Illinois Press, 1989.

McMillen, ed. *Remaking Dixie: The Impact of World War II on the American South*. Jackson: University Press of Mississippi, 1997.

Murray, Albert. *Stomping the Blues*. New York: McGraw-Hill, 1976. Novelist and social critic Murray's history of jazz influenced, among others, the musician and composer Wynton Marsalis in his efforts to give jazz the attention it deserves as one of the most important forms of American artistic expression.

O'Brien, Michael. *The Idea of the American South, 1920–1941*. Baltimore: Johns Hopkins University Press, 1979. The soundest and most provocative postmodern explanation of why the South is regarded as a place separate and distinct from the rest of America.

Orser, Charles E., Jr. *The Material Basis of the Postbellum Tenant Plantation: Historical Archaeology in the South Carolina Piedmont*. Athens: University of Georgia Press, 1988. Historical archaeology—the investigation of such aspects of material culture as settlement patterns, personal possessions, housing, and other physical objects—complements and sometimes corrects the memorial and written record of the past. Orser's investigation is based on several years of work at the site of a large plantation, Millwood, that was active

during the time of slavery and after the Civil War.

Osterweis, Rollin G. *The Myth of the Lost Cause, 1865–1900*. Hamden, Conn.: Archon, 1973.

Owsley, Frank Lawrence. *Plain Folk of the Old South*. Baton Rouge: Louisiana State University Press, 1949.

Peterson, Merrill D. *The Jefferson Image in the American Mind*. New York: Oxford University Press, 1960.

Reed, John Shelton. *The Enduring South: Subcultural Persistence in Mass Society*. Lexington, Mass.: Lexington Books, 1972. Reed's early book on the South is indicative of his continuing research on the subject: he continues to keep track of what allows the region to retain its individualized character.

Scott, Ann Firor. *The Southern Lady: From Pedestal to Politics, 1830–1930*. Chicago: University of Chicago Press, 1970.

Scott, ed. *Unheard Voices: The First Historians of Southern Women*. Charlottesville & London: University of Virginia, 1993.

Shapiro, Henry D. *Appalachia on Our Mind: The Southern Mountains and Mountaineers in the American Consciousness, 1870–1920*. Chapel Hill: University of North Carolina Press, 1978.

Smith, Stephen A. *Myth, Media, and the Southern Mind*. Fayetteville: University of Arkansas Press, 1985.

Stampp, Kenneth M. *The Era of Reconstruction, 1865–1877*. New York: Vintage, 1965.

Tindall, George Brown. *The Ethnic Southerners*. Baton Rouge: Louisiana State University Press, 1976.

Vandiver, Frank E., ed. *The Idea of the South: Pursuit of a Central Theme*. Chicago: University of Chicago Press, 1964.

Wilson, Charles Reagan. *Baptized in Blood: The Religion of the Lost Cause, 1865–1920.* Athens: University of Georgia Press, 1980.

Wilson. *Judgment and Grace in Dixie: Southern Faiths from Faulkner to Elvis.* Athens: University of Georgia Press, 1995.

Woodward, C. Vann. *American Counterpoint: Slavery and Racism in the North-South Dialogue.* Boston: Little, Brown, 1971.

Woodward. *The Burden of Southern History.* Baton Rouge: Louisiana State University Press, 1960. One of the most interesting arguments for differences between the South and the rest of the United States; the "burden" of Southern history, it turns out, has given the South the opportunity to be more in tune with the rest of the world than with the rest of America.

Woodward. *The Strange Career of Jim Crow,* third edition. New York: Oxford University Press, 1974.

Wyatt-Brown, Bertram. *Honor and Violence in the Old South.* New York & Oxford: Oxford University Press, 1986. An abridgment of Wyatt-Brown's *Southern Honor: Ethics and Behavior in the Old South* (1982).

Wyatt-Brown. *Yankee Saints and Southern Sinners.* Baton Rouge: Louisiana State University Press, 1985.

Zinn, Howard. *The Southern Mystique.* New York: Knopf, 1964.

THE WPA GUIDES TO THE SOUTHERN STATES

Federal Writers' Project of the Works Progress Administration. *Alabama: A Guide to the Deep South.* New York: Richard R. Smith, 1941. Revised edition, edited by Alyce Billings Walker. New York: Hastings House, 1975.

Federal Writers' Project of the Works Progress Administration. *Arkansas: A Guide to the State.* New York: Hastings House, 1941. Reprinted as *The WPA Guide to 1930s Arkansas,* with an introduction by Eliott West. Lawrence: University Press of Kansas, 1987.

Federal Writers' Project of the Works Progress Administration. *Florida.* New York: Oxford University Press, 1939. Reprinted as *The WPA Guide to Florida,* with an introduction by John I. McCollum. New York: Pantheon, 1984.

Federal Writers' Project of the Works Progress Administration. *Georgia: A Guide to its Towns and Countryside.* Athens: University of Georgia Press, 1940. Reprinted as *Georgia: The WPA Guide to its Towns and Countryside,* with an introduction by Phinizy Spalding. Columbia: University of South Carolina Press, 1990.

Federal Writers' Project of the Works Progress Administration. *Kentucky: A Guide to the Bluegrass State.* New York: Harcourt, Brace, 1939. Reprinted as *The WPA Guide to Kentucky,* with a foreword by Thomas D. Clark. Lexington: University of Kentucky Press, 1996.

Federal Writers' Project of the Works Progress Administration. *Louisiana: A Guide to the State.* New York: Hastings House, 1941. Revised edition, New York: Hastings House, 1971.

Federal Writers' Project of the Works Progress Administration. *Mississippi: A Guide to the Magnolia State.* New York: Viking, 1938. Reprinted as *Mississippi: The WPA Guide to the Magnolia State,* with an introduction by Robert S. McElvaine. Jackson: University Press of Mississippi, 1988.

Federal Writers' Project of the Works Progress Administration. *North Carolina: A Guide to the Old North State.* Chapel Hill: University of North Carolina Press, 1939. Reprinted as *North*

Carolina: The WPA Guide to the Old North State, with an introduction by William S. Powell. Columbia: University of South Carolina Press, 1988.

Federal Writers' Project of the Works Progress Administration. *South Carolina: A Guide to the Palmetto State.* New York: Oxford University Press, 1941. Reprinted as *South Carolina: The WPA Guide to the Palmetto State,* with an introduction and appendices by Walter B. Edgar. Columbia: University of South Carolina Press, 1988.

Federal Writers' Project of the Works Progress Administration. *Tennessee: A Guide to the State.* New York: Viking, 1939. Reprinted as *The WPA Guide to Tennessee,* with an introduction by Jerrold Hirsch and a foreword by Wilma Dykeman. Knoxville: University of Tennessee Press, 1986.

Federal Writers' Project of the Works Progress Administration. *Texas.* New York: Hastings House, 1940. Reprinted as *The WPA Guide to Texas,* with an introduction by Don Graham. Austin: Texas Monthly Press, 1986.

Federal Writers' Project of the Works Progress Administration. *Virginia: A Guide to the Old Dominion.* New York: Oxford University Press, 1940. Reprint, Richmond: Virginia State Library and Archives/Virginia Center for the Book, 1992.

LITERARY PERIODICALS
MAGAZINES PUBLISHED DURING THE SOUTHERN RENAISSANCE

Double Dealer (New Orleans), 1921–1926.

Fugitive (Nashville), 1922–1925.

Pseudopodia (Clayton, Ga.), 1936–1937; continued as *North Georgia Review,* 1937–1941. Edited by the Georgia novelist and memoirist Lillian Smith, a courageous foe of racial and political injustice.

Reviewer (Richmond), 1920–1925.

Southern Review (Baton Rouge), 1935–1942. Cleanth Brooks and Robert Penn Warren were editors for the journal during this period. It was revived in 1965 and still publishes with some emphasis upon things Southern.

Year Book of the Poetry Society of South Carolina (Charleston), 1921–1926.

CONTEMPORARY JOURNALS

Several scholarly journals publish critical work on the Southern Renaissance and Southern literature in general, including *American Literature* (Duke University). One is more apt to find Southern subjects treated with great regularity in *The Mississippi Quarterly: The Journal of Southern Culture* (Mississippi State University), *The Southern Humanities Review* (Auburn University), *The Southern Literary Journal* (University of North Carolina at Chapel Hill), and *The Southern Quarterly* (University of Southern Mississippi). Both *The Sewanee Review* (University of the South) and *The Georgia Review* (University of Georgia) were traditionally associated with the Southern Renaissance: Allen Tate and Andrew Lytle served as editors for the former, and John Donald Wade founded the latter. These two journals still publish the work of Southern writers and essays on Southern subjects.

INDEX